Questions of Faith

RELIGION IN THE MODERN WORLD

Series Editors: Paul Heelas and Linda Woodhead, *Lancaster University*

Editorial Advisor: David Martin, *Emeritus Professor, London School of Economics*

Founding Editors: John Clayton, *University of Boston*, and Ninian Smart, *formerly of University of California – Santa Barbara*

The **Religion in the Modern World** series makes accessible to a wide audience some of the most important work in the study of religion today. The series invites leading scholars to present clear and non-technical contributions to contemporary thinking about religion in the modern world. Although the series is geared primarily to the needs of college and university students, the volumes in **Religion in the Modern World** will prove invaluable to readers with some background in Religious Studies who wish to keep up with recent thinking in the subject, as well as to the general reader who is seeking to learn more about the transformations of religion in our time.

Published:

Don Cupitt – *Mysticism After Modernity*
Paul Heelas, with the assistance of David Martin and Paul Morris – *Religion, Modernity and Postmodernity*
Linda Woodhead and Paul Heelas – *Religion in Modern Times*
David Martin – *Pentecostalism: The World Their Parish*
Steve Bruce – *God is Dead*
David Smith – *Hinduism and Modernity*
Peter Berger – *Questions of Faith*

Forthcoming:

Juan Campo – *Pilgrimages in Modernity*
Bronislaw Szerszynski – *The Sacralization of Nature: Nature and the Sacred in the Global Age*

Questions of Faith

A Skeptical Affirmation of Christianity

Peter L. Berger

Blackwell Publishing

BLACKWELL PUBLISHING
350 Main Street, Malden, MA 02148-5020, USA
9600 Garsington Road, Oxford OX4 2DQ, UK
550 Swanston Street, Carlton, Victoria 3053, Australia

First published 2004 by Blackwell Publishing Ltd

4   2005

Library of Congress Cataloging-in-Publication Data

Berger, Peter L.
    Questions of faith : a skeptical affirmation of Christianity / Peter L. Berger.
    p. cm.
    Includes bibliographical references and index.
    ISBN 1-4051-0847-9 (alk. paper) – ISBN 1-4051-0848-7 (pbk. : alk. paper)
    1. Apostles' Creed. 2. Theology, Doctrinal – Popular works. I. Title.

BT993.3.B47 2004
238'.11 – dc21

                                                                        2003044373

ISBN-13: 978-1-4051-0847-8 (alk. paper); ISBN-13: 978-1-4051-0848-5 (pbk. : alk. paper)

A catalogue record for this title is available from the British Library.

Set in 10 on 12.5 pt Meridian
by SNP Best-set Typesetter Ltd, Hong Kong
Printed and bound in the United Kingdom
by TJ International, Padstow, Cornwall

The publisher's policy is to use permanent paper from mills that operate a sustainable forestry policy, and which has been manufactured from pulp processed using acid-free and elementary chlorine-free practices. Furthermore, the publisher ensures that the text paper and cover board used have met acceptable environmental accreditation standards.

For further information on
Blackwell Publishing, visit our website:
www.blackwellpublishing.com

Contents

Preface

This book is an exercise in what used to be called "lay theology." That is, its author is not a professional theologian, and the intended audience is assumed to consist, in the main, of similarly unaccredited people. If some professional theologians should read it, they will undoubtedly find various errors and misinterpretations in the discussion of religious thinkers and doctrines. That is a risk that must be taken by a lay person who ventures into a field in which he is not academically accredited. Evidently, I think that the risk is worth taking. And if I look at the works that many professional theologians have regaled us with in recent years, I become even more convinced that a lay intrusion into their precincts is fully justified.

The structure of the book is very simple. Each chapter (with the exception of a couple of excursi) is based on a phrase of the Apostles' Creed. This document, alas, does not date from the time of the Apostles. It was composed early on in the history of the western church, probably in Rome, and was subsequently adopted in the east as well. It is the most compact statement of Christian faith and, along with the Nicene Creed, the one that is most often recited in worship. Obviously it does not cover everything that Christians have believed. But it covers most of it and is thus a convenient guide for a *tour d'horizon* of Christian beliefs.

My subtitle combines the words "skeptical" and "affirmation." This is not an oxymoron. My argument is skeptical in that it does not presuppose faith, does not feel bound by any of the traditional authorities in matters of faith – be it an infallible church, an inerrant scripture, or an irresistible personal experience, and takes seriously the historical contingencies that shape all religious traditions. Nevertheless, my argument eventuates in an affirmation of Christian faith, however heterodox. Of course the reader will be free not to follow me to this conclusion.

In the name of honest advertising, I should state my own location on the theological map. I feel uncomfortable with all available theological labels and ecclesial affiliations. My biographical roots are in Lutheranism, and I would still identify myself as Lutheran, albeit with great reservations. I attend services in an Episcopal church, not because I am in any sense on the road to Canterbury, but because the two Lutheran churches located at convenient distances from my home are impossible for opposite reasons (one belongs to the Missouri Synod, which adheres to a quite stifling orthodoxy; the other is a parody of "political correctness," which, if anything, is even more stifling). I most feel at home in the tradition of liberal Protestantism, going back (in attitude, not in substance) to Friedrich Schleiermacher, because this tradition embodies precisely the balance between skepsis and affirmation that, for me, defines the only acceptable way of being a Christian without emigrating from modernity. I should emphasize, however, that I do not consider this book to be a liberal Protestant manifesto. Readers who do not so locate themselves may find themselves able to go along with me at least part of the way. Some of my best conversations in recent years have been with Catholics – the kind who are prone to say, "I am Catholic, *but . . .*"

This "but" is important. Quite a few years ago, in a book by that title, I used the phrase "the heretical imperative" to describe the situation of religious believers in the contemporary world. The Greek word *hairesis*, from which the English "heresy" derives, means "choice." That is, a heretic is one who picks and chooses from the tradition, retaining some parts of it and giving up other parts. I argued (correctly, I continue to think) that such exercises of choice are inevitable in a situation in which no religious tradition is any longer taken for granted. The individual now *must* make choices. And even if he defines himself as an orthodox adherent of this or that tradition, that too is the result of a choice. This situation is both liberating and burdensome. All in all, I think that this is good. I cannot see how taken-for-granted religion is superior to religion that is chosen. Kierkegaard, in his passionate attack on the taken-for-granted Christendom of the Danish established church of his time, urged us to become "contemporaneous" with Jesus. That is hardly feasible. The Christendom which he attacked hardly exists anymore (certainly not in Denmark). Its taken-for-granted status has been exploded by modernity and pluralism. What this means, however, is that in a strange way we have become "contemporaneous" with the earliest Christians, who also existed in the exuberantly pluralistic world of late Graeco-Roman civilization, and for whom Christian faith was possible only as a deliberate act of choice. I don't think that we should deplore the fact that our situation, in this particular aspect, is similar to that of Paul as he preached in the *agora* of Athens, where a multitude of gods competed with each other.

Some sympathetic readers of the manuscript of this book have pointed out that I do not engage with much of contemporary theology. I acknowledge the point. But the purpose of this book is not to comment on this or that theologian, contemporary or other. I refer only to such theologians as are directly pertinent to the argument I try to make. Put simply, the book explains how one contemporary individual, skeptical in temperament and reasonably well informed, manages to affirm the Christian faith.

This book was written over a period of about two years, in moments of time snatched from other busy activities as a social scientist. Conversations with a number of people helped me in this enterprise. I will here mention only three. Brigitte Berger, as with other books of mine, was the by no means passive audience of what she likes to call *Dichterlesungen*. Robert Arida (of Holy Trinity Orthodox Cathedral in Boston) and Claire Wolfteich (of Boston University's School of Theology) were very helpful in introducing me to authors and modes of theological thought with which I was previously unacquainted.

Peter L. Berger
Boston, Autumn 2002

Chapter One

"I believe . . ."

This is a book on questions of religious faith. If one has no faith, is there any reason why one should be interested?

Leave aside for the moment the question of why one may have faith: There are good reasons why many people go through life, often very successfully, without faith. It is more difficult to see how one could fail to be *interested* in the matter. Religious faith, in whatever form, always involves one fundamental assumption – namely, that there is a reality beyond the reality of ordinary, everyday life, and that this deeper reality is benign. Put differently, religious faith implies that there is a destiny beyond the death and destruction which, as we know, awaits not only ourselves but everyone and everything we care about in this world, the human race and the planet on which its history is played out, and (if modern physics is correct) the entire universe. One can reasonably say that one does not believe in such a transcendent destiny; it is less reasonable to say that one is not interested in it. Religion implies that reality ultimately makes sense in human terms. It is the most audacious thought that human beings have ever had. It may be an illusion; even so, it is a very *interesting* one.

Most of the time, in the course of ordinary living, we assume that reality is what it appears to be – the physical, psychological, and social structures that provide the parameters of our actions. The philosopher Alfred Schutz called this "the world-taken-for-granted." There are exceptional individuals who question this taken-for-grantedness by way of intellectual reflection, individuals like Socrates or Einstein; they are quite rare. For most people ordinary reality is put in question by something that happens to interrupt the flow of ordinary living. Often what happens is something bad – illness, bereavement, loss of social status, or some other individual or collective calamity. But the taken-for-grantedness of everyday reality can also be put in question by some very good things: an intense aesthetic experience, or falling in love, or being awed by the birth of one's first child. Either way, suddenly, it becomes clear that there is more to reality than one had previously assumed. Minimally, this is what is meant by experiences of transcendence. Such experiences are not yet religious – atheists and agnostics too become ill, get to be parents, become intoxicated by music or by love. But one could call these experiences "pre-religious": By relativizing ordinary reality they open up the possibility of a reality – or, perhaps, of many realities – that are usually hidden. One takes the step from a pre-religious to a religious perception of transcendence when one believes that the reality that lies beyond ordinary experience means well by us. Again, one need not believe this. But it is certainly *interesting* to consider the possibility.

I used to know a psychoanalyst who was a very orthodox Freudian. We had a number of conversations about religion. He found it hard to understand that an intelligent person (he generously allowed that I was such a person) could be religious. He, so he said, had been a convinced atheist as far back as he could remember, and he was sure that religion was nothing but a comforting illusion. I asked him once whether he ever had any doubts about this conviction of his. He said no, he never had any doubts. Then he hesitated and said, actually yes: He had moments of doubt about his atheism every time he listened to the choral portion of Beethoven's Ninth Symphony, the chorale based on Schiller's "Ode to Joy." Thornton Wilder, in his novel *The Ides of March*, puts a similar thought into the mouth of Julius Caesar. Wilder's Caesar says that he never believed in the gods (he only performed the religious rituals demanded of a public official in Rome because he thought them to be politically useful). But Caesar too admitted to occasional doubts about his atheism. This happened in some moments in the midst of battle or of some important political actions when he had the feeling that a greater power was guiding him. It also happened during the so-called epileptic aura, the acute sense of ecstasy which typically occurs just before a grand-mal attack.

On the other hand, if one has faith, why should one ask questions about it?

There are people who have faith without feeling the need to reflect about it. Sometimes one refers to this kind of faith as "child-like," but it is not necessarily something that one should look down upon. These are often people who have grown up in a social environment in which their particular faith is taken for granted, or they have had a powerful experience which confirmed their faith and which retains its power in their memory. Or perhaps the capacity for unquestioning faith is simply a part of a certain personality type; in religious terms one could then say that such faith is a gift. The value one ascribes to reflection will determine whether one envies such people or thinks that they are missing something important. Be this as it may, most human beings (and by no means only intellectuals) feel constrained to reflect about their experiences and beliefs, if only to relate different experiences and beliefs to each other in such a way that they make overall sense. If reflection becomes systematic, one can describe this activity as theorizing. Obviously any aspect of human experience and belief can become an object of reflection. Religion is no exception. The simplest definition of *theology* is to say that it is systematic reflection about faith.

The word "theology" comes out of Christian usage and people in other traditions (such as Judaism or the religions of India) do not like to use it (often because they associate it with an overly cerebral approach to religion or because they want to distance themselves from the repressive dogmatism which, unfortunately, has been a recurring habit among Christians). However, in the simple sense in which theology has just been defined it will necessarily occur in every religious tradition, from the most sophisticated to the most primitive. A Jew might not want to attach the label "theology" to the highly sophisticated theorizing permeating the Talmudic literature, but in the aforementioned sense it is a specific sort of theologizing that goes on there (even though, with its rootage in practical considerations of religious law, it is different in character from the evolution of Christian doctrine). The same goes for the monumental theoretical edifices constructed in the course of Hindu and Buddhist history. But even in so-called primal religions – that is, traditions without sacred texts or bodies of learned religious functionaries – some sort of theorizing goes on. Thus mythology – the stories about gods and other supernatural beings – is also a very distinctive type of theoretical reflection. In other words, theology occurs whenever there is a systematic attempt to reflect about faith. For anyone who identifies with a particular tradition this reflection will be some sort of dialogue between this tradition and the individual's experience of faith. Needless to say, the present book is just such an exercise.

Scholars will differ as to the date at which full-blown theological systems first appeared in the development of Christianity – certainly no later than the time when the early Church Fathers felt it necessary to spell out their beliefs in the confrontation with Hellenistic philosophy. But there is theology – or, more precisely, a number of theologies – already in the New Testament, and not only in the letters of the Apostle Paul and the Johannine texts. Even in the Synoptic Gospels, which tell the story of the life of Jesus, there are theological considerations that shape the telling of the story (for example, in relating events to prophecies in the Hebrew scriptures). Thus theology has been a very important feature of Christian history from the beginning. Over the centuries this process of reflection had to take account of different theoretical interlocutors: rabbinical authorities, Greek philosophers, teachers of Gnosticism and other esoteric doctrines, the powerful rival of Islamic thought, more recently the manifold theoretical expressions of modernity.

In a general way, therefore, doing theology today is not fundamentally different from what it was at any time since the early Christians had to make sense of the events around the life of Jesus. Nevertheless, there is something distinctive about the modern situation, and it is useful to recognize this: Modernity progressively undermines the social environments which support taken-for-grantedness, in religion as in everything else that people believe. This is not the place to elaborate on this important phenomenon, but the basic reason for it can be stated quite simply: People take their beliefs for granted to the extent that everyone around them does the same. Put differently, beliefs appear to be self-evident if there is a more or less unified social consensus about them. Modernity, through some of its most basic processes (such as mass migration, mass communication, urbanization), undermines this sort of consensus. The individual is increasingly confronted with many different beliefs, values, and lifestyles, and is therefore forced *to choose* between them. Choice requires at least rudimentary reflection. Religious choice, then, requires at least rudimentary theologizing.

To use a philosophical term, modernity *problematizes*. There is an old American joke (admittedly not a very good one) that nicely illustrates what is meant by this term. A soldier returns from the war. He used to be a great talker, but now he just sits and does not speak. His family is worried about him, and everything is done to make him comfortable. At the dinner table his mother gives him the food he likes best and, because she knows that he likes to put a lot of salt on his food, she places a large salt shaker next to his seat. One day she forgets, and the salt shaker is at the other end of the table. The soldier looks around, then says: "Will someone please pass the goddam salt shaker." Everyone is very happy – the returned warrior seems to have overcome the trauma that must have caused his long silence. The mother passes the salt shaker to him and says: "Son, I'm so happy that you are speaking to us again. Why didn't you speak before?" He answers: "There was no problem before."

A sociologist can say that modernity problematizes beliefs because of the high degree of *pluralism* it creates in the social environment of modern people: Where there is a plurality of beliefs, and where the individual is therefore compelled to make choices between them, a higher degree of reflectiveness becomes unavoidable. This fact has far-reaching consequences in every area of human life. Among other things, it means that religious certainty is harder to come by. In a sense then, every reflective person, if concerned with religion at all, must become a sort of theologian. And this has yet another consequence: More than ever before, theology today should not be left to the professional theologians (even leaving aside the regrettable fact that very frequently the latter talk only to each other). Minimally, there should be a dialogue between professional theologians and others who lack such credentials. Obviously again, this book is an expression of this view.

But why should one have faith in the first place?

The verb "should" is often understood in a moral sense, as when one says, for example, that one should help people who are in trouble or that one should respect the dignity of every person. The same implication is often found in religious language: Thus one is told, in sermons or other religious pronouncements, that one *should* have faith, conversely that lack of faith (or unbelief) is a moral failure, a sin against God. This is not a very plausible proposition. If God exists, He has not made it very easy to believe in Him – the world is full of terrible things that, on the contrary, make it easy *not* to believe in Him (or at least not to believe that He is benign). What is more, assuming that God is as omniscient as He is supposed to be, He knows this, and therefore will not hold it against us if we do not manage to have faith. The verb "should" in the above question, then, is to be understood, not as a moral injunction, but simply as a request for an explanation: Are there good reasons to have faith?

There is a venerable tradition in Christian thought proposing proofs for the existence of God. The high point of this tradition can be found in medieval scholasticism, when Thomas Aquinas and other Christian philosophers put forth elegant, closely argued proofs of this kind. One can still learn from these arguments, but, at least since their critique by Immanuel Kant, it has become very difficult to accept them as the proofs they purport to be. But one does not have to be a student of Kant, or for that matter a philosopher of any persuasion, to realize that faith cannot be demonstrated like a mathematical theorem or even supported in probabilistic terms like a scientific hypothesis. If it could, it would not be faith: One believes that which one does not *know*. Unbelief is the unwillingness to step beyond what one knows with certainty or even with a reasonable degree of probability. This is not a moral failing; on the contrary, it may be a morally admirable attitude of intellectual integrity. By no means is it implied here that *faith* is a moral failing or a lack of intellectual integrity (as has been said by many critics of religion, who have seen it as a cowardly flight from the harsh realities of life, as in Marx's characterization of religion as an "opiate"). Still, one should be able to explain why one is willing to make that step into the unknown which constitutes the act of faith.

Of course, as has been suggested before, the question does not appear in its sharpest form as long as faith is taken for granted in the individual's social environment (although in all periods of history there have been breakdowns of taken-for-grantedness as a result of either individual or collective events). The question has become very sharp in modern times. Thus it makes sense that, close to the beginning of modern history, Pascal made his famous statement about faith as a wager. We cannot know whether faith is true or not, but it is reasonable to bet that it is: If it turns out to be true, we will be gloriously vindicated; if it turns out to be untrue, we will have lost nothing (indeed, we will not be around to draw a conclusion). This probably suggests an overly intellectual understanding of faith, as if it involved the verification of a hypothesis (actually, Pascal held a much more nuanced view). But the term "wager" is helpful. Faith is indeed a sort of wager. Put simply, when one decides to have faith, one bets on the ultimate goodness of the world; conversely, one bets that annihilation is not the ultimate fate of everything one holds dear in the world.

Luther used a play of words, in Latin, when he described faith (*fides*) as trust (*fiducia*). Luther, unlike Pascal, only stood on the threshold of a modern sense of reality, and the trust he had in mind was not so much in the existence of God (which, it seems, he never doubted) but in God's grace. But we can take on his wordplay in a sharper, more modern sense: Faith is trust in the goodness of the world. In our experience there are many indications that the world is a meaningless chamber of horrors and that all human aspirations will end in an abyss of nothingness. But there are also signals of another destiny, a destiny in which one could invest hope – in the wonders of the universe and in the magnificent possibilities of the human condition. I think that my Freudian friend had something like this in mind when he mentioned Beethoven's Ninth Symphony. Let me put it this way: *Faith is to bet on the ultimate validity of joy.*

Probably the most cited Biblical passage dealing with faith is from the eleventh chapter of the Letter to the Hebrews, which begins with the eloquent sentence: "Faith is the assurance of things hoped for, the conviction of things not seen." There then follows a long list of Biblical characters who acted out of faith, and the Christian community to which the letter is addressed is urged to follow their example. A little later in the chapter it is said that "whoever would draw near to God must believe that he exists and that he rewards those who seek him," yet for most if not all the characters listed – such as Noah, Abraham, and Moses – the question was not whether God exists, but rather whether to have faith in what God told them to do. That is, God spoke to them, and their faith was a response to this divine address. With all due respect for this New Testament text, one must regretfully conclude that it is not terribly helpful to the contemporary individual who hovers between belief and unbelief (and, insofar as such individuals existed in earlier times, the text would not be very helpful to them either) – quite apart from the tension that exists between "faith" on the one hand and two other nouns in the text, namely "assurance" and "conviction": If I'm convinced, why do I need to have faith? Perhaps the author of the text intended this tension, as expressing a central paradox of faith. But this paradox can only be appreciated from within the act of faith; it is not helpful to anyone who is still contemplating the act, who asks whether one should have faith in the first place.

But that is the question that is being discussed here. It is the question of all those who find themselves in a situation where God has *not* spoken – or, if it seems that He may have spoken, one cannot really be sure about this. Put differently, the problem for faith in this situation is the profound fact of *God's silence*. I think that this silence ought to be taken with utmost seriousness, in which case the question of faith must be addressed in ways other than the one suggested by the aforementioned text.

There could be many starting points for what one might perhaps call an argument from silence. I choose a very modern author, Simone Weil (1909–43), the idiosyncratic French philosopher whom Leslie Fiedler, an American admirer of hers, aptly described as a "saint in an age of alienation": "At a time like the present, incredulity may be equivalent to the dark night of Saint John of the Cross if the unbeliever loves God, if he is like the child who does not know whether there is bread anywhere, but who cries out because he is hungry" (Simone Weil, *Waiting for God*, p. 211f). And a little earlier she writes: "The danger is not lest the soul should doubt whether there is any bread, but lest, by a lie, it should persuade itself that it is not hungry. It can only persuade itself of this by lying, for the reality of its hunger is not a belief, it is a certainty."

Perhaps only a French philosopher could have written these lines! What we have here is a sort of Cartesian reduction to certainty from within the situation of unbelief, which is the silence in which God has not spoken. Only after this reduction has taken place, Weil suggests, can a journey of faith begin. Let me quickly say that to accept Weil's starting point need not imply agreement with her description of the rest of the journey (a point to be taken up presently). But the starting point is helpful, at least for those who also find themselves in an "age of alienation."

Looking at Simone Weil's biography, one can easily see why Leslie Fiedler described her as he did. Offspring of an agnostic Jewish bourgeois family, she finished secondary school at age fifteen, was a brilliant graduate of the elite Ecole Normale Supérieure, and became a teacher of philosophy. She reflected the *Zeitgeist* to the extent of rebelling against her bourgeois background and defining herself as some sort of socialist, but even in this rebellion she took the most radical path possible. To be in solidarity with the working class, she started work in a factory, something she was singularly unsuited for. She went to Spain to join the Republican army during the Civil War, but had barely arrived there when she fell into a boiling cooking pot and had to be sent back to France. When the Germans occupied the north of France she became a refugee in the south, and worked on the farm belonging to her protector, evincing similar ineptitude. It was during this period that she became converted to Catholicism, but she refused to be baptized – not because of any loyalty to Judaism (which she never understood or was interested in understanding), but because she was offended by the in-group coziness of the Catholic community and felt that she had to remain in solidarity with all the outsiders, particularly all those who could not believe. She subsequently escaped to England, where she had a job with the Free French government set up there. She put herself on a diet corresponding, she thought, to the food ration available in occupied France, an act which probably contributed to her final illness. She died at the age of 34.

Awkward, stubborn, in perennial poor health, Simone Weil appears to us as a Quixotic figure, in some ways a modern incarnation of a classical Christian type, that of the holy fool. Perhaps it is just for this reason that she is paradigmatic of a thoroughly modern mind confronting faith – that is, confronting the silence of God. As the title of one collection of her writings aptly summarizes it, her basic stance was one of "waiting for God" – as she put it in a Greek phrase, *en hypomene* – "in patience" (the Greek word is stronger). It is in this stance that she finally claimed to have attained a kind of certainty. In other words, she did not stop at the minimal certainty pointed to in what I have called her Cartesian reduction. It seems to me, though, that Weil's starting point is also helpful for those who cannot replicate her entire journey.

Weil reduces the question of God to the point where the only indication of His presence is my suffering from His absence. It is, as it were, a point of double silence: The silence of God who does not speak, and my own silence in the face of His. Language cannot express either silence; both silences are speechless. The reference to John of the Cross shows that Weil was well aware of the fact that she was placing herself in a long tradition of Christian spirituality, most of it mystical in character – the so-called apophatic tradition (literally, the speechless tradition), which in turn is related to the mode of theologizing known as the *via negativa*. The key proposition here is that God cannot be apprehended through human language or conceptual thought.

At the beginnings of this tradition stands a rather mysterious figure, that of the so-called Pseudo-Dionysius, also known as Dionysius the Areopagite. An author writing in Greek, probably in Syria around the year 500 CE, he took on the name of an individual reported in the New Testament as having been converted by the Apostle Paul in Athens (a common practice in classical antiquity, not meant to deceive but to indicate an identification with a tradition). Despite the uncertainties of his historical location and the highly controversial character of his thought (he was clearly influenced by Neo-Platonism and his Christian orthodoxy has been quite suspect), Dionysius has had an immense influence over centuries of Christian history. The opening lines of his *Mystical Theology* give a good idea of why he has been called the father of the apophatic tradition:

> For this I pray; and Timothy, my friend, my advice to you as you look for a sight of the mysterious things, is to leave behind you everything perceived and understood, all that is not and all that is, and, with your understanding laid aside, to strive upward as much as you can toward union with him who is beyond all being and knowledge. (Colm Luibheid, trans., *Pseudo-Dionysius*, p. 135)

Compare this with a text almost a millennium later, from the fourteenth-century anonymous Middle English author of *The Cloud of Unknowing*:

> Though we cannot know him we can love him. By love he may be touched and embraced, never by thought . . . Let your loving desire, gracious and devout, step bravely and joyfully beyond it and reach out to pierce the darkness above. Yes, beat upon that thick *cloud of unknowing* with the dart of your loving desire and do not cease come what may. (William Johnston, ed., *The Cloud of Unknowing*, p. 54f)

John of the Cross, the sixteenth-century Spanish mystic whom Weil refers to, stands in the same tradition with his famous metaphor of the "dark night of the soul." And indeed the same themes can be found in mystical traditions outside Christianity. There is the near-universal proposition that ultimate reality cannot be grasped by language or in concepts. The Upanishads (arguably the most splendid texts of classical Hinduism) expressed this in the formula *neti, neti* – "not this, not this" (that is, the ultimate reality is not this, nor that), and the same idea probably reached its most sophisticated expression in the Madhyamika philosophy of Mahayana Buddhism. Equally widespread is the proposition that the mystical journey begins in a darkness in which all being, including the being of the self, is abandoned. It finds different formulations in Jewish and Muslim mysticism, as well as in the great mystical schools of Hinduism, Buddhism, and Taoism. But if the journey begins in silent darkness, it also ends in another kind of speechlessness, when the self has attained union with the ultimate. Speech, language, and conceptual thought are, so to speak, intermediate stations on the journey between God's absence and His overpowering presence. I think it is correct to place Simone Weil, despite her Catholic beliefs, into this context of trans-cultural mysticism.

I have several difficulties with this. First of all, given the consensus on these themes in what may be called a mystical internationale, what remains here of the distinctive Biblical God? It is no wonder that so many of the great mystics in the monotheistic traditions – Judaism and Islam as well as Christianity – were tottering on the outer boundaries of these traditions (to the recurring dismay of the guardians of orthodoxy). More important, this mystical journey may begin in uncertainty, but it ends in certainty: But what if the uncertainty persists? And equally important, a crucial part of the journey is the abandonment of self: But what if one refuses to abandon it? The discovery of the autonomous self (which is synonymous with the discovery of freedom) is arguably the greatest achievement of Western civilization, from its twin roots in ancient Israel and ancient Greece. Is that discovery to be reclassified as a gigantic mistake? But if the human self is the most precious reality in the world, is the ultimate reality to be understood as somehow less than that? If there is any claim to moral achievement in Western history, it is in the recognition of the infinite value of every human being: Can I conceive of a God who negates this value? I think not.

For these reasons, then, I would rather not follow Weil to the end-point of her thinking. I prefer to stay, at least for now, at the point to which she came with her aforementioned reduction, and to ask how one can proceed from there without embarking on the great mystical journey. I will use the first person singular – not with any autobiographical or con-fessional intent, but in order to make the account graphically clear.

I confront God's silence, I am determined to *bear* that silence, I refrain from trying to deny its reality by prematurely speaking into it. I too remain silent, and I wait – *en hypomene*. At the same time, I acknowedge that I find God's silence intolerable, even offensive. I refuse to deny *either* God's silence or my hunger for the silence to be broken. And then I find myself compelled to address – to speak into – that silence nevertheless. This, I suppose, could be called the primeval form of prayer – addressing the silent God, from whose absence I suffer. I'm not sure of the chronol-ogy of these two postures – the posture of my being silent and the posture of breaking my silence; perhaps this is a sequence that repeats itself, or perhaps, paradoxically, the two postures are simultaneous.

And then I can begin to reflect, and I decide to reflect by looking at human reality without, for the moment, making any religious assumptions – that is, I will reflect *etsi Deus non daretur*, "as if God were not given." I then find that prayer, in one form or another, is a universal human phenomenon. Possibly the most comprehensive study of prayer is the great work with that title by Friedrich Heiler (*Das Gebet*). One can read it with a mounting sense of depression. Over the ages human beings have spoken into the silence – in simple words, in elaborate ceremonies, chanting, singing, dancing, offering sacrifices, beating drums, and playing on every sort of musical instrument – an endless cacophony of yearning sound. Could it be that there never was an answer? Weil is right: There is no way of denying the hunger. Could it be that this hunger is all there is?

Weil and all the mystics agree that one can proceed from such uncertain prayer to a blissful sense of certainty. Let it be stipulated that this progression has been plausible to some individuals (perhaps those whom Max Weber called the "religious virtuosi"). Most human beings have not been so lucky, and, within the present argument, I must place myself in that underprivileged company. Perhaps, at some point in my life, I too might attain certainty. In the meantime, if I am honest, I must acknowledge my uncertainty. I must cultivate what perhaps might be called an "interim spirituality." This further implies that I must reject the various alleged certainties that are on offer in my social situation, although, because of my hunger, they are very tempting.

In the situation in which we find ourselves in the modern world there is a multitude of such offers, not all of them religious. In the Christian context, there are three principal offers of certainty – by way of the institutional Church, of the Bible, and of spiritual experience. I am promised certainty if I throw myself into the welcoming arms of the Church. In principle, this could be any church, though it is the Roman Catholic Church that makes this offer in the most magnificent manner: The infallible Church provides me with an invulnerable certainty. Most Protestants do not think of their churches in this way. The great Protestant offer of certainty is by way of an inerrant Bible: If I cling to the text, my own spirituality can attain a sort of inerrancy. And cutting across all confessional boundaries is the offer of certainty by means of an inner experience – from the great ecstasies of the mystics to the conversion experiences of "born again" Protestantism (one may think here of the rich hymnody of the Methodist tradition and of American revivalism – "I know that my redeemer liveth") to the ecstasies of Pentecostalism, which is arguably the most dynamic religious movement in the world today. It seems to me that each of these alleged "methods" toward certainty, while they could always be questioned, have been particularly put in question by modern critical thought – the Church by both history and the social sciences, the Bible by modern critical scholarship, and subjective ecstasies of all kinds by the findings of psychology: The Church is demonstrably fallible, the Bible is full of errors, and my ecstasies are highly vulnerable to psychological inquiry. If I am to have faith, that faith must not be based on what, if I am honest, I am constrained to call false or at least doubtful certainties. I think that this proposition touches on the deepest level of what the Reformers meant by saying that we are saved by faith alone – *sola fide*. Be this as it may, as I contemplate the act of faith, I do so while I still wait for God to break His silence.

However, even if God has not spoken to me in the way in which, supposedly, he spoke to Abraham or Moses, I can find in human reality certain intimations of his speech, signals (unclear though they are) of His hidden presence. These signals are not "proofs," but they are indications that, *if* I have faith, I can relate that faith to a number of powerful human realities. I have previously mentioned the experience of joy – that joy, mightily expressed in Beethoven's Ninth Symphony, which seeks eternity. There are other signals – the human propensity to order, which appears to correlate with an order in the universe beyond humankind (a man locked up in an attic can do mathematics and, as he looks out from his attic, he finds that the universe is mathematically ordered), the immensely suggestive experiences of play and humor (especially the experience of the comic as a metaphor of redemption), the irrepressible human propensity to hope (which implies a rejection of the finality of death), the certainty of some moral judgments (which imply a moral order beyond the relativities of human history), and, last but not least, the experiences of beauty (I would propose that the landscape of, say, Lake Como is an argument for the existence of God). I have long argued that one could construct an "inductive theology" that would begin with an analysis of these "signals of transcendence" (which could also be called glimpses of the presence of God in human reality). But that is another story.

These considerations do not lead to the temple of faith in a direct, incontrovertible manner. But they place me in a sort of antechamber of that temple. It is in that antechamber that I confront the traditions that claim to be revelatory of God, including that tradition that spans Sinai and Calvary. Augustine had an interesting formulation in this connection: *Nullus quippe credit aliquid, nisi prius cogitaverit esse credendum* – "no one indeed believes anything, unless he previously knew it to be believable." In other words, there is a movement from the *credendum* to a *credo* – reflection as an antecedent of the act of faith. Barring direct experiences such as the mystics rightly or wrongly claim, this *credo* comes out of my response to a particular story that is communicated to me by other human beings, some living, some long dead. The story comes to me as a sort of rumor of God. I hear the story and, in an act of faith, I respond to it by saying "yes!"

As far as Christian faith is concerned, this story comes to me through the tradition that begins in ancient Israel, a tradition I may encounter by reading the relevant texts or by hearing it through the spoken words of preachers or other interlocutors. I will say "yes!" to it insofar as it connects with the rest of my experience of reality, though that connection will never be beyond any possible doubt. Eric Voegelin, in *Order and History*, his work on the philosophy of history, made the rather strange statement that Israel discovered God. Looked at in empirical terms, that is a startling but accurate statement. In the perspective of faith, however, it is evident that this discovery could not have occurred unless God had allowed Himself to be so discovered. This implies that God chose to reveal Himself, not everywhere, but in particular places and at particular times. One can then say, however hesitantly, that God's silence has not been absolute.

Chapter Two

"... in God"

When the Apostles' Creed affirms belief "in God," of course, it has a very specific divinity in mind – in classical Christian diction, "the God of Abraham, Isaac, and Jacob, the Father of our Lord Jesus Christ." That was by no means to be taken for granted in those early days of Christian history when, probably in the cosmopolitan milieu of Rome, the Creed was first formulated. Then as now, a host of other gods are on offer in the religious marketplace. The question, then as now, is quite simple:

How does this God relate to all these other gods, and why should we believe in Him over against all the others?

Christianity emerged in a situation, at the height of the Roman empire, which was remarkably similar in its religious pluralism to our situation today, at least in the large cities of the empire. Then as now, belief in the God of the Biblical tradition could not be taken for granted (by contrast to some later periods of Christian history, when the Church had established a more of less efficient monopoly, so that its faith had acquired a taken-for-granted quality). Arguably, though, religious pluralism today is unique in both its intensity and its extensiveness. There is nothing mysterious about this. It is the result of all the powerful forces of modernity – urbanization and migration, throwing people with the most diverse backgrounds into close proximity with each other, together with mass literacy and the media of mass communication, which allows access to the beliefs and values of people virtually everywhere. Thus every major bookstore in Europe and America, and increasingly elsewhere, contains inexpensive books giving reasonably reliable information about the major religious traditions of human history. And the electronic media, capped by the Internet, provide even easier access to every conceivable religious phenomenon. This situation has thrown down a serious challenge to every institution with an absolute truth claim. It also presents both a great opportunity and serious difficulties to reflective individuals struggling to locate themselves in this emporium of religious possibilities. An author describing the explosion of new religious movements in Japan in the wake of World War II called it "the rush hour of the gods." This phrase can serve to describe the present religious situation, not only in Japan but in the countries that used to be thought of as belonging to "Christian civilization."

Both Protestant and Catholic theologians have paid increasing attention in recent years to this challenge, and ecclesiastical bodies (including the World Council of Churches and the Vatican) have set up agencies to engage in a sustained dialogue with other religious traditions. By now there is a large literature dealing with this issue, and it cannot be the purpose here to give an overview of this literature. It has become conventional to distinguish between three major theological approaches to the issue, labeled (not too felicitously) "pluralist," "exclusivist," and "inclusivist." The "pluralists" have gone furthest in renouncing Christian claims to absolute truth; the "exclusivists" continue to assert these claims in more or less feisty tones; the "inclusivists" (surprise!) take an in-between position, insisting on the unique character of Christian faith but remaining open to the truth claims of other traditions. Let me say right off that, if pushed to the wall, I must place myself with the "inclusivists," though I don't like the label (quite apart from its sounding like the political rhetoric of American liberalism, it suggests that nothing at all is to be excluded and that is a recipe for terminal mushiness). But before I spell out what I would regard as a reasonable version of "inclusiveness," it would be useful to take a closer look at the "pluralists," since they represent the most radical but also the most intellectually stimulating response to the multiplicity of religious options available today.

Probably the most prominent representative of the "pluralist" school is the British theologian John Hick, who, coming out of a Protestant background, has worked out in an impressive number of publications a "theology of religions" which leaves every kind of Christian orthodoxy far behind. Hick calls for a "Copernican revolution" in theology: We must accept, he proposes, that our own tradition is not the center around which all reality revolves; rather we must see the center as being the ultimate reality itself, fully perceived by no single tradition, though the traditions revolve around this center, each providing a specific though limited vision of the center. We must recognize that (as the title of one of his books has it) "God has many names." All religious traditions affirm a transcendent and benign reality. That is their common core, but they approach it in very different ways. For Christians this approach is by way of Jesus, though Hick insists that the incarnation is a myth and that the trinitarian doctrine that has expressed it theologically must be abandoned (except perhaps as a heuristic tool). Christian faith, then, must be resolutely non-absolutist.

To make these points, Hick makes use in an interesting way of a concept derived from Buddhist thought – that of *upaya*. The Sanskrit term is usually translated as "skilfull means," an awkward phrase. The intention, though, is quite clear: An *upaya* is an aid, be it an experience or a conceptual tool, which is helpful on the path toward ultimate reality. It is, as it were, a crutch for those who are not yet very advanced on this path; as such, it can be freely left behind when one has acquired the skill necessary for moving on further. I don't want to be unfair to Hick, but he seems to say that the entire Biblical tradition, all of Judaism and Christianity, should be understood as an *upaya* – useful to those who, through an accident of birth, have become accustomed to this tradition, but by no means to be taken as a definitive affirmation of truth. Hick himself confesses that he could not imagine himself as ever giving up his particular Christian *upaya* – a surprising statement from someone who has spent many years in trying to enter into the universe of discourse of non-Christian traditions. Hundreds of thousands of Western converts to Buddhism, not to mention converts to Christianity and just about every other faith, suggest that the accident of birth is not as compelling as Hick makes it out to be. Even the central Biblical affirmation that God is a personal being, a being who speaks and acts, is not definitive in Hick's view: He recognizes the sharp divergence among religious traditions on the question of whether the ultimate reality is to be understood in personal or impersonal terms, but that question too should be, as he says, "shelved."

Hick is somewhat uneasy about what appears to be an equal acceptance of any and every expression of human religiosity. He would not like to bestow the status of *upaya* to, say, the Mesoamerican cults of human sacrifice. He then proposes what is essentially a moral test: Religious traditions are more or less "true" to the extent that they help human beings to overcome self-centeredness and to become open to love others. Thus he proposes that the major traditions are "more or less equally fruitful in saintliness, producing extraordinary men and women whose spirit and lives make God more real to the rest of us" (*Disputed Questions*, p. 155).

What is wrong with this argument?

The metaphor of the "Copernican revolution" in our thinking about religion is immediately appealing. It implies a rejection of fanaticism and of all parochial views of the world, and no one would want to quarrel with this attitude. However, what is wrong is the notion of truth that is also implied in Hick's approach. There appears to be the assumption that just about any "planet" can serve as a platform from which to contemplate the "sun" of the ultimate reality (with the possible exception of Aztec sacrificial altars). But what if, to stay within Hick's metaphor, some of the "planets" are not facing the "sun" at all? What if they are looking the other way and mistakenly identifying the "sun" with a passing meteor? Put simply, Hick's approach is too "inclusive" and, in this, it relativizes the conception of truth to the point where it becomes meaningless. He clearly sees this problem and for this reason introduces a criterion for distinguishing "true" from "untrue" religion – the criterion of whether a tradition induces its adherents to cultivate selflessness and altruism. But this is a purely moral criterion, which reduces the notion of "truth" to a sort of social utilitarianism. The historical record shows that some of the greatest religious figures engaged in morally dubious behavior – some were downright monstrous – while agnostics and atheists have been morally admirable. To see the weakness of Hick's criterion, all one has to do is to transfer it from religion to, say, physics: Is one to accept or reject a discovery in physics on the basis of a physicist's moral qualities? Does the theory of relativity depend on Einstein's having been a nice man? If religion has anything to do with *reality* – a reality that transcends the human world, as Hick strongly insists – then the test of its being true does not depend on the "saintliness" of its representatives.

Perhaps the trouble here comes from the experience described by Hick in an autobiographical piece in which he describes how he moved to his present position from a narrow Evangelical Protestantism. It was the experience of coming into contact with all varieties of non-Christians in an increasingly pluralistic Britain – Muslims, Hindus, Sikhs, and so on. Many of them were morally admirable people, and so Hick found it increasingly impossible to view them as heathen, existing in some sort of metaphysical darkness. He felt compelled to say *yes* to the traditions to which they adhered. Again, no one would want to quarrel with the inter-religious tolerance and respect that often comes from such encounters. It is morally much to be recommended. But it is *not* a criterion of truth. I would argue that in inter-religious dialogue it is just as important to know when to say *no* as when to say *yes* – and it is possible to say *no* without for a moment giving up respect for the interlocutor to whom one is saying it.

"Exclusivism" has become a relatively rare stance, at least in academically respectable circles in Western countries, though it continues vigorously among academically unaccredited conservative Protestants and Catholics. In twentieth-century theology the individual most often cited in support of this stance is Karl Barth, though the relevant citations come mostly from his earlier period – he mellowed considerably in his later

years. Occasionally, though, there are theologians who take an "exclusivist" position, though they will usually give at least a nod in the direction of inclusivity. A good example in recent years is Carl Braaten, a
Lutheran theologian, who in 1992 published a book with the program-
matic title *No Other Gospel! – Christianity among the World's Religions.*
Braaten is certainly no fanatic, but the titles of a sequence of his chapters give a good idea where he stands: "Absoluteness is a Predicate of
God's Kingdom"; "Christ Alone is the Heart of the Church's Message",
and – here comes the nod toward inclusivity – "Christ is God's Final, not
the Only, Revelation." (This last phrasing is strongly reminiscent of the
classical Muslim position on other religious traditions: They too had their
prophets, but the Quran is the "seal of prophecy.")

Let me confess that I have a lot of sympathy for this type of robust
assertiveness. It is more appealing than the fixed smile of ecumenical
politeness. But, and here I must agree with Hick, this assertiveness
becomes progressively implausible as one seriously encounters the traditions of others – not because their representatives are nice people, but
because one is impressed by the insights into reality which these traditions embody. It also becomes implausible as one comes to understand
the empirical conditions under which one's own tradition was formed.
This latter challenge to religious absoluteness is the massive consequence
of modern historical scholarship (of which more in a moment).

The theologians most often cited in support of an "inclusivist" position
are the Protestant Paul Tillich and the Catholic Karl Rahner. I would not
identify myself fully with the approach of either one: I have great difficulty accepting Tillich's notion of God as the "ground of being," and
Rahner's "inclusion" of other traditions by calling their adherents
"anonymous Christians" strikes me as being patronizing (though I'm sure
that this was not Rahner's intention). I would, though, identify with the
spirit in which these positions were constructed. Be this as it may, my
purpose here is not to engage in detailed exegeses of this or that theologian. I will presently outline my own understanding of inclusivity. Before
I do that, I want to emphasize that the issue of other truth claims is far
from new in the history of Christian thought, however pressing the issue
has become in the pluralistic situation of contemporary religion.

A great drama in intellectual history took place in the nineteenth
century, with a veritable explosion of historical scholarship on the origins
and development of religious traditions. At the core of this drama was
Biblical scholarship, which made it more and more difficult to look upon
the Biblical texts in the terms of Christian and Jewish orthodoxy. Rather,
the immense contingencies under which these texts were produced
became very clear. This is all the more impressive when one reflects upon
the fact that much of this scholarship came out of Protestant theological

faculties, especially in Germany. It was a unique event in the history of religion, with scholars turning all the tools of critical inquiry on the sacred texts of their own tradition – an act of impressive intellectual courage. The inevitable result of these endeavors was to relativize the authority of these texts. This was especially troubling to Protestants, who had made the Bible the sole authority for Christian belief and life (the Reformation principle of *sola Scriptura*). Catholics were more troubled by what historical scholarship discovered about the origins of ecclesiastical institutions.

Ernst Troeltsch was a German Protestant theologian for whom this challenge (he called it that of "historicism") was at the center of his work. In 1901 he published a very influential work with the telling title *The Absoluteness of Christianity and the History of Religions* (an English version was published in 1972). Troeltsch devoted himself to other topics (notably the work best known in the English-speaking world, *The Social Teachings of the Christian Churches*), but he always returned again to the issue discussed in *Absoluteness*. Just before his death in 1923 he wrote a lecture (it was to be delivered in Oxford and was published posthumously) under the title "The Place of Christianity among the World Religions," in which he somewhat modified his view of the distinctiveness of Christianity.

Troeltsch lucidly summed up the question posed by "historicism": "How can we pass beyond the diversity with which history presents us to norms for our faith and for our judgments about life?" (1972 translation of *Absoluteness*, p. 61.) His answer to the question was highly sophisticated, but it came down to a key proposition: Christianity was unique as a "personalistic religion" – that is, as a religion that had at its core a view of God as person and that consequently gave ultimate validity to the personhood of human beings. As he put it: Christianity gives "the only depiction of the higher world as infinitely valuable personal life that conditions and shapes all else" (p. 112). It should be observed that Troeltsch was aware that the same could be said about Judaism and Islam; he claimed Christianity as superior to them for reasons that are not convincing but that need not concern us here. What I find most important in his approach is, precisely, the insight that the Biblical tradition emphatically validates the infinite worth and dignity of the human person. Needless to say, this insight has had immense moral consequences, but it is not only a matter of morality. Rather, it is an insight into the relation between the human condition and the ultimate constitution of reality. It was summed up by Luther in his statement that God addresses man and that man exists as long as God continues to address him. In other words, there is an ontological antiphony between the personhood of God and the personhood of human beings. And I think that Troeltsch was correct in seeing *this* as a crucially distinctive quality in Biblical religion.

However, he also proposed that this core insight cannot be held immune to the relativities of history: "Faith may regard Christianity, therefore, as a heightening of the religious standard in terms of which the inner life of man will continue to exist. But we cannot and must not regard it as an absolute, perfect, immutable truth . . . The absolute lies beyond history and is a truth that in many respects remains veiled" (p. 115). I suppose that one could call Troeltsch's position a sort of "relative absoluteness" – an oxymoron which, nevertheless, expresses his nuanced view of the matter. I find this position eminently plausible, even if, almost a century later, Troeltsch's language and conceptual apparatus would need some modifications (for example, in his rather cavalier treatment of the other two great monotheistic traditions).

But the problem of how to relate the God of the Biblical tradition to all the other gods is much older than the troubles of modern theology. It recurs in both the Hebrew Bible and the New Testament. It preoccupied the early apologists for Christianity. I will mention only one of those, indeed one of the earliest – Justin Martyr, who wrote in Greek in the second century CE. His question, *au fond*, was how the truth of Socrates could be reconciled with the truth of the Gospel. To answer this question he coined the suggestive concept of the *Logos spermatikos* – loosely translatable as the Logos who sows His seeds. Already the Gospel of John, in its preamble, made the immense jump of appropriating for the Christian faith the Stoic idea of the Logos, the universal reason upon which the world is based, identifying it with the cosmic Christ. One could say that, in doing this, the author of the Gospel incorporated not only Greek philosophy but the entire world of Greek religion – all the gods were, so to speak, sucked into the gigantic work of redemption centered in Christ. This Logos has been present from the beginning of creation and, while He was revealed most fully to Israel and in Jesus, there is no corner of reality in which He is not present and has always been present. For Justin the "seeds" of this Logos are also "seeds" of truth. Thus, by way of the *Logos spermatikos* Socrates in some way knew Christ or, more precisely, participated in the truth of Christ. It is not implausible to extend this metaphor to "include" all the manifold worlds of human religion.

But be all this as it may, there still remains the basic question:

If our situation forces us to choose between the gods, since no god can any longer be taken for granted, why should we choose the Biblical God?

The word "choose" will grate on the ears of believers. Within the perspective of faith it is *God* who chose *us*, and our choice is a feeble response to His. But in this argument we are not yet in the perspective of faith; we are still asking how and why we should enter this perspective. This replicates the position outlined in the preceding chapter. It is the position of all those to whom no direct access to transcendent reality has been given – that is, those to whom God has not spoken directly. To proceed as if He had (which is the procedure implied by most advocates of orthodox or neo-orthodox schools of religion) is to base one's religious existence on a lie. It seems plausible to propose that, if God exists, He would not want us to lie.

The sacred scriptures of the three great monotheistic traditions are full of stories in which God speaks directly to human individuals. It is safe to assume that, for these individuals, the question of why they should choose this God would have been an absurd one. They *knew*, with overwhelming certainty, that *God* had chosen *them*. Thus we must assume that there was no doubt in the mind of Moses as he heard the voice coming out of the burning bush, of Paul as Christ stopped him on the road to Damascus, or of Muhammad as the angel spoke to him on Mount Hira. There is no way in which historical scholarship can ascertain "what really happened" on these momentous occasions; the historian can only record their enormous consequences.

The rest of us – the metaphysically underprivileged, as it were – can stand in awe of these apparent manifestations of divine presence. But we must also acknowledge that God has not spoken to us in such a direct manner. His address to us, if that is what it is, comes to us in a much more indirect manner. It is always *mediated*. It is mediated through this or that experience (the sort that I have subsumed under the heading of signals of transcendence), and most importantly it is mediated through encounters with the scriptures and with the institution that transmits the tradition. It is the latter mediations which give meaning to our own experience. For example, I stand in wonder as I look upon a particularly beautiful landscape and say to myself, in the words of a well-known Protestant hymn, "the hand that made thee is divine." But it is unlikely that I would say this if I had not previously encountered the idea of creation in the Bible or in the worship of the church. What happens then is that a *nexus* comes about between my own experience and the tradition.

I'm not sure that "nexus" is the best term to use here. But it tries to describe what I consider to be a very important step in the development of faith. It comes close to what Paul Tillich called "correlation," but that term suggests a rather cerebral process, and that would be misleading in the present argument. It also comes close to what Max Weber called "elective affinity" (using the term *Wahlverwandschaft*, which comes originally from Goethe, who meant by it an emotional affinity between individuals), but that is too broad a concept for what I have in mind. Perhaps

I can put it this way: The nexus comes about when I relate the tradition to my own experience and am compelled to say, *"yes, yes* – this fits!"

Now I must assure the reader: I'm not handing back my credentials as a sociologist. I'm well aware of the relativities of time and space, of my location in a particular history and a particular society. Thus my nexus with the Biblical tradition would probably not occur if I were, say, a Tibetan monk looking upon this impressive landscape. In that case, this or that Buddhist interpretation would come to mind, and it would have nothing to do with the idea of creation. However, as I have proposed before, one should not exaggerate the irresistibility of the accident of birth. Many Christians have become Buddhists, and vice versa. In the contemporary situation of widespread religious diversity, Buddhism is *available* to Christians or Jews in the Western world as it has never been before; conversion to Buddhism is an empirically real possibility, and with this conversion a very different response to the beautiful landscape becomes an option (it might, for example, be seen as a temptation to desist from the renunciation that leads to enlightenment). But in any case genuine insights are not necessarily invalidated by placing them in a historical or social context. We can say confidently that Einstein would not have revolutionized modern physics if he had been born as a contemporary of the Buddha or as a Tibetan peasant. This proposition, though, does not invalidate Einstein's contributions to physics.

All these references to choices may suggest the idea that there is a near-infinite range of such choices. That is not the case. A contemporary American Christian or Jew may choose to become a Buddhist, may even choose to become a Tibetan monk (if only in California), but is very unlikely to choose adherence to the bloody gods of ancient Mesoamerica. If one goes back far enough in the religious history of every human culture, one comes upon an interesting fact – that everywhere there is a remarkably similar substratum of experiences and ideas that I would call the mythic matrix. I'll come to that in a moment. However, in terms of what I would call intellectually serious religious options, there are two pivotal choices – between two mighty streams of religious development, one coming out of south Asia, the other out of west Asia. One may use shorthand terms for this: The two pivots are Benares and Jerusalem – the holiest city of Hinduism, on the outskirts of which the Buddha preached his first sermon, and the city where the Jewish temple stood, where Jesus died and was resurrected, and from which Muhammad ascended to heaven. I deliberately use here the language of Jewish, Christian, and Muslim faith, because seen from the vantage point of Benares these three traditions are so close to each other that they appear as one single counter-option. To say this is in no way to overlook the important differences between these three west Asian traditions, and it will be necessary to return to these at some point. For the rest of this chapter, though, the fact that I stand in the Christian tradition is more or less irrelevant; I think that a Jew or a Muslim could identify with my argument without much strain. The three traditions embody what Richard Niebuhr aptly called "radical monotheism," and as such share a common perspective on the nature of God, on the world as His creation, of history as an arena of His actions, and, last but not least, on the human condition and the nature of the self. And in all of this they are highly distinctive in comparison with the great traditions which originated on the Indian subcontinent.

Both streams of religion emerged out of the mythic matrix in what Eric Voegelin, in his great and finally incomplete attempt to write a comprehensive philosophy of history, called "leaps in being." The mythic matrix perceives reality as a unified whole. The boundaries are fluid and permeable between what we would call the natural and the supernatural, between human beings and the spirit world, between human beings and animals. In this mythic reality the human individual experiences and understands himself as being part of the cosmic whole. Religious rituals are designed to restore the connection with this cosmic harmony whenever it is disturbed. It would be a mistake to see this worldview as being left behind once and for all. It is curiously replicated in the development of children – every child lives in a mythic world before being socialized into what we now consider reality – and it also resurfaces in certain forms of psychosis. But it is also available to adults with perfectly respectable psychiatric profiles. Throughout history, in all cultures, the mythic matrix has again and again reasserted itself, typically to the great annoyance of the guardians of the official definitions of reality. In the contemporary Western world, much of what has come to be called New Age spirituality is such a resurgence of the mythic matrix. Its attractiveness lies, precisely, in the aforementioned perception of human existence as part of a sheltering cosmic harmony, in which all tensions and contradictions are resolved.

One could also call the mythic matrix a "polytheistic" view of reality, but this term is slightly misleading because the experience of a cosmic whole antedated the arrival of the gods. Still, the mythic matrix was well caught in the exclamation of the early Greek philosopher Thales of Miletus – "The world is full of gods!" Against this, the very heart of the west Asian religious experience is in the passionate assertion that "God is one!" In the early stages of that experience (still traceable in the oldest layers of the Hebrew Bible) the existence of other gods was not denied outright, but the one God, who had revealed Himself to Israel, allowed no competition from them and was infinitely more powerful. Eventually the very existence of all other gods was denied. The oneness of God is affirmed in the basic Jewish confession of faith, the Shema – "Hear, oh Israel, the Lord is our God, the Lord is one." Christianity did not recant this faith, and a central concern of the christological controversies in the early Church was to ensure that the affirmation of Christ's divinity not be understood as undermining the monotheism of the Jewish tradition: Whatever else it may be, the doctrine of the trinity does *not* propose the existence of three gods. Islam, arguably more singlemindedly than the other two monotheistic traditions, insists on the oneness of God and repudiates any idea that might throw doubt on it.

What is the nexus here? It seems to me that it emerges from two experiences. One is the result of perceiving the world as reflecting a tremendous creative intelligence, which can only be ascribed to a single creator. The other is the result of detecting the same voice as it comes to me through the tradition, a voice that can only come from one single source. Needless to emphasize, this nexus does not have the quality of a "proof" – no nexus does – but it mediates between my experience of reality and what the tradition says about it. On the other hand, to affirm the oneness of God – be it in Jewish, Christian, or Muslim terms – does not necessarily lead to the proposition that all the experiences and ideas associated with the mythic matrix are pure illusions. The one God who created the world is free to manifest Himself in any part of His creation, and the mythic consciousness may therefore contain valid perceptions of His presence. Once more, the idea of the *Logos spermatikos* could be useful in what one might call a theology of the mythic matrix. Perhaps luckily, this cannot be a task for this book.

As the monotheistic traditions confront what I have called the Benares option, they will above all encounter the mighty streams of Hinduism and Buddhism (the latter incomprehensible without the background of the former). This is by no means to disparage the other great traditions of eastern Asia, notably Confucianism, Taoism, and Shinto, as well as the primal folk religions that underlie all of them. But I don't think that these raise questions for Jerusalem that are not raised, mostly in a more interesting way, by Hinduism and Buddhism. And a key question is the following:

Why should one conceive of God as a person?

Conceptions of the ultimate reality as a personal God and as an impersonal entity are to be found in all religious traditions. But it is a fair generalization that the traditions pivoted on Jerusalem greatly favor the former, those pivoted in Benares the latter. Is God a person, who therefore speaks and can be addressed in personal terms? Or is the divine a reality beyond all personhood, neither speaking nor reachable by human speech? This is a very fundamental question, and it cannot be "shelved," as John Hick suggests. Nor is it helpful to say (as some religious thinkers have said) that He, or It, is both or is neither. Of course the ultimate reality cannot be captured in humanly constructed categories such as "personal" or "impersonal," but I want to know whether this reality is in any way capable of interacting with me in a way that does not negate my own personhood (in which, understandably, I have a considerable stake).

If God is a person, I can assume that He can address me and that in turn I can address Him. An impersonal ultimate reality is beyond any such "I/thou" relationship (as Martin Buber called it); it can only be reached if I leave behind all vestiges of my empirical self, and this is precisely what all religious teachers of this viewpoint (notably many of the great mystics) have strongly advocated. This viewpoint negates what I have earlier described as the primordial religious gesture, that of *prayer*. If the ultimate reality is impersonal, I can try to reach it through meditation, through all sorts of spiritual and even physical exercises, but it makes no sense *to pray* to It. The urge to pray is so powerful that it can be found in all traditions, including those whose most sophisticated representatives taught that the ultimate reality is impersonal. Thus Vedanta, arguably the most sophisticated form of Hinduism, conceived of the ultimate reality as impersonal, but masses of ordinary Hindus have continued to pray to this or that personal deity (in Hinduism the generic term of this type of personal devotion is *bhakti*). Thus the central schools of Buddhism have taught that the ultimate reality (*nirvana*, often described as "nothingness" or "emptiness") is utterly beyond personhood, but masses of ordinary people, especially in Mahayana countries, pray to very personal redeemer figures (the *Bodhisattvas*, who have attained enlightenment but have forgone the move into *nirvana* out of compassion for all "sentient beings" left behind). Both in Hinduism and in Buddhism one can observe this dichotomy between (in Max Weber's terms) the "religious virtuosi" and the "religion of the masses." In the west Asian traditions the conception of God as person is central on both levels. Ernst Troeltsch was correct in seeing this feature as distinctively Christian (though, it should be added, it is just as distinctively Jewish and Muslim). The Biblical God both speaks and listens. And the ultimate destiny of human beings is an eternity of this interaction, not an ocean of divinity in which all selves are dissolved.

I will tell a personal story here (I have told it elsewhere, but I do not assume that readers of this book have read other writings of mine!). On my first trip to India I was in Calcutta, on my way to visit a religious scholar, when I encountered a Hindu funeral procession. It is a shocking sight for a modern Westerner, since there is no coffin – the corpse, in this instance an old man, lies exposed on a wooden plank. There was a rather small number of mourners in the procession, and some of them were chanting. When I reached the house of the scholar, I told him of the experience, and something made me ask him what they would be chanting on such an occasion. He said that it would probably be a passage from the second chapter of the *Bhagavad Gita*, which he then proceeded to recite, first in Sanskrit, then in English. I had been familiar with the passage, but I had not known that it was used at funerals. When I returned to my hotel room I looked it up in a copy of the *Gita*, which the hotel management had put in the room along with a Gideons' Bible. The passage goes as follows:

> Even as a person casts off worn-out clothes and puts on others that are new, so the embodied Self casts off worn-out bodies and enters into others that are new. Weapons cut It not; fire burns It not; water wets It not; the wind does not wither It. This Self cannot be cut nor burnt nor wetted nor withered. Eternal, all-pervading, unchanging, immovable, the Self is the same for ever. This Self is said to be unmanifest, incomprehensible, and unchangeable. *Therefore, knowing It to be so, you should not grieve.* (my italics; Swami Nikhilananda, trans., *The Bhagavad Gita*, p. 20)

It is clear what this "It" is – the innermost self, the *atman*, which Vedanta Hinduism identified with the *brahman*, the ultimate and impersonal reality. The two are identical, as the famous formula of the Upanishads put it: *Tat tvam asi*, "you are that." The truth, which is supposed to console any mourner, is that this *atman* travels from one incarnation to another, none of which finally matters, until (if the proper acts of renunciation are followed) it merges with the *brahman* – as all streams end in the ocean.

I reread this passage in my hotel room and was once again impressed by its power. But I also reflected that, if I had been one of the mourners in the funeral procession, I would not have been consoled. I asked myself why. Then I thought of one word from the Greek New Testament, the word *ephapax*. When I was back home I looked it up in a concordance. It means "once and for all" and it occurs in the Letter to the Hebrews, where it refers to the "once and for all" quality of Christ's redemptive sacrifice. But I hadn't thought of Christ at all in my Calcutta hotel room. Rather, I thought of the infinite worth of *this* person, *this* body, *this* world. And I would not be consoled by a religious message – indeed, would not be personally interested in it – unless it recognized the unique value of these empirical realities. Which is why I thought of a word from the New Testament, which contains the message of the personal God, who created this world and this embodied individual, and who promises that both have an eternal destiny that does not negate them. In other words, I found myself saying *no* to the consolation of the *Gita*, and in this *no* I found a nexus with the Biblical tradition.

This *no*, however, need not imply that the experience underlying the worldview of the *Gita* is simply an illusion. The experience in which the self loses itself in an ocean of universal being is found not only in Hinduism but in mystical movements throughout all religious cultures. It would be both presumptuous and implausible to propose that this experience is nothing but several millenia's worth of illusion. Similar to the aforementioned question about the epistemological status of the mythic matrix in the light of Biblical faith, the question here concerns the status of this particular experience. The question was asked again and again when mystical movements arose in the context of the monotheistic traditions. Meister Eckhart, arguably the greatest Christian mystic, distinguished "God" (that is, the personal God of Biblical revelation) and "Godhead" (that is, the impersonal divinity of mystical experience). The latter had priority over the former, in Eckhart's view: "God becomes and disbecomes." This view, understandably, led to the condemnation of Eckhart by the medieval Church authorities. Other Christian mystics, like John of the Cross or Teresa of Avila, were more cautious. Analogous questions were raised in response to Jewish and Muslim mystics. And interestingly one finds similar questions in other traditions, whenever an impersonal cosmic divinity was counterposed to personal redeemer figures. In Mahayana Buddhism, where there has been the ongoing problem of reconciling devotion to personal *Bodhisattvas* with the impersonal goal of renunciation, there arose the idea of the "two bodies" of the Buddha – the *rupakaya* ("body of form"), which is the form taken by Buddhas of personal redemption, and the *dharmakaya* ("body of truth"), which is the form in which a Buddha attains the ultimate impersonal reality. The terminology suggests that the original intention, similar to Eckhart's, was to give the higher epistemological status to the latter form. However, there have been Buddhist schools, possibly those closer to the "religion of the masses," who took the opposite position. In other words, it is possible to assert that both experiences are true – the experience of the personal God who speaks and in doing so bestows ultimate validity to the human self, and the experience of the impersonal ocean of divinity in which the human self dissolves. The question then is which of these two experiences has primacy.

I have suggested that, in the context of Biblical faith, there must be something like a theology of the mythic matrix. There is also the need for a theology of mystical experience. There are rich resources for this in the history of Christian, Jewish, and Muslim thought. It seems to me that a key insight for this reflection will once more have to be the silence of God. Perhaps the impersonal speechlessness of the mystical experience will then have to be understood as the silence before God speaks – or, if you will, the vastness of the universe waiting for God's word. I will have to leave it there.

If an essential nexus between the Biblical tradition and my own experience is the veridical status of the self, then the most radical challenge to this comes indeed from Buddhism. This is not only because the ultimate reality in most Buddhist schools of thought is impersonal (*that* Buddhism shares with most traditions building on mystical experience), but because one of the core doctrines of Buddhism is the denial of the reality of the self. Thus selflessness is not only a moral imperative – "lose the love of self so as to be open to love others" – but an epistemological thesis: "begin the path to enlightenment by perceiving the self to be an illusion." (This distinction, incidentally, helps to see the fatuous character of some recent efforts to construct a universal ethic in which Buddhist "compassion" is equated with Christian *agape*. I would argue that, despite some similarities on the level of practical activities, the two have very little to do with each other, indeed are almost opposites.)

The first step in the enlightenment of Gautama Buddha was the understanding of what Buddhist tradition called the Three Universal Truths. In the words of the Pali canon (the basic text of the Theravada school) these are *a-nichcha* (all reality is impermanence), *dukkha* (all reality is suffering), *an-atta* (all reality is non-self). What was taken for granted here was the Hindu cosmology of *samsara* – the endless cycle of rebirths and thus the endless repetition of suffering. The Buddha was by no means the only Hindu teacher who saw redemption as the escape from this dreadful cycle; so did, for an important example, the Vedanta school. But his view was more radical, especially in its denial of the reality of the self. The Three Universal Truths served as the starting point of his program of redemption. The cause of suffering is desire, he taught, that desire which creates *karma* (the cosmic law by which every deliberate action has consequences that stretch far beyond any particular incarnation), which in turn leads to imprisonment in the cycle of rebirths. Only the extinction of desire can bring about the extinction of suffering and thus escape from the horror of *samsara*. The Noble Eightfold Path is the basic program for the attainment of this goal, a careful discipline of renunciation. At its conclusion one achieves *nirvana*. However that final state is interpreted (there are different Buddhist versions of it), it is marked by the complete abandonment of self.

It is important, I think, to understand the liberating quality of this program. One encounters it very quickly in any contact with Buddhist spirituality. It is characterized above all by tranquillity. It can be found in the stillness of the Buddhist shrines of the Deer Park outside Benares, especially if one arrives there from the tumultuous religious life on the banks of the Ganges – the noise of the three-hundred-thousand gods of the Hindu pantheon giving way to a profound Buddhist stillness. Perhaps the most impressive expressions of this stillness are to be found in the Buddhist aesthetic of Japan – in the stone gardens of Kyoto, in the tranquil gestures of the tea ceremony, in the quiet concentration of Zen meditation halls. I think it is this quality, more than any other, which has attracted converts from the all too busy West.

To give up the tensions and contradictions of the self is a great emotional relief. But the Buddhist doctrine of *an-atta* is also attractive intellectually. I would go further than that: If one abandons the hypothesis of God, *etsi Deus non daretur*, this doctrine becomes eminently plausible. It seems to me (this is not an original observation) that modern psychology and modern neurology have put in question the notion of the autonomous self, which has been widely perceived as, among other things, the crowning achievement of Western civilization. This self is, of course, more than an idea. It is also a lived experience and, in the biography of every individual, an ongoing achievement. Early in the twentieth century the Austrian philosopher Ernst Mach declared that, in the light of modern science, the self is not "salvageable." I think that nothing that has happened since has falsified Mach's proposition. This does not deny, of course, that millions of people continue to believe in and to experience themselves as autonomous beings. And, of course, this has vast social and political consequences, as in the international movements for human rights and democracy. This does not necessarily falsify the proposition that all of it is based on a great illusion. Western Buddhists in particular are struggling to combine their religious beliefs with a commitment to human rights and democracy. It is a strain, because it is difficult to see how an illusionary self can have rights. Be this as it may, a recurring theme in Western thought for the last hundred years has been the attempt to salvage the self which Mach pronounced to be unsalvageable.

I'm not alone among those for whom both the idea and the experience of the self is central to the sense of reality, not least because of its moral and political implications. For people of my generation this attained the status of certainty in the compelling necessity to say *no* to totalitarianism and to its monstrous inhumanity. This means saying *no* to every denial of the autonomous self, because that is tantamount to a denial of the reality of freedom. This *no* must then be said to every version of freedom-denying scientism; it must also extend, with all due respect, to the Buddhist understanding of *an-atta*. And here is yet another vitally important nexus between the Biblical tradition and my own experience.

In the perspective of Biblical faith the self is not an illusion, neither is the empirical world, because both are creations of God. It is possible to affirm this faith in a threefold *no* to the Buddha's Three Universal Truths: All reality is *not* impermanence, because at its heart is the God who is the plenitude of being in time and eternity. All reality is *not* suffering, because God's creation is ultimately good and because God is acting to redeem those parts of creation, especially humanity, where this goodness has been disturbed. And all reality is *not* non-self, because the self is the image of God, not because it is itself divine but because it exists by virtue of God's address. As to this self, its destiny is not dissolution in some cosmic impersonal reality, but rather a journey toward God.

Historical scholarship will never be able to establish just what occurred in the deserts of the Middle East, when some tribes of Semitic nomads encountered a God who was radically different from all the gods of the surrounding cultures. In the act of faith one is constrained to say that God revealed Himself to Israel in a unique way, and out of that revelation came whatever followed in later centuries. To say this, however, is not to deny *a priori* that God may have revealed Himself at other times and in other places; on this, Troeltsch had it right. Drawing the boundaries of revelation is a perilous business. And I don't think that it is an urgent task. It is sufficient to be grateful for what has been given to us in this particular tradition, and then to remain open to whatever may come to us from other sources.

Chapter Three

"... the Father Almighty"

This phrase in the Creed describes the essential qualities of the God who is being affirmed. Yet there is an immense tension between the noun and the adjective. There is God who is like a father, God who cares, God to whom one can pray. And there is God who is omnipotent and, in terms of our experience, uses His power very sparingly. Human beings have called upon God down the centuries, crying out for His help in the most extreme situations of pain and terror – and, over and over again, the cry went unanswered. It is a simple fact of experience that prayers remain unanswered, even when voiced by or on behalf of the most innocent victims. Now, believers repeatedly assert that their prayers were indeed answered and that they were delivered from whatever calamities they sought deliverance from. Upon reflection, however, this makes the tension even worse: Why does God answer some prayers and not others? If anything, this makes the case of the victims, whose prayers were *not* answered, even more unbearable.

As one reflects about this portion of the Creed in our time, one is inevitably confronted with the feminist challenge to the masculine gender attributed to God. This challenge raises interesting questions, among others the question of the social location of symbols and the question of whether symbols can be freely changed. However, as for as the tension between God's benevolence and His omnipotence is concerned, these questions are not relevant. Let it be stipulated, for the sake of the argument, that God could just as well be addressed as mother – "the Mother Almighty." The tension would remain exactly the same. One of the great female mystics in Christian history, often cited by feminist theologians, was Julian of Norwich (we will return to her at the end of this chapter). She frequently referred to God as mother; at the same time she was consumed by the question of how God can allow suffering and evil. In other words, the problem of theodicy (literally, the problem of the justice of God) cannot be liquidated by feminist language.

The problem is very old indeed. It recurs again and again, not only in theological reflection, but more importantly in innumerable crises of faith in the lives of ordinary believers:

How can God, who is supposed to be both all-good and all-powerful, preside over a world full of innocent suffering and unpunished evil?

Suffering and evil are universal facts of the human condition, but the problem they pose for religious faith is obviously sharpest if the ultimate reality is understood in terms of monotheism. The three so-called Abrahamic traditions – Judaism, Christianity, and Islam – have had to grapple with the problem from their very beginnings. The facts of suffering and evil, however painful they may be in human lives, pose less of a *religious* problem in pantheistic or dualistic traditions in which the ultimate reality is understood either in impersonal terms or in terms of a cosmic struggle between good and evil divinities.

The question of the justice of God resonates throughout the Hebrew Bible. In the earlier period of Israelite history the question was posed communally rather than individually: If God has established a covenant with the people of Israel, why is this people so often abandoned to this or that calamity? There is, of course, a powerful current of Biblical thinking which explains the calamities as punishment for the sins of the people, but when these calamities took on unbearable forms and when they afflicted those who seemed innocent of any wrongdoings, this explanation began to wear thin. Faith in the covenant then affirmed that God's power would *eventually* be exercised on behalf of His people, and it is this affirmation which led to the notions of the Messiah, who would establish God's reign of justice, and of a day of judgment at the end of history. In other words, the problem of theodicy was solved in terms of eschatology.

As the Israelite religious consciousness developed, the question of God's justice also turned toward the suffering of individuals. It is powerfully addressed in many of the Psalms. But, of course, its classical formulation is in the Book of Job. Ever since, Job has been the prototype of the perfectly innocent victim of every conceivable kind of misfortune. The arguments of Job's friends, to the effect that his suffering should be understood as punishment for his sins, are decisively rejected. Two solutions are suggested by the text – that Job suffered to test his faithfulness, and that his suffering is redemptive through his praying for his misguided friends. Both these solutions resonate through the subsequent history of Jewish and Christian theodicy. Job's own attitude is one of complete submission to the will of God, as expressed in the classical formula "the Lord gave, and the Lord has taken away; blessed is the name of the Lord." And God's own answer, coming "out of the whirlwind," is a proclamation of His enormous power, with which no argument is possible: "Shall a fault-finder contend with the Almighty?" And Job, once again, accepts. There is then the rather unconvincing, almost Hollywood-like happy end, with Job's fortune being fully restored; a majority view among Biblical scholars is that this ending was added to the text at a later time.

One reads the Book of Job with mixed feelings. On the one hand, it constitutes a deeply moving testimony to the persistence of trust in God in the face of adversity. But on the other hand God's final answer to Job presents God in a way that is morally troubling. It is as if God said to Job: "Look how strong I am! So just shut up!" If this were the attitude of a powerful human being, one would morally condemn it, and the person who accepts it would be diagnosed as a masochist (or, if you will, as a victim of the "Stockholm syndrome," the phenomenon of hostages identifying with their captors). The classical answer to such musings, of course, has always been that one may not apply human standards to God. It is an unconvincing answer: Can one affirm a God who contradicts the moral standards that apply to human beings, who (impossible thought) is morally inferior to the best human beings? Yet Job's submission to God, even if it may strike one as a sort of metaphysical masochism, has been the paradigmatic Jewish, Christian, and Muslim response to suffering and evil. Through the centuries Judaism has understood suffering as an occasion to bless God's name (*kiddush hashem*). And the very word "Islam" is derived from the Arabic word for submission (*'aslama*). The same may be said for most of Christian thought and piety.

John Hick, before he turned his attention to the Christian attitude to other religions (in which capacity we encountered him in the preceding chapter), wrote a useful book on the development of Christian theological reflection about the problem of theodicy (*Evil and the Love of God*). He distinguishes between two principal versions of Christian theodicy, which he calls the Augustinian (expressed classically by the great Latin Church Father Augustine) and the Irenaean (referring to Irenaeus, a second-century Greek theologian and bishop). Augustine grounded his theodicy in the idea of freedom: God created free beings, who are then capable of willfully misusing this freedom. (He had, of course, human beings in mind, but he also envisaged some sort of primordial catastrophe involving angels who misused their freedom and fell into evil.) Irenaeus' theodicy proposed that evil is allowed by God so as to make possible a more perfect creation. One might say that these two approaches indicate important differences between Western and Eastern Christianity, the former strongly focused on the phenomenon of sin, the latter more focused on the cosmic dimension of the divine/human drama. But, in Hick's words, "both alternatives acknowledge explicitly or implicitly God's ultimate responsibility for the existence of evil" (p. 264). In the words of an Eastern liturgy referring to original sin, "O fortunate crime, which merited so great a redeemer" – the "fortunate crime" (in its Latin version, *felix culpa*) as the necessary precondition of Christ's great work of redemption.

It seems to me that both traditions of theodicy are abstract to the point of repulsiveness, and both are vulnerable to the charge that they envisage a God whose moral quality seems to be less than that of even moderately admirable human beings. But it is the abstraction that is most disturbing. The most concrete case questioning the goodness of God is that of a suffering child: *No theodicy is tolerable that cannot be reiterated in the face of a suffering child, either to the child directly or to those who love the child and are helpless to end the suffering.* This is the searing insight expressed in Dostoyevsky's *The Brothers Karamazov* by Ivan Karamazov, a paradigmatic rebel against the Biblical God – he cannot accept a God who accepts the torment of an innocent child. It seems to me that any credible theodicy must confront and indeed embrace Ivan's outrage.

I find it interesting that most approaches to theodicy, at least in Christian thought and especially in what Hick calls the Augustinian tradition, focused on suffering caused by the evil deeds of human beings. But suffering brought about by natural causes is actually much more common. And the child dying of a painful disease challenges the notion of a God both all-good and all-powerful even more sharply than the murdered child: Put simply, it is more difficult to absolve God in the former case.

For the moment, however, let us focus on suffering caused by the evil deeds of human beings. This is, to be sure, a timeless problem. From the beginning of the human presence on earth, history has been an ongoing massacre, mostly of the innocent, with only brief periods of respite and uneasy peace. While it is important to keep this in mind, in our own time the Holocaust has been a revelation of absolute evil, as absolute as it can ever get. There has been a good deal of debate as to whether the Holocaust has been a unique event (a debate that has often been politicized). It seems to me that a historical perspective will suggest that the Holocaust both was and was not unique: It was unique in the systematic brutality of its execution, an industrial death machine devoted to the annihilation of an entire people; it was not unique in that it stands in a long line of mass murders, a line that, alas, has not come to an end. This debate, however, is not really germane to the issue of theodicy under consideration here. It is estimated that, among the victims of the Holocaust, there were about one million children, many of them killed with a cruelty that is unbearable to visualize. The Holocaust then poses the question of theodity in the sharpest possible way: *How could God permit the murder of one million Jewish children?*

Is *this* question any different from the question of how God can permit the cruel murder of a single child? Again, it is and it is not. Ivan Karamazov was right in asserting that the suffering of even one child challenges the notion of a benevolent God. But the sheer numbers of Holocaust victims, and the manner in which they died, poses the issue of theodicy with a sharpness that is almost impossible to avoid. For Jews it has been *the* central issue of faith. It has been less so for Christians, though it should be (at least for Christians in the orbit of Western civilization, within which this horror took place). Christians reflecting on theodicy in the context of the Holocaust should avoid premature Christological responses to it, and not only out of respect for the victims and for Jewish sensitivities: The Jewish responses to the Holocaust should be accorded priority because they pose the issue of theodicy in the most immediate and sharpest manner.

In the immediate wake of World War II there was little reflection about the wider import of the murder of European Jewry. There were more pressing practical concerns – for the care of the survivors, for the support of the new state of Israel, and for measures to prevent a recurrence of such events (as in the definition of genocide as a crime under international law). And, of course, there was the stunning effect of the events themselves. Widespread reflection only began in the 1960s, possibly spurred by the Eichmann trial and other (belated) prosecutions of Nazi war criminals. Since then an entire literature has sprung up. Obviously it is not possible to go into this in any detail, but we will look at some major approaches.

Eliezer Berkovits (*Faith after the Holocaust*, 1973) relates the Holocaust to the Book of Job, then points out that we, who were not there, are not Job – we are only Job's brothers. Therefore, we must first listen to those who *were* there. But their voices are not unanimous: Some lost their faith and cursed God; others kept their faith to the end, in the age-old Jewish tradition of *kiddush hashem*. Berkovits insists that we must respect both responses. This insistence is morally compelling, but it is not clear how it helps in confronting the burning issue of God's inaction in the face of the Holocaust.

Among some Orthodox writers there has been the assertion that the Holocaust was a divine punishment for the sins of the Jews; only recently it was repeated by a leading rabbinical authority in Israel. Unfortunately, this position is not without antecedents in the Hebrew Bible (though it was rejected in the Book of Job). One can only say that, in the face of the murdered Jewish children, this position is humanly and morally obscene. It is not far from the equally obscene assertion, by some Christians, that the Jews were being punished for their rejection of Christ. One can only reject, passionately, the notion that God willed the actions of the Nazi murderers.

Steven Katz (*Post-Holocaust Dialogues*, 1983) proposes a useful four-fold typology of Jewish religious responses to the Holocaust:

One: The Holocaust compels a repudiation of the Biblical God. This position was stated most starkly by Richard Rubenstein: There is now a void where God used to be. Having said this, Rubenstein goes on to say that continued Jewish existence is humanly valuable, while his own religious position is phrased in vaguely mystical terms with a marked affinity with New Age thinking. Neither Rubenstein's claims for the value of a non-theistic Judaism nor his mystical affirmation of nothingness need concern us here. His position is important because it states with great honesty that, after the Holocaust, it is no longer possible to believe in God.

Two: A very influential position has been that of Emil Fackenheim. It is summed up in his statement that one must not give Hitler a "posthumous victory" by giving up on Judaism and the Jewish people. There is now a "sacred obligation to survive," to be especially expressed by support for the state of Israel.

Three: There has been the position, eloquently stated by Ignaz Maybaum, that the Jews were suffering vicariously for the sins of mankind. This proposition is linked to the image of the suffering servant in the Book of Isaiah. A very disturbing corollary (explicitly stated by Maybaum) is that even Hitler must be seen as an agent of God.

Four: The aforementioned Eliezer Berkovits refers to the traditional Jewish idea of God who sometimes "hides His face" (*hester panim*), an act of hiding that is mysteriously linked to God's redemptive actions. This hiding supposedly ended with the birth of the state of Israel.

Rubenstein's position is clearly an option; it is, if you will, the most direct amplification of Ivan Karamazov's outcry against God in the context of the Holocaust. But I think that, for all those who are not prepared to give up on the Biblical God, none of the other three approaches will finally convince. Against Fackenheim one could argue that giving up on Judaism and Jewishness may be one practical way of avoiding a repetition of future genocides directed against Jews. And the sacralization of the state of Israel is a morally ambiguous exercise. Be this as it may, the instrumentalization of murdered children for any purpose whatsoever – be it the legitimation of a political cause, or this or that divine plan of redemption – is finally both morally and theologically offensive.

Thus all four positions enumerated by Katz are unsatisfactory to anyone who wants to cling to the Biblical God even after the Holocaust.

A rather unusual and at least partly more persuasive response can be found in an essay by Hans Jonas, who writes both as a philosopher and as a believing Jew ("The Concept of God after Auschwitz," in Michael Morgan, ed., *A Holocaust Reader*, pp. 259ff). Jonas asserts flatly that we cannot have it both ways: We must give up *either* the notion of God's benevolence *or* the notion of His omnipotence. To do the former is inconceivable: It would be tantamount to worshipping Satan. Therefore, in some way, we must do the latter. Jonas proposes two ideas to this end, neither of them new, but both attaining new relevance in the context of the Holocaust. One idea is that of the *suffering God* – that is, God does not stand outside the suffering of His creation, but in a mysterious way undergoes it Himself. Jonas relates this idea to an intriguing tradition in Jewish mysticism, propagated by the kabbalistic school of Isaac Luria, according to which God underwent a painful contraction (*tsimtsum*) in order to make room for the creation, so that God must be seen as suffering from the beginning of creation. (It is not without interest that Lurianic mysticism developed after an earlier great catastrophe in Jewish history, the expulsion of the Jews from Spain.) The other idea suggested by Jonas is that of the *becoming God* – that is, God has not yet achieved His full being and is still in a process of painful becoming (this idea has been developed philosophically by Whitehead and his followers). The second idea would seem to be in direct contradiction to the Biblical conception of God, and it is difficult to see how it could be incorporated within Jewish (or Christian) faith. But the idea of the suffering God is one of compelling power, linking up with a number of Biblical themes (again, Isaiah's suffering servant may be relevant here, though the reference of that text, probably, was not to God but to the people of Israel). The idea, of course, leaves us with the problem of *why* there has been this limitation of God's power that makes His suffering necessary. Jonas confesses that "all this, let it be said at the end, is but stammering." True enough. But, even if only in a stammering manner, we cannot help reflecting about the meaning of these events for our faith.

Only a word about the Christian responses: They are relatively scarce and, if anything, even less helpful for the present issue than the Jewish responses. They mostly exhibit three themes: Confessions of guilt for the anti-Jewish tradition in Christianity (going all the way back to portions of the New Testament); a rejection of so-called "supersessionism" (that is, of the idea that the New Testament supersedes the Old – against this, it is affirmed that God's covenant with Israel continues to be valid); and a strong commitment to Christian opposition to any form of anti-Semitism (which often includes a rather uncritical support for the state of Israel, including its claim to the Holy Land on the ground of a divine warrant). All these themes are worthy of discussion. None of them are of any help on the issue of theodicy.

The idea of a suffering God implies a temporary limitation of God's omnipotence. It must be temporary, or God would not be the one who disclosed Himself in the Biblical tradition. This further implies a mysterious flaw in the creation, a countervailing power that causes both evil and suffering – a flaw that can only be repaired by God's own suffering, by His participation in the agonies of His creation. It goes without saying that all speculation about the origin and nature of this flaw can only be extremely hesitant (a 'stammering" indeed). But two further implications can be stated: The notion of a power opposing God will probably have to be personalized, as it was from early on in the figure of Satan – and one may say that *this* notion has gained credibility in the context of the more-than-human evil manifested in the Holocaust. And further, the flaw in the creation cannot be limited to human history – for there is the immense pain driving the evolutionary process long before human history began, with entire species of animals suffering and being swept into oblivion by the inexorable selection of biological evolution. In other words, the flaw in the creation must have a meta-historical, perhaps even a cosmic dimension – and so, it follows, must the process of its redemptive repair (which, in Jewish mysticism, has been called *tikkun*).

The most unbearable scene in Elie Wiesel's book *Night,* the memoir of his experiences in the Nazi death camps, is the description of the agonizing execution of a child which he and his fellow-inmates were forced to watch. As the child was slowly dying on the gallows, a fellow-inmate whispered to Wiesel: "Where is God?" Wiesel replied: "He is there, on the gallows." I do not pretend to know just what Wiesel meant at that moment. But there are two ways of understanding his reply. One could understand it in Rubenstein's sense: God died here – that is, it is no longer possible to believe in Him. Or one could understand it in Jonas' sense: God died here – that is, He participated in the agony.

I will allow myself a final comment here. Understandably, almost all religious reflections about the Holocaust have focused on its victims: How can one conceive of God in the face of their suffering? But one may also reflect about God in the face of the perpetrators of this suffering: How can one conceive of God dealing with the Nazi murderers? And here another Biblical tradition becomes highly relevant – the affirmation of God who, beyond history and at its end, will judge the living and the dead. Put differently, Biblical faith must hold out the promise of heaven for all the victims of history; Biblical faith must also hold out the promise of hell for their murderers. In an earlier work I have called this the argument from damnation for the existence of God.

Of the three monotheistic faiths, it is Islam that has put the strongest emphasis on the day of judgment, and this despite the fact that every chapter of the Quran begins with the formula "In the name of God, the compassionate, the merciful" (*bismillah al-rahman al-rahim*). I hope that neither Jews nor Christians will be offended if I conclude with a Quranic passage (sura 82, headed "The Cataclysm" in N. J. Dawood's translation, p. 16):

> When the sky is rent asunder; when the stars scatter and the oceans roll together; when the graves are hurled about; each soul shall know what it has done and what it has failed to do. – O man! What evil has enticed you from your gracious Lord, who created and proportioned you, and moulded your body to His will? – Yes, you deny the Last Judgement. Yet there are guardians watching over you, noble recorders who know all your actions. – The righteous shall surely dwell in bliss. But the wicked shall burn in Hell-fire upon the Judgement-day; they shall not escape. – Would that you knew what the Day of Judgement is! Oh, would that you knew what the Day of Judgement is! It is the day when every soul will stand alone and God will reign supreme.

Looking at religious responses to the Holocaust has inevitably centered attention on suffering caused by the evil deeds of human beings. This is fully justified. But it is very important to stress, once again, that the question of theodicy is raised in what is possibly an even sharper form by suffering due to the ravages of nature. It is sharper because here it is not possible to ascribe the cause of suffering to the misuses of human freedom. At least the Augustinian version of theodicy collapses here, unless one wants to propose the free actions of some angelic beings who fell from a state of grace long before the beginnings of human history on earth (a proposition that came to be embodied in the myth of Lucifer). Put simply: The child tormented by disease puts the blame more directly on God than the child tormented by murderers. And this only takes account of human beings afflicted by an evidently flawed nature. But there is also the vast domain of animal suffering, which has been the accompaniment of biological evolution for millions of years. To say this is not to endorse the claims of current ideas about animal rights that equate the latter with human rights. But anyone who has looked into the eyes of a dying dog will understand that it is necessary to question God about this suffering as well.

Evolution is lavishly wasteful of life. Each step in the evolutionary process leaves behind hecatombs not only of individual animals but of entire species. If one looks at this process in teleological terms, as a dramatic progression culminating in the appearance of *homo sapiens*, then it is reasonable to ask whether the enormous cost can be justified: Is *this* the best that a benevolent and omnipotent creator could come up with?

We have previously considered how a beautiful landscape seems to proclaim the agency of a creator. Let this thought stand. But one should also be mindful of the world of suffering concealed by this landscape. As one looks out over the magnificent vistas, say, of the great lakes of northern Italy, one might not see any dying animals. But they are there all the same. One only has to dig one's feet into an anthill.

A popular cliché, elevated into alleged wisdom by various schools of philosophy, proposes that suffering and death should be accepted because they are "natural." This proposition must be emphatically rejected. On the contrary, it is "nature" – in the sense of the biological order of things – that is unacceptable. Death in particular is a brutal denial of the very essence of being human. Indeed, one could turn the proposition around and say that death denies the essential "nature" of man, which intends being and consciousness. Death is an affront, and to accept is to participate in the affront. It is precisely the "naturalness" of death that must be refused. Every credible theodicy must incorporate this refusal.

Do these considerations lead to a satisfactory theodicy? Of course not. Indeed, the very phrase is an oxymoron and a morally offensive one at that. But it seems to me that what emerges is at least a certain line of thinking about theodicy. To sum up, it is a line of thinking that involves the cosmos as well as history. It must not blame man for all the suffering in the world. Paradoxically, it points to two seemingly contradictory ideas about the relation of God to His creation – God as suffering within the world, and God as the judge in the future of this world. Both cosmos and history then appear as arenas of an immense drama of catastrophe and redemption. God is engaged in a struggle against the flaws within creation, possibly in a struggle with a cosmic antagonist who has caused and who wills these flaws. But the struggle is not open-ended: God's power will eventually reassert itself, the creation will be repaired (*tikkun*), and, in the words of the Quran, God will reign supreme. It is part of the dignity of man that, precisely because of his freedom, he can participate in this struggle.

Every well-rounded theory on these matters – Augustinian, Irenaean, or what-have-you – is bound to be unsatisfactory, even morally offensive. In the face of agony and terror we must cry out, and our theorizing, as Hans Jonas put it, can only be a kind of stammering. Finally, unless one chooses to abandon faith, there is no alternative to holding on to the trust that was at the heart of the original act of faith – both if one is in the midst of suffering oneself, or if one is overcome by the suffering of others (as Eliezer Berkovits put it, whether one is Job or only Job's brother).

Before ending this chapter (itself an exercise in stammering) let us step back from the horrors of history and nature, returning to the original act of trust in which all faith originates. This is the astounding affirmation that God, who created all the galaxies, did so out of love – in Dante's words, the love that moves the stars. This is an affirmation before and beyond all theorizing. In that sense, it is a childlike act.

In my youth I knew a very admirable man, a German Protestant pastor, who was very absent-minded. He kept losing and misplacing things – his keys, his wallet, important papers, even his sermon notes. His wife once mentioned that, whenever such an incident occurred, she and her husband would go down on their knees and pray to God to help them find the misplaced object. At the time I thought that this was quite absurd: How could God be bothered with such trivialities? Later I thought that this was no more absurd than the belief that God could be bothered by matters which to us appeared to be much weightier: Seen from beyond the distant nebulae, the fate of the nation, say, would appear to be no less trivial than the pastor's lost keys. Faith proposes that God pays attention to both.

Julian of Norwich, perhaps more than any figure in the long history of Christian mysticism, was focused on the proposition that the essence of God is love. This is why she referred to Him as mother (rather than for the reasons that modern feminists have been interested in her). She was some kind of nun, though she apparently lived by herself as a so-called anchorite. In 1373 she had a series of revelations, which she called "showings." She subsequently wrote them down in a longer and a shorter version. They do not make for easy reading. A modern reader has difficulty placing himself in her medieval worldview and he will wonder about the psychological makeup underlying her experiences. Yet it is possible to shelve these modern difficulties and to appreciate what she was trying to say. And everything she says relates to her view of God as love.

Her most amazing "showing" is the following:

He showed me something small, no bigger than a hazelnut, lying in the palm of my hand, and I perceived that it was as round as any ball. I looked at it and thought: What can it be? And I was given this general answer: It is everything which is made. I was amazed that it could last, for I thought that it was so little that it could suddenly fall into nothing. And I was answered in my understanding: It lasts and always will, because God loves it; and thus everything has being through the love of God. (*Showings*, trans. Edmund Colledge and James Walsh)

It is as if in this vision Julian saw the entire universe as God must see it – infinitely small, no bigger than a hazelnut. And she understood that it can fall into nothingness at any moment, unless it is sustained by an infinite love.

Yet Julian was deeply troubled by the presence of sin and pain in this world, and by what she perceived as the pervasive power of the devil. She answered these troubles in the passage that is most frequently quoted from her writings: "And so our good Lord answered to all the questions and doubts which I could raise, saying most comfortingly: I may make all things well, and I can make all things well, and I shall make all things well, and I will make all things well, and you will see yourself that every kind of thing will be well" (ibid., p. 229).

I daresay that it is not accidental that this passage reads like a lullaby. These are exactly the words that a mother will use to comfort a crying child, today as in fourteenth-century England: "all will be well, all will be well." God speaks to Julian in the words of motherly love, and in doing so He bestows ultimate validity to the reassurances of every human mother.

A little later on there is a very moving passage in which Julian ponders the fate of the devil and all others relegated to damnation: How can all things be well if there will be those in hell throughout eternity? It appears that Julian would like to believe that they too will eventually be embraced by God's love (this is the doctrine of universal salvation or *apokatastasis*), but, as a loyal daughter of the Church, she is not supposed to believe this: "And all this being so, it seemed to me that it was impossible that every kind of thing should be well, as our Lord revealed at this time. And to this I had no other answer as a revelation from our Lord except this: What is impossible to you is not impossible to me. I shall preserve my word in everything, and I shall make everything well" (ibid., p. 233). One could say that, almost elegantly, Julian dismisses the possibility that her thinking is leading her into heresy.

It is worth quoting the final passage of Julian's *Showings*:

So I was taught that love is our Lord's meaning. And I saw very certainly in this and in everything that before God made us he loved us, and love was never abated and never will. And in this love he has done all his words, and in this love he has made all things profitable to us, and in this love our life is everlasting. In our creation we had beginning, but the love in which he created us was in him from without beginning. In this love we have our beginning, and all this shall we see in God without end. (ibid., pp. 342f)

Chapter Four

"... Creator of heaven and earth"

The Hebrew Bible begins with the lapidary statement that God made heaven and earth, implying that everything we know as the world is of His making, that He is not part of this world that is His creation but that He stands outside it. Even leaving aside for the moment the daunting problem of theodicy discussed in the previous chapter, this leaves open an enormous question:

What is the relation between God and the world?

In terms of religious thought (and not only in the Biblical tradition) this has been the question of God's transcendence and/or His immanence. And included in this question is that of the relation of human beings both to God and to the world.

As was pointed out earlier in this book, if one goes back far enough in the history of religion, in just about any human culture, one comes upon the curious fact of what I have called the mythic matrix – a near-universal conception of continuity between the human individual, the human world (what we today call society, with all its institutions), the biological and physical world (what we now call nature), and the world of spirits and gods (in our parlance, the world of the supernatural). It is a conception of reality in which all borders are fluid and permeable. And it is not just a conception in the sense of an intellectual construction (though it is that too), but it is a form of experience: Human beings existing in the mythic matrix not only understood reality as such a continuum, but they *lived* in such a reality. The border between the human individual and others was fluid, in that the individual was not experienced as a sharply delineated self, but rather as connected with everyone in a particular collectivity (clan or tribe) and with the non-human environment of that collectivity (one may think here, for example, of the relation between American Indians and their totem animals). Social institutions were understood and experienced as linking human beings with an all-embracing cosmic order. What we would consider to be supernatural agencies, including the gods, ongoingly intervened and penetrated the ordinary realities of human life. One may argue whether this mythic matrix made people happier than they are today, but it certainly made them less solitary. The life of the individual unfolded within a clearly demarcated order in which individual choices were sharply limited by what was understood as destiny.

One should not exaggerate the uniformity of early cultures, but there is solid evidence for the universality of what Eric Voegelin, in his ambitious attempt at a philosophy of history (in his multi-volume work *Order and History*), has called "cosmological civilizations," all marked by the aforementioned continuity. Such archaic civilizations stretch from China to India to the Near East to the Mediterranean littorals to Mesoamerica, and all were built upon the foundations of pre-literary (if you will, "primitive") cultures. Put simply: The dawn of human history is pervasively mythic (which is why the term "matrix" seems appropriate).

In all the civilizations just enumerated (with the possible exception of Mesoamerica) there occurred what Voegelin called "leaps in being" – that is, ruptures in the human – cosmic continuum. New borders and differentiations now made an appearance. Inevitably this also meant that human beings became more solitary – or, which amounts to the same thing, more individuated. Again put simply: Human individuality arises out of the collapse of the mythic order. With this also arises a new quest for the meaning of existence. The ruptures of the mythic order took different forms in different parts of the world – for example, with Confucianism in China, with Buddhism and the Vedanta in India. What came to constitute Western civilization was rooted in two ruptures occurring independently on two opposite shores of the Mediterranean, in ancient Greece and in ancient Israel. Voegelin called these, respectively, the discovery of reason and the discovery of God. It was the achievement of Christianity to merge these two streams of experience and thought. The achievement took centuries to reach full fruition, but it is already foreshadowed in the prologue to the Gospel of John, which identified the Hellenic notion of rational order, the *Logos*, with the Biblical God incarnate in Christ. To say that this was an achievement is to make a historical statement, not necessarily to endorse it. But the many critics who have bemoaned the "alienation" of modern man, and who have then blamed the Judaeo-Christian tradition for it, are at least partially right: If you don't like "alienation," you can rightly blame the Jews and the

Christians for it (though you should be reminded that the Greeks must share in the blame). Let me quickly add that, while acknowledging the historical argument, I do not share in the lamentation: "Alienation" is the precondition not only of individuality, but of anything that can reasonably be called freedom. And *that* is not something that I'm willing to bemoan.

Needless to say, it cannot be our task here to follow Voegelin into the intricacies of a philosophy of history. Rather, let us return to the Biblical version of the great rupture, which is already encapsulated in the statement that God created the world, which implies His transcendence and thus negates the mythic continuum. Biblical scholars disagree about innumerable things, but most of them agree that even the earliest layers of Israelite religion show a marked difference from all the other cultures the ancient Near East. The latter were all "cosmological," in Voegelin's sense of the term, in that the gods permeated both the natural and the social worlds. Sacred sexuality expressed this permeation most eloquently: The same sacred energies pulsated through human fertility and the fertility of nature, and these energies could be directly experienced by way of institutions such as temple prostitution and ritual orgies. The spokesmen of the God of Israel, be they priests or prophets, vociferously rejected all these practices and the understandings of reality underlying them, and Israel was prohibited from having anything to do with them. I think it would be a mistake to see in this some sort of repressive "puritanism": It was not sexuality as such that was being put down here; it was *sacred* sexuality. When it came to ordinary (if you will, "secular") sexuality, ancient Israelites were rather a raunchy lot (as can be verified by many a prurient adolescent, who searched for the "good parts" in the Hebrew Bible). Be this as it may, the God of Israel could not be reached through the natural rhythms of human sexuality or of nature. Rather, the relation between God and Israel was constituted by a *covenant* – that is , a treaty – with specific obligations and rights incurred by the human "signatories." This treaty was rooted, not in nature, but in history – the history of God's mighty acts, notably in the exodus from Egypt, the revelation of the law on Sinai, and the taking of the promised land. Put simply, the relation between God and Israel was "unnatural" in the most literal meaning of this word.

Biblical scholarship has shown the extent to which Israel absorbed ideas and rituals from the surrounding cultures, but it consistently changed them to fit into its very peculiar religious worldview. It did so by *historicizing* them. To take just one important example, the feast of tabernacles (*sukkot*) almost certainly derived from an ancient Semitic fertility cult, in which people moved into these tents and celebrated the fertility of the soil in rituals that, we may safely assume, had a decided

X-rated quality. Israel changed this festival into a commemoration of a historic event – the dwelling of Israel in the desert, following the exodus from Egypt – and it removed from the festival any trace of what one could accurately call "redeeming prurient interest" (alas, nothing there for thrill-seeking adolescents). Max Weber was, I think, correct in seeing this development as one of "rationalization": When the world is denuded of the pervasive presence of supernatural agencies, it becomes, at least potentially, subject to rational manipulations by human agency. Weber also called this development a "disenchantment" of the world (the German term is *Entzauberung* – literally, "de-magicalization"). The mythic matrix was indeed an "enchanted" world (Weber also spoke of a "magic garden"); Israel took a gigantic step out of this enchantment, with consequences that reverberated through all the centuries that followed.

This development was painful. It still is. The mythic matrix is the "home world" of all of us, in terms not only of historical origins but of the biography of every individual. The world of childhood is an "enchanted" world, and all of us retain a lasting nostalgia for it. We cannot pursue here the intriguing fact that the development of consciousness seems to replicate the development of the organism – here too "phylogenesis" seems to replicate "ontogenesis" (the terms refer to the curious way in which the individual organism. from conception on, seems to mirror the sequence of biological evolution). Be this as it may, the Hebrew Bible itself recounts the perduring attraction of pre-Israelite ideas and practices, always pilloried as apostasy by the spokesmen of the God of Israel. The attraction continued through the centuries, to our own day (in phenomena such as New Age spirituality). One can speak of an "eternal return" of the mythic matrix. or one could say that the Baalim of ancient Canaan are with us still (and, contrary to the claims of feminist theorists, they can be of either gender – mother goddesses have no monopoly to the claim of mythic restoration). The powerful lure of the mythic matrix is not difficult to explain; it lies in the promise of a rescue from solitariness and of the restoration of a warm, all-embracing sense of belonging, of at-home-ness in reality. The promise is not false. It can indeed be fulfilled. It is important to point out, however, that its price is the surrender of individuality and freedom.

To reiterate: The Biblical vision of reality presents us with a God beyond nature, and man is "in the image of God" precisely by sharing this "unnatural" quality. Put differently, nature is not normative in any sense – that is, to say that something is natural in no way implies any sort of moral approval (a point made in the preceding chapter, in the context of a theodicy that refuses to accept death just because death is a natural event). Human beings, of course, are part of nature, in that they are biological organisms and products of biological evolution. Yet there is an essential element, call it what you will, within man that transcends nature. It is the element that constitutes the core of individuality, the agent of freedom and the bearer of rights. Philosophers have argued for centuries about the relation between the natural and the meta-natural components of human existence, as in the endless debates over the so-called body/soul problem. Once again, this is a vast area into which we cannot venture here. Suffice it to say that the Biblical vision of reality sets up two related but distinct boundaries – between God and nature, and between man and nature. The question that concerns us here is the former boundary. And it should be emphasized once again that this is not only, or even primarily, a theoretical question, to be negotiated by philosophers and theologians. More basically, it is a question of lived *experience*: Just as archaic people experienced the world in terms of the mythic matrix, so individuality, freedom, and alienation are experienced in the lives of countless ordinary people on the other side of the great historic ruptures.

On the one hand, the world is presented as God's creation in the Biblical vision. On the other hand, within that vision is a realistic recognition of the pain and finitude present in the natural order of things. It is this realism which must have motivated the inclusion in the Hebrew Bible of the Book of Ecclesiastes, with its almost despairing portrayal of human existence: "Vanity of vanities, says the Preacher, vanity of vanities. All is vanity." And on to the melancholy reflection: "There is no remembrance of former things, nor will there be any remembrance of later things yet to happen among those who come after." This is a vision of reality far removed from the consoling order of the mythic matrix. The gods are far away, if they exist at all, and even the God of Israel does not offer any easy consolations.

Is God then utterly transcendent, with no traces of His presence within the created world? There is a positive answer to this question in different versions of dualism, going back to the dualistic vision of ancient Zoroastrianism (which, interestingly enough, continued for centuries in the religious consciousness of Iran, even after its conversion to Islam). In Christian history its classical expression was in Gnosticism, which looked upon this world as utterly void of goodness, indeed the creation of a malevolent deity – the good God was to be reached by abandoning this world altogether. In less radical and more orthodox versions this vision survives in various ascetic movements within both western and eastern Christianity. And one could make the argument that Calvinism, in its radical emphasis on the transcendence of God, has a certain affinity with this sort of dualism (as witnessed by its deep hostility to the body). Yet all these approaches are in great tension with the root Biblical affirmation that this world is God's creation. The creation account in the first chapter of Genesis thus ends with the statement: "And God saw every-thing that he had made, and behold, it was very good." Could it be that nothing remains of this divine goodness in the created world? Or must there not rather be some way of balancing God's transcendence with a recognition of His continuing immanence in the world?

Within the three great monotheistic traditions (and always in tension with the official guardians of the traditions) there have been two princi-pal ways of conceiving and allegedly experiencing God's immanence. The first way has been to find God in the depths of the human self. This, of course, has been the path of interiority characteristic of most of the great mystics. The other way has been to find God in the wonders of nature. It is this latter celebration of immanence that is more directly relevant to the topic of this chapter.

In Christian history one of the most impressive such celebrations was that of Francis of Assisi, beginning with his visionary experiences in 1224. The celebration is eloquently expressed in his famous "Canticle of Brother Sun," a wonderful hymn to God's presence in nature. Francis addresses the sun and the wind as brothers, the moon as sister, and so on through the wonders of nature, all celebrated as tokens of God's presence. It is in the same vein that Francis is supposed to have preached to animals, also perceived as co-celebrants of God's glory in the natural world. It is important to point out that Francis, though he can be described as a mystic, is far removed from those mystics (such as his contemporary Meister Eckhart) who claim to experience union with God. Nor does Francis identify nature with God. Rather, he praises God *for* and *through* the wonders of nature (both prepositions are implied in the word he uses in medieval Italian, *per*). One can distinguish between religious thinkers who stress the unity between God and world, and those who stress the difference. Ewert Cousins, an eminent scholar of the Franciscan move-ment, has suggested that Francis' approach should be described as "unity-in-difference." The phrase is not terribly elegant, but it helps to clarify what Francis was about. Cousins describes this very eloquently:

> We can compare the Franciscan experience of God's reflection in the uni-verse to the experience one has within a Gothic cathedral. The sunlight pours through the great stained glass windows in a brilliant array of colors. The cathedral is illumined with blues, reds, greens, yellows in intricate designs – a kaleidoscope of colors and forms. The circular rose windows and the vaulted windows of the nave and apse become aglow with a riot of colors that are at the same time as harmonious as a symphony. In a similar way Francis saw God reflected in creatures: in brother sun and sister moon, in brother fire and sister water, in the power of the wolf and the gentleness of the dove. The fecundity of God is revealed in the variety of

creatures – from the grandeur of the heavens to the simplicity of a fly. The pure rays of the divinity penetrate into the universe, which acts as a prism refracting the light into a myriad of colors. (Cousins, *Bonaventure and the Coincidence of Opposites*, p. 46)

Bonaventure, another Italian, was born shortly before Francis' climactic vision and as a child was supposedly cured from a serious illness by a miracle performed by Francis. Be this as it may, Bonaventure became head of the new Franciscan order and a distinguished teacher at the University of Paris. He sought to weave the Franciscan experience into a sophisticated theological system, which had a far-reaching influence beyond his own time. A key element of this system was an integration of the ideas of God's transcendence and immanence, which Cousins believes to be centered in the notion of the "coincidence of opposites" (the phrase was coined later by Nicholas of Cusa, but Cousins argues that Bonaventure is its original source – many features of Bonaventure's system can be traced back all the way to Neo-Platonism, but this intellectual history need not concern us here).

Bonaventure's thought was deeply Trinitarian, full of speculation about the relations between the three persons of the Trinity. The Father is understood to be the source of everything, an infinite fountain of fecundity (*fontalis plenitudo*). In the interrelation between Him and the other two persons of the Trinity, this infinite fecundity was already active long before the creation of the world, which Bonaventure understood to be primarily the work of Christ, the second person. Ewert Cousins has tried very valiantly to make these speculations relevant to modern concerns, relating them to such recent thinkers as Whitehead and Teilhard de Chardin. I have not found these arguments very persuasive, and in any case it is not easy for anyone today to enter fully into Bonaventure's intellectual discourse. However, it is not necessary to assent to his Trinitarian theology in order to grasp his essential point – namely, that the fecundity of God is rooted in His very being and precedes the creation, which is not necessary for Him but which is one product of His infinite fecundity.

All created things are already present from eternity in God's inner being. Everything, including every feature of the world and every living being in it, pre-exists as an "exemplar" in God's mind. The created world, then, is filled with the "vestiges" of these "exemplars" – pale reflections, as it were, of the divine plenitude. This is how Bonaventure puts it in two passages of his major work, *The Soul's Journey into God*: "Concerning the mirror of things perceived through sensation, we can see God not only through them as through his vestiges, but also in them as he is in them by his essence, power and presence" (Ewert Cousins, trans.,

Bonaventure: The Soul's Journey into God). And again: "All the creatures of the sense world . . . are shadows, echoes and pictures of that first, most powerful, most wise and most perfect Principle, of that eternal Source, Light and Fulness, of that efficient, exemplary and ordering Art. They are vestiges, representations, spectacles proposed to us and *signs divinely given* so that we can see God" (ibid., pp. 75f – my italics).

"Signs divinely given": I think that this phrase expresses compactly Bonaventure's understanding of the relation between God and the world. And we can follow him in this attempt to reconcile God's transcendence and immanence, over and beyond the (to us) strange-sounding metaphysics in which the phrase is embedded. We can, perhaps, place ourselves imaginatively in the Italian landscape of Bonaventure's lifeworld – say, on the shores of Lake Como, which I have suggested is in itself an argument for the existence of God. This landscape is not God, and we cannot merge with God by means of some romantic or mystical immersion in it. God transcends the world and all its realities. Nor must we forget the horrors that lurk beneath and behind the beauty of the landscape – horrors that we discussed in the preceding chapter. Animals continue to suffer and die throughout this landscape, in addition to the horrors perpetrated by human beings over the centuries in and around it. Nevertheless, nevertheless – we look upon this scene and we perceive, precisely, "signs divinely given." Signs of what? The answer is obvious: Signs of God's presence in His creation.

A more contemporary way of expressing this idea would be to say that the world is sacramental. The Anglican Book of Common Prayer defines a sacrament as "a visible sign of an invisible grace." The phrase, of course, is meant to refer to the two classical Christian sacraments of baptism and communion. But it may also serve to refer to the signs of God's presence in the visible, empirical world. The history of Christianity has many examples of such sacramental thinking. But it should be pointed out that the problem of reconciling God's transcendence and immanence is not only a Christian one. It is shared by the other two monotheistic traditions. Of the three, arguably, Islam has maintained the most radical conception of God's transcendence (at least in part out of opposition to what it understood to be the Christian doctrine of the Incarnation). Yet there is a Muslim saying that God is as close to us as the gland in our throat!

The Hebrew original of the first sentence of the Book of Genesis has "heaven" in the plural – *shamaim*, "the heavens." Undoubtedly the ancient author of this text had in mind a cosmology that modern science has made impossible to accept – some sort of three-layered universe, with earth in the middle between an upper region populated by various spiritual beings and a netherworld where the dead led a shadowy existence (possibly in the company of sinister demonic entities). I don't think that we ought to be troubled by the difference between this cosmology and our own, at least not in the context of thinking about God as creator. For the Biblical author as for ourselves, earth is not the only world. There are many worlds. The important point is that God created all of them – God created all there is. Yet earth, the world of human existence, is the locale of a specific drama of redemption in which, for the Biblical author, God's revelation to Israel played a central part.

At the same time it cannot be denied that the universe disclosed by modern astronomy gives us a different feeling for the human world than animated earlier generations, even those much closer to us in time than people in the ancient Near East. Pascal, in a famous statement, described man as standing at the midpoint between nothingness and the infinite. Both poles in this putative continuum have expanded immensely since Pascal wrote these words. Astronomy has opened up a vista of a universe within which our earth and its solar system are like specks of dust – a universe of galaxies and super-galaxies, exploding stars, "black holes," "dark matter" – with dimensions of time and space that can be described mathematically but which exceed the capacity of the human imagination. There is here, indeed, an intimation of infinity. And at the other pole, the one that seems to verge on nothingness, there is the mysterious world of sub-atomic particles, moving in ways that have driven even hard-boiled physicists to speak in the language of poetry and mysticism – a world, this one infinitely small, which exists within the body of every human individual. I'm not sure whether this modern cosmology makes it either more or less difficult to believe in God as creator. Thus a sense of human insignificance and vulnerability may have been just as pressing for a nomad spending a night alone in the desert under the stars as it is for a modern individual in a nocturnal vigil behind a telescope (perhaps even more so, since the nomad's chances of surviving the night were substantially less).

At the entrance to the planetarium of the Museum of Natural History in New York there is a huge sphere representing the known universe. Next to it is a little ball representing the solar system. Here, indeed, the latter appears to verge on nothingness. Around that sphere is an equally huge circular plate marking the chronology of the universe, from its beginning in the alleged "big bang," to the beginnings of our galaxy and the solar system, to the beginnings of biological evolution on earth, to the appearance of the human species and the beginnings of recorded history. Even the last two events combined are almost invisible, so insignificant are they in the chronology of the universe. All of this is with reference to the known universe studied by modern science. Yet even beyond this is the question of *other* universes, beyond or alongside this vast agglomeration of galaxies – a question which has even been raised by contemporary physicists exploring the mysteries of "dark matter," though the question is not new in human metaphysical speculation. A venerated text of Mahayana Buddhism, *The Holy Teaching of Vimalakirti*, opens with a sort of convention of many hundreds of thousands of gods and *Bodhisattvas* – each one representing a distinct universe (or Buddha-field). The idea of many worlds, many more than the physical universe we know, has a long history in the thought of India, as has the idea of immense cycles of time within which human events are barely notice-able, fleeting moments.

The vastness of space and time, whether apprehended by way of modern science or Indian metaphysics, leads easily to a sense of awe. This is certainly, if not necessarily, compatible with the notion that behind this vastness is a cosmic intelligence, which designed it and which is perhaps guiding it toward some sort of culmination. The religious history of India demonstrates that one can profitably meditate upon this vastness, pos-sibly acquiring a consoling tranquillity as a result. Meditation is one thing, prayer is quite another. I can rather easily imagine that the universe, indeed any number of possible universes, can be ascribed to an immense intelligence brooding over it, even that this intelligence must have the qualities that we associate with a person. What I find much more diffi-cult to imagine is that this cosmic intelligence has the least interest in the fate of human beings – let alone my own fate. Let me put it this way: As I contemplate the distant nebulae, *how can I bring myself to pray?*

I doubt very much whether an intellectually satisfying answer can be given to this question. Whatever may be the farthest reaches of the uni-verse, it is within the human lifeworld, in all its pitiable finitude, that I must choose between an affirmation of ultimate meaning or a resigna-tion to ultimate meaninglessness. If I reaffirm the former, I can do no more than return to the original decision of faith – faith in the validity of joy, holding on to those "signs divinely given" that I once glimpsed and that I can recall in memory.

Chapter Five

"I believe in Jesus Christ, his only Son, our Lord"

As one moves from the first to the second article of the Apostles' Creed, the theological ground shifts: One leaves the common ground of the three great monotheistic traditions into specifically Christian territory. Indeed, one directly confronts the central "scandal" of Christian faith, already noted as such by the Apostle Paul – namely, the affirmation of faith in the person of Jesus. Seen in a Jewish or Muslim perspective, this is an affirmation very close to if not identical with blasphemy against the one God evoked in the first article. Seen in the perspective of the south and east Asian traditions, it is an expression of an utterly parochial particularism.

Just what is it that, supposedly, "I believe" in? Clearly it is not a belief in the *existence* of Jesus, a Jew from Nazareth. This Jesus is a human individual, as such not an object of faith but of historical scholarship, just like any other individual who lived in ancient times. As with all objects of historical scholarship, the life of Jesus is researchable, with all the ambiguities, probabilities, and puzzles that afflict the historian. It makes no sense to say that one *believes* in this figure from history, unless one means by this that one believes that he indeed existed – which no serious historian has doubted. But even a statement of "belief" in this latter sense is not a statement of faith in a religious sense, but rather a statement of very strong probability.

Rather, the credal affirmation refers to the linkage of the Jewish name of Jesus, the man from Nazareth – Yeshua ha-Nozri – with the titles appended to the name: "Christ," "Son of God," "Lord." Biblical scholars and theologians have quarrelled endlessly as to the precise origins and meanings of these titles – "Christ," the Greek translation of the Hebrew term "Messiah," the anointed one; "Son of God," a phrase with multiple roots in the traditions of Jewish eschatology; "Lord," possibly a term coming from the world of Hellenistic religiosity. But whatever may be the genealogy of these titles, they clearly give to Jesus an immense significance in the drama of redemption. Thus there is also an immense tension between the name and the titles. It leads to a seemingly simple question, but one with extraordinarily complicated ramifications:

What is the relation between the Jesus of history and the Christ of faith?

The question was present from the beginning of Christian history, already in Jesus' lifetime, as when he asked his disciples "who do you say that I am?," and persistently from the beginnings of the community that remained after his departure from this world. One might actually say that this has been the key question throughout the centuries of Christian history ever since. But the question attained a novel sharpness with the coming of modern historical scholarship, as the critical apparatus of this scholarship was let loose on the New Testament. Again and again, both in the lives of Biblical scholars (many of whom were, or at least started out as, Christian theologians) and among those who read their works, the puzzles of scholarship led to crises of faith. I have sometimes asked myself how a gynecologist could manage to have sexual intercourse; by the same token, one could ask how a New Testament scholar could be a Christian. It is remarkable that considerable numbers of such scholars have remained believing Christians.

Who was the historical Jesus?

The modern quest of the historical Jesus is commonly dated from 1778, when Hermann Reimarus (this one not a theologian, but a professor of oriental languages in Hamburg) published a paper entitled "On the Intention of Jesus and His Disciples." Reimarus portrayed Jesus as a failed political prophet, executed as such by the Roman authorities, whose body was stolen from the tomb by his followers, who then began to construct a myth around him. Christianity is then to be understood as an endless amplification of this myth. This was a thoroughly debunking approach. Many of its details are untenable as a result of later research, but Reimarus is important because he insisted with great clarity that the historical Jesus was very different from the Christ of faith.

The historical scholarship of the New Testament flourished throughout the nineteenth century, mostly within Protestant institutions and in the context of liberal theology. Most of this effort, unlike Reimarus', did not intend to debunk Christianity as such, but rather to debunk orthodox views of Christianity. The intention was to give faith a sound his-

torical foundation, even if this meant leaving behind many of the orthodox doctrines of Protestantism and indeed of all the major Christian communities. This period is now commonly called the "old quest" or the "first
quest" of the historical Jesus. Needless to say, there were many divergent
views during this period, but there developed a widespread consensus
that historical scholarship cannot support orthodox views of Jesus. The
consensus was surpassed in an influential work by Martin Kaehler, *The
So-Called Historical Jesus* (1896): We cannot know the historical Jesus,
because all the New Testament accounts of him are intended to proclaim
the Christ of faith; therefore, faith must be independent of the results of
historical scholarship.

It is undoubtedly correct that all the relevant texts are expressions of
faith. Even the Synoptic Gospels are not exercises in objective historical
scholarship, but rather express distinctive (and by no means uniform)
theological viewpoints. This simple fact obviously presents the Christian
theologian with a great difficulty. Some years ago I had a long conversation with a prominent Protestant theologian, who insisted that Christian
theology cannot divorce itself from history and, at least as far as Jesus is
concerned, must leave itself vulnerable to the results of historical scholarship. I expressed respect for the courage of this position, but said that
I did not see how this could be done. We then talked about the Resurrection of Jesus. My interlocutor spoke of the many references to this
event in the New Testament. In that, of course, he was correct. But he
then was carried away to the rather astounding statement that the
Resurrection of Jesus was an event as fully documented as any in ancient
history. As I kept saying that none of the accounts of the Resurrection
constituted objective evidence, that they were all partisan documents, he
became quite irritated. He asked: "Just what kind of evidence would you
want?" I replied: "One single police report." That was the end of this particular conversation.

A turning point of this drama of reason and faith came in 1906, when
Albert Schweitzer published a highly critical account of the history of
New Testament scholarship (the English translation of his book, published in 1910, had the title *The Quest of the Historical Jesus*). The book had
a powerful influence. Schweitzer argued that nineteenth-century scholarship had falsely modernized and thus distorted the historical Jesus,
mostly by moralizing his message so as to make it palatable to the modern
liberal mind. Jesus was not a teacher of morality, but an eschatological
preacher, who expected the imminent end of the world and the establishment of a supernatural kingdom centered on his own person. But this
historical Jesus is irrelevant to Christian faith in the twentieth century.
What is important to modern Christians is "Jesus as spiritually within
men." Thus, in his own way, Schweitzer returned to Reimarus'

dichotomy between history and faith. Having established this to his own satisfaction, and that of many of his readers, Schweitzer went off to his famous (and not uncontroversial) career as a medical missionary in Africa, leaving behind something of a scholarly mess.

The period between 1906 and 1953 represents a sort of hiatus in the quest of the historical Jesus, at least in the sense of a theologically useful quest. New Testament scholarship, of course, continued, with many impressive results, but most of this scholarship was divorced from overt theological constructions. Schweitzer had been amazingly successful. Two important twentieth-century Protestant thinkers were particularly influential in their efforts to separate the Christ of faith from the Jesus of history – Rudolf Bultmann and Paul Tillich – respectively, a great New Testament scholar and a systematic theologian. We shall return to them presently.

A "new quest" or "second quest" is often dated from 1953, when Ernst Kaesemann gave a lecture entitled "The Problem of the Historical Jesus" (of all places at a gathering of Bultmann's former students – many an academic's career is founded on a repudiation of his teacher!). Kaesemann argued that Bultmann's skepticism about any attempt to reconstruct what really happened in the life of Jesus was too extreme. To be sure, the New Testament texts must be seen as propaganda documents, but the historian can still work through these documents (as well, of course, any other relevant materials he can dig up – often literally, since archaeology has played an increasingly important role here), in order to come closer to the actual events. In the following years there appeared a flurry of new works on Jesus.

Some would now speak of a "third quest" of the historical Jesus, from the beginning of the 1980s, partly spurred by the aforementioned archaeological discoveries (such as the discovery and subsequent analysis of the so-called Qumran texts). The general tendency of this renewed quest has been to put Jesus more firmly in his *Jewish* context. Needless to say, *that* has not been terribly comforting to Christian theologians either.

This literature is intellectually fascinating, but going into its details is foreclosed by both the limitations of space and of my own competence in this area. But one thing is very clear indeed: It is futile to expect definitive results from this scholarship. (This in no way implies a criticism: Historical scholarship is *never* definitive, as each generation of scholars sets about eviscerating the works of their predecessors. For example, just think of the centuries-old debates over the causes of the decline and fall of Rome.) We now have almost as many portrayals of Jesus as there have been scholars producing them. Thus Jesus has been portrayed as an eschatological prophet (E. P. Sanders), as a prophet of social change (Gerd

Theissen), an exorcist (Graham Twelftree), a "Galilean Hasid" (Geza Vermes), and even as a "peasant Jewish cynic" (John Dominic Crossan) – not to mention the more fanciful psychoanalyitc, Marxist, and feminist portraits. The lay person delving into this literature may be intellectually fascinated, but any such person wanting definitive answers can only give up in exasperation. A simple lesson here can be stated as follows: If you want any kind of certainty, religious or otherwise, don't expect it from historians!

Still, despite many disagreements, there is near-complete consensus among New Testament scholars (including most of those who would adhere to some kind of Protestant or Catholic orthodoxy) about one point: *Neither Jesus himself, nor his immediate followers, nor the Synoptic Gospels thought of him in terms of the Church's later teachings* – that is, as divine, as the second person of the Trinity, or as the being affirmed in the great historic creeds. To be sure, such ideas can already be found within the New Testament, notably in the Pauline and Johannine texts, but they almost certainly represent later developments. It may be arguable that these ideas, expressing a "high Christology," were there from early on in some implicit form, perhaps even in the mind of Jesus himself, but this is not what the scholarly consensus would suggest. Later in this book we will look at another great drama, that of the Christological controversies in the early Church. But for now what emerges is a *theological* necessity (a necessity, that is, if one wants of affirm Christian faith without a sacrifice of intellect): The necessity of freeing affirmations of faith from the quicksands of historical scholarship.

Liberal Protestantism, in whose service much of nineteenth-century New Testament scholarship toiled, responded to the aforementioned necessity in its own way. This response still resonates in many Christian circles today, even among Catholics who view themselves as "progressive" and especially among people who define themselves as "spiritual" (that is, as being religious while keeping distant from any particular church). The approach here is to view Jesus as a *teacher*, or as an *exemplar*, or perhaps as both. Jesus has been hailed as the teacher of a superior morality by many who dismissed any claim as to his divine or supernatural status. In other words, what is emphasized is his alleged moral message, not his person or his actions (including especially his purported miracles). The core of the Christian message then becomes the Sermon on the Mount. Even within the churches there are many people who take this view; Nancy Ammerman, an astute sociological observer of American religious life, has termed these people "Golden Rule Christians." Or, alternatively, Jesus can be viewed as the exemplar of a spiritually and morally superior way of living – as, say, in the "gentle Jesus" image of so many liberal

Protestant Sunday school texts. Of course, the understanding of Jesus as an admirable teacher and/or exemplar can be shared by people who do not consider themselves Christians at all. An important case of this was Mahatma Gandhi, who never ceased to be a pious Hindu but who claimed that his non-violent method was inspired by Jesus.

If one understands Jesus in this way, one can be rather insouciant about the results of historical scholarship. The teachings and the personal example can be admired or emulated regardless of what the historians may have to say about the individual from whom they derive. The Buddhist comparison is instructive in this regard. Historians have been able to find out relatively little about the Indian prince who, according to the traditional texts, started the Buddhist enterprise. Yet this fact hardly bothers any practicing Buddhist. The focus of the latter's religious life is not the historical person of Prince Gautama who supposedly attained Enlightenment centuries ago, but rather it is to seek Enlightenment today. Even if historians might one day conclude that Gautama never existed at all, this would make no significant dent in the belief that the teachings and the spiritual path traditionally ascribed to him can serve as a guide to the attainment of Enlightenment.

There is no compelling reason why one could not look upon Jesus in the same way as Buddhists look upon the founder of their tradition. The trouble with this is that, in order to do so, one must not only free oneself from the shifting results of historical scholarship but must pretty much ignore the latter altogether. For the New Testament makes clear that the Jesus proclaimed by it was not primarily a teacher of moral wisdom and was not an exemplar at all. It is important to note that Paul, whose genuine letters (which are not all to whom his name has been attached) are the oldest texts in the New Testament, showed no interest in Jesus' teachings – the interest is almost exclusively in his status as redeemer. As far as modern scholarship is concerned, it has been able to show that Jesus' moral teachings were very much in the Jewish tradition and not all that original, though they had distinctive emphases (as in the concern for marginalized people in the society of his time). What is more, even the morality contained in the Sermon on the Mount makes little sense if taken out of the context of Jesus' preaching of the imminent coming of the Kingdom of God – that is, the morality is eschatological in character and does not offer guidance for ordinary life in this world. Nor does the New Testament present Jesus as an exemplar to be emulated. In any case, with the exception of a saint here and there, no ordinary person could live by the principles of the Sermon on the Mount – or, more precisely, could not live very long. Ferdinand Mount, an acerbic British writer, has called the Sermon a most admirable one – but one suitable only for bachelors – one might add, for bachelors who expect the world to end tomorrow. Let me put it this way: *If Christianity is a moral project, it is not a very interesting project.*

Rudolf Bultmann proposed what is probably the most radical solution, within the context of Christian theology, of the problem of how to relate faith to the historical figure of Jesus. He is still considered to have been one of the foremost New Testament scholars of the twentieth century, the author of many books of continuing importance. While his scholarly work goes back to the 1920s, his theological influence came to the fore after World War II. During the Third Reich Bultmann was associated with the Confessing Church, the movement that resisted Nazi influences within the Protestant church – a fact that, quite apart from his scholarly achievements, gave him a certain moral authority after the war. In the final years of that war Bultmann wrote a paper on what he called the necessity of "demythologizing" the New Testament (the German term is a neologism as unattractive as its English translation). No theological publications were possible at that time, and the paper was circulated privately. It was published soon after the war and unleashed a violent debate. It was summarized in five volumes, published in German between 1948 and 1955, edited by Hans-Werner Bartsch under the title *Kerygma and Myth*. An English translation soon appeared and carried the debate beyond Germany. In a way, the debate has not ended.

Bultmann maintained that the worldview of the New Testament was thoroughly mythological, by which he meant that it understood the world as being ongoingly penetrated by supernatural forces, foremost among them Christ as a supernatural being. This worldview, he further insisted, was not acceptable to the modern mind. If the Christian message (the proclamation of the Gospel, called the *kerygma* in New Testament Greek) was to be understandable to modern people, it would have to be freed of its mythological trappings and translated into a non-mythological language. Bultmann thought that this could be done. The language for this "demythologizing" project he took from existential philosophy, notably that of Martin Heidegger. On these philosophical grounds human existence can be understood as being alienated from its true nature. The kerygma announces the possibility of being freed from this alienation and transposed into a new being of authenticity. Traditional Christian symbols could then still be used, but they are given a meaning divorced from their New Testament supernaturalism. Bultmann believed that his project was possible within the context of the Protestant church, indeed that it offered the latter a new lease on life in the modern world. While his project was very different from the moralism of liberal theology, it provided a sanctuary from the anxieties caused by historical scholarship: Christian faith, which is faith in the kerygma, is made independent of the shifting results of the historian's work.

The rough outline of Bultmann's project was already visible in writings of his prior to World War II. For example:

> *Jesus Christ confronts man in the kerygma and nowhere else* . . . It is therefore illegitimate to go behind the kerygma, using is as a "source" in order to reconstruct a "historical Jesus", with his "messianic consciousness", his "inner life", or his "heroism". That would be merely "Christ after the flesh", who is no longer. It is not the historical Jesus, but Jesus Christ, the Christ preached, who is the Lord. (Bultmann's italics; *Faith and Understanding – I*, p. 241)

And in an earlier essay, this revealing personal note:

> I have never yet felt uncomfortable with my critical radicalism; on the contrary, I have been entirely comfortable. But I often have the impression that my conservative New Testament colleagues feel very uncomfortable, for I see them perpetually engaged in salvage operations. *I calmly let the fire burn* [my italics], for I see that what is consumed is only the fanciful portraits of Life-of-Jesus theology, and that means nothing other than "Christ after the flesh". (ibid., p. 132)

One line is worth repeating here: "I calmly let the fire burn"! Bultmann the theologian can calmly watch as the fire produced by Bultmann the historian burns up the assumptions of orthodox doctrine. The kerygma, which is the real locale of Christian faith, here and now, is sovereignly independent of whatever modern scholarship can dig up from the past. Bultmann reiterates that neither Paul nor John had any interest in the teachings of Jesus, or for that matter any other aspect of the historical Jesus. Rather, their focus is on the *event* of Jesus, which is only revealed (at least for Paul) in his Resurrection.

It is worth noting that, in his rejection of all the positions of liberal Protestantism, Bultmann here shows the influence of Karl Barth. Going farther back, Bultmann shows his Lutheran roots. He repeatedly quotes Melanchthon: "To know Christ is to know his benefits." This is a variant of Luther's own insistence that the Christ of faith is the Christ who is there *for me* – "*Christus pro me.*" This should not be misinterpreted as some sort of egocentrism, rather to be understood as an honest acknowledgment that I cannot escape the cognitive limitations of my own situation in time and space.

Rather than delving into the turbulence of the debate over Bultmann's manifesto on demythologization, I propose looking at a curious and revealing essay written later in Bultmann's life. Bultmann was asked, in his capacity as a prominent New Testament scholar, to comment on the lapidary credal statement adopted by the newly formed World Council of

Churches at its inaugural assembly in Amsterdam. The statement announces that "the World Council of Churches is composed of churches which acknowledge Jesus Christ as God and Savior." Bultmann's response is contained in a lecture delivered at a theological conference in Switzerland in 1951 (published in his *Essays Philosophical and Theological*).

If asked whether this formulation is in accordance with the New Testament, Bultmann states that, basically, he would have to say, "I don't know." The formulation is ambiguous. But more importantly, the New Testament does not give a clear-cut answer. He makes some comments on the ambiguity of the term "savior," but he then focuses on the question whether the New Testament understands Jesus Christ as God: "Neither in the Synoptic Gospels nor in the Pauline Epistles is Jesus called God; nor do we find him so called in the Acts of the Apostles or in the Apocalypse" (ibid., p. 275). There are several passages where God and Christ are mentioned closely together, but these do not imply identity between the two. The only unambiguous passage is in John 20:28, where Thomas addresses Jesus as "my Lord and my God" (and, as with much of John's Gospel, there is the question of when this passage is to be dated). Only in the Apostolic Fathers does one find unambiguous references to Jesus Christ as "our God." All other titles given to Jesus in the New Testament understand him as being subordinate to God – such as "Messiah," "Son of Man," "Son of God," even "Lord" (*kyrios*, which Bultmann ascribes to Hellenistic influences).

My reading of Bultmann is as follows: God was seen as *present* in Jesus during his lifetime, and dramatically so after the event called the Resurrection. The early Christian community worshipped Jesus as a "divine figure," Bultmann says, "as *theios* we might most conveniently say in Greek – and so as a god, but not simply as God" (ibid., p. 279). He is always distinguished from God the Father. And none of the titles given to Jesus are meant to refer to his "nature" (*physis*), but to his revelation as God's word to us – again, the *Christus pro me*.

And here is the key statement is this essay (p. 287):

> It may be said that in him God is encountered. The formula "Christ is God" is false in every sense in which God is understood as an entity which can be objectivized, whether it is understood in an Arian or Nicene, an Orthodox or a Liberal sense. It is correct, if "God" is understood here as the event of God's acting. But my question is, ought one not rather avoid such formulae on account of misunderstanding and cheerfully content oneself with saying that he is the Word of God?

The later Christological formulations, from the Council of Nicaea on, are then understood by Bultmann as due to the need to cast Christianity in the language of Hellenistic thought, and as such not binding on us today.

This is an impressive, not to say elegant intellectual exercise. Just as Bultmann is "comfortable" with all the explosive findings of modern historical scholarship, so he "cheerfully" leaves behind all the agonizing Christological debates of the early Church. What is wrong with Bultmann's project? I would suggest that two things are wrong with it: Its view of the modern mind is too narrow, and his view of mythology is too broad. In his foundational essay on demythologization, Bultmann states that people today, who use radio and electricity and who when ill make use of modern medicine, cannot accept the miracles (and thus the entire "mythological" worldview) of the New Testament. This is not a theological but a *sociological* statement – and there is very little empirical evidence for it. The sociologist of contemporary religion can show that, with the exception of rather limited groups (prominent among them people with higher education in the humanities and social sciences), modern people are very capable indeed of accepting all sorts of miracles and full-blown "mythological" worldviews. Put simply, mythology is alive and well in the modern world. But Bultmann's view of mythology itself is too broad. It encompasses every intrusion of transcendent reality (of the supernatural, if you will) into the world of human experience. In other words, it encompasses just about everything that most people have understood as religion. Curiously, as some of Bultmann's critics have pointed out, it *excludes* what he calls the "event" of God's presence in Jesus and in the kerygma. Should this not also be called "mythological"? If so, nothing remains of Christianity beyond a somewhat eccentric philosophical understanding of the alienation or inauthenticity of the human condition, liberation from which could (and has been) just as well expressed in non-Christian language.

But there is also something very right about Bultmann's project: Faith cannot be based on any historical construction. My faith in Christ can only be based on the recognition of "Christ for me." Let me put this in the language I suggested earlier in this book: I do indeed encounter this Christ in the kerygma, but this encounter will only be meaningful to me if I can find the *nexus* between it and my own experience of reality. And this nexus cannot dogmatically exclude whatever Bultmann chose to call "mythology."

Paul Tillich, unlike Bultmann, was a systematic theologian. Like Bultmann, he came out of the milieu of German Protestantism and was influenced by the eruption of Barthian theology in the 1920s as well as by existential philosophy. Unlike Bultmann, he emigrated to America, where his major theological opus was produced after World War II. His solution to the problem of the historical Jesus was quite similar to Bultmann's, though perhaps even more radical in its formulation. I will only cite some passages from the second volume of Tillich's magisterial three-volume theological system (*Systematic Theology*), the volume tellingly entitled "Existence and The Christ."

According to Tillich, Christian faith brings about, or is supposed to bring about, a change in human existence which he called the "New Being": "Christianity is what it is through the affirmation that Jesus of Nazareth, who has been called 'the Christ', is actually the Christ, he who brings the new state of things, the New Being" (ibid., p. 97). Not a very elegant sentence, but clear enough: As with Bultmann's project, Tillich's proposal is that Christ should be understood as the symbol which effectively mediates a new form of human existence. But Tillich must also face the problem of how this Christ relates to the Jesus which historical scholarship has tried to understand.

Tillich is in agreement with the view that the historian's attempt to discover the "real" Jesus beyond the kerygmatic sources has not succeeded: "The attempt of historical criticism to find the empirical truth about Jesus of Nazareth was a failure. The historical Jesus, namely, the Jesus behind the symbols of his reception as the Christ, not only did not appear but receded farther and farther with every new step" (ibid., p. 102). And further:

> The search for the historical Jesus was an attempt to discover a minimum of reliable facts about the man Jesus of Nazareth, in order to provide a safe foundation for the Christian faith. This attempt was a failure. Historical research provided probabilities about Jesus of a higher or lower degree. On the basis of these probabilities, it sketched "Lives of Jesus". But they were more like novels than biographies; they certainly could not provide a safe foundation for the Christian faith. Christianity is not based on the acceptance of a historical novel; it is based on the witness to the messianic character of Jesus by people who were not interested at all in a biography of the Messiah. (ibid., p. 105)

The resultant position is, once again, a reiteration of a very Lutheran understanding of "Christ for me":

> One must say that participation, not historical argument, guarantees the reality of the event upon which Christianity is based. It guarantees a personal life in which the New Being has conquered the old being. But it does not guarantee his name to be Jesus of Nazareth. Historical doubt concerning the existence and the life of someone with this name cannot be over-ruled. *He might have had another name.* (ibid., p. 114; my italics)

Or, one might add, he may not have existed in history at all! And perhaps the sharpest statement of this view: "The New Being is not dependent on the special symbols in which it is expressed. It has the power to be free from every form in which it appears" (ibid., p. 165).

Tillich's theological system is one of impressive philosophical sophistication, and I cannot claim the competence of fully evaluating it. However, it seems to me that it is similar to Bultmann's project in that it effectively immanentizes the "Christ event" – that is, it becomes an event *within* human existence in this world, a symbol of the existential transformation which Tillich called the "New Being." Leave aside the point that the precise nature of this transformation remains rather nebulous. More importantly, one must ask, if this transformation can be brought about with a variety of symbolic representations, why could one not, say, substitute the symbolism of Mahayana Buddhism, with the name of this or that *Bodhisattva* replacing the name of Jesus Christ? What is lost here is not just the connection with the historical Jesus, but also with the cosmic process of redemption with which Christian faith has associated the person of Jesus Christ (which, no doubt, Bultmann would subsume under the inadmissible category of "mythology"). All the same, I must agree with Tillich, as with Bultmann, that this faith cannot be based on the ever-shifting ground of historical scholarship.

Where does all this leave us?

Despite all the differences between New Testament scholars, there are some statements about Jesus as a historical figure that one can make with a high degree of probability. He was a charismatic preacher and miracle-worker, proclaiming the coming of a Messianic kingdom, understood in essentially Jewish terms as the rule of God over all nations. He also appeared to have believed that this event was imminent, and that in some way it was already being inaugurated by him and somehow connected with his person. His teaching remained within the context of Jewish piety and as such was largely unoriginal, though it placed unusual emphasis on God's fatherly compassion, especially as directed toward the poor and the despised. This teaching, however, must also be seen in the perspective of the imminent advent of God's kingdom – that is, it refers to the eschatological future rather than to the empirical present. Thus the Beatitudes, the core of the Sermon on the Mount so much cherished by those who would see Jesus as the teacher of a new morality, all refer to the future kingdom. Jesus did not intend to set up a new moral code to replace the Jewish Torah. Even so, his activity, especially in and around the Jerusalem sanctuary, upset the Jewish religious authorities (as religious authorities have always been upset by charismatic preachers). It is also reasonably clear that he did not understand his activity to be a political one, though it was so understood by the Roman colonial government, which could not care less about intra-Jewish religious squabbles but which was alert to any potential threat to its precarious hold on a turbulent province. Thus it was as a political rebel ("king of the Jews") that Jesus was executed on a Roman cross.

Thus the critics of the liberal view of Jesus, from Albert Schweitzer on, have been correct that the New Testament account does not support that view – that is, does not support the view of Jesus as the teacher of an innovative morality or as a spiritual exemplar – at least insofar as neither he nor his immediate disciples intended anything like this. On the other hand, the liberal New Testament scholars, from the early nineteenth century on, were also correct in stating that the New Testament account does not support the way in which orthodox Christians have viewed Jesus – neither he nor the Apostles, probably not even Paul, would have assented to the Christological affirmations of, say, the Nicene Creed.

If the story of Jesus had ended with his death, what interest would there be in it? Perhaps as a moving episode of Quixotic failure and fatal misunderstanding, but hardly more than that. Søren Kierkegaard suggested that Christians should become contemporaneous with Jesus, by which he meant that Christians today should, as far as possible, imagine that they were actually present as Jesus went about his activities in Galilee and elsewhere. It seems to me that this is a perilous suggestion. Would we have liked him? I rather doubt it. Nor does the bulk of his followers, in all the centuries since then, offer much inspiration. One can make a very plausible historical argument to the effect that many of the moral insights we cherish today, notably those concerning human rights, have Christian roots. Having achieved those insights, however, there is no compelling reason why we should have to share the religious assumptions on which they were originally based. If morality is what Jesus was all about, then what we owe him is a gesture of historical gratitude, and no more. We can also note that, with admirable exceptions here and there, Christians over the centuries have not been famous for their moral excellence. One is reminded here of Nietzsche's quip, that he would find the redemption promised by Christianity more credible if the Christians looked more redeeemed. And if Jesus is to be understood as an exemplar of the spiritual life, there are indeed individuals who have tried to live up to this aspiration. They are the ones commonly called saints. Some of them were indeed admirable. Many of them, I suspect, would not be very likeable if we were actually contemporaneous with them. In any case, to admire individuals for their personal qualities or actions need not imply agreement with their worldviews, religious or other. In our own time there have been very admirable Communists, for example in the resistance movements against Nazism, but to acknowledge the admiration does not obligate us to give credence to Marxist ideology.

With this I come to the central proposition of this chapter: *An affirmation of faith in Jesus Christ hinges on the Resurrection as an event, not in human existence or consciousness, but in the reality of the cosmos.* Put differently: *Not Good Friday but Easter morning is pivotal for Christian faith.* This was succinctly put by the Apostle Paul: "If Christ has not been raised, then our preaching is in vain and your faith is in vain" (1 Corinthians 15:14). And one can go a step further: *Only through the Resurrection is Jesus perceivable as the Christ – that is, as cosmic redeemer, and as victor over all the evils and sufferings of this world.*

We will have to return in greater detail to the Resurrection as an event later in this book. But some observations are necessary at this point of the argument: More so than with any other portion of the New Testament accounts, there is no way in which historical scholarship can establish "what really happened" (which, as Leopold von Ranke put it, is the aim of historical scholarship). But whatever the historians may be able to say about what occurred in Jerusalem on that day, Christian faith cannot be held hostage to their findings. Faith in the Resurrection is faith in a pivotal shift in the cosmic drama of redemption, not in (let us say) a televisable occurrence in a Judean graveyard. Obviously, the perception of this shift, first by Jesus' mourning followers and ever since by believing Christians, took place *through and around* this occurrence. But the perception is not dependent upon the empirical circumstances of the occurrence. A sort of science-fiction exercise of the imagination may be useful here. Suppose that, at some time in the future, scientists may be able to retrieve images of past events from light projected from earth to outer space. Suppose further that such retrieval could be pinpointed in such a way as to allow actual viewing (perhaps on special television sets) of particular occurences in past history. And then suppose that one would see (as Reimarus thought) that some of the disciples made off with Jesus' body in the early hours of the third day, and a little later that one would see the women looking with amazement on the empty tomb. Or, alternatively, suppose that one would be able to see that Jesus did not really die on the cross, that he revived and took off from wherever his unconscious body had been laid – and, who knows, lived quietly to an old age, having prudently given up any charismatic activities. Would these television images destroy faith in the Resurrection? I think not. With a little straining I could put my opinion on this in a formula derived from Lutheran theology: The Lutheran view of the eucharist is that Christ is present "in, with, and under" the physical elements of bread and wine, but without the empirical nature of these elements being miraculously changed. By analogy, one might say that the cosmic event of the Resurrection took place "in, with, and under" the occurrences in Jerusalem at that time, but the event was not and is not dependent on "what really happened" empirically. (All analogies limp, but I find this one suggestive.)

Historical scholarship (at least at a time when trans-galactic television is not yet available) *can* establish one important fact: More or less immediately after Jesus' crucifixion, which must have been a shattering event to his followers, some of them became triumphantly convinced that he had been resurrected from the dead and that he was again present among them, not as a resuscitated corpse (the Resurrection narratives do not resemble, say, the account of the raising of Lazarus), but as an enormously powerful spiritual being. It is *as such a being* that Jesus of Nazareth became the Christ of faith. This was so for the surviving disciples of Jesus as it was for Paul, in the dramatic reversal between Good Friday and Easter. I am proposing that this is equally so for us many centuries later: In the light of Easter the life of Jesus takes on an entirely different meaning. It is now seen as the extreme humiliation, the *kenosis*, of God within the world, culminating in the agonizing death of Jesus. This kenosis would be utterly unbearable, tantamount with the ultimate defeat of God, if it were not for its being a prelude to the victory of Easter. Only in the light of Christ the victor does the kenotic Jesus acquire redeeming significance. At that point, however, the kenosis of God in Jesus embraces every tragedy and frailty of Jesus' empirical life – even, perhaps, whatever personal frailty we might have discovered if we had indeed been contemporaneous with him. I will risk a possibly offensive statement: The kenosis of Jesus' mundane life would simply be accentuated if it turns out that he was not an especially likeable person – and that kenotic fact would then also be swallowed up (*aufgehoben*, if you will) in the transcendent event of the Resurrection.

Let me return, then, to the language I used earlier: What is the *nexus* here? It is precisely in the dramatic tension and link between Good Friday and Easter, between kenosis and cosmic victory. And this brings us back to the tension we discussed earlier in the context of theodicy – the tension between the benevolence and the omnipotence of God. Kenosis is the utmost stretch of the benevolence, the Resurrection the utmost expression of the omnipotence. I have suggested that the agonizing problem of theodicy can only be addressed ("solved" would be an inappropriate word to use here) if God is perceived as suffering within creation; if that suffering is understood, however falteringly, as necessary for the redemption of a flawed creation; and if God is also perceived as the one who, at the end of time, will be judge and ruler of all. It hardly needs emphasizing that we stand here before a mystery, that any language used to conceptualize it will be a kind of stammering. Christian faith affirms the mystery, and in that affirmation I can say that I believe in Jesus Christ.

The mystery (Paul called it the "scandal") stands at the core of Christian faith. Christian theologians have been stammering about it ever since – often, unfortunately, in tones of highly implausible certitude. The attempt to articulate the mystery characterizes all post-Easter Christology. Inevitably, I think, it pushed Christian thought toward an understanding of Christ as pre-existing the earthly life of Jesus (already expressed eloquently in the preamble to the Gospel of John) and as post-existing this life. Thus Christ, as the redeeming power of God, was affirmed as having been with the Father since before the creation of the world. And he was affirmed as continuing to be active beyond his empirical life span – raised from the dead, ascended to heaven, and destined to return in glory to establish the kingdom he announced. These affirmations imply redemption as a cosmic event, as a breaking-in of God's power into this world.

It should now be reasonably clear where I would agree with Bultmann's and Tillich's way of dealing with the historical Jesus – that is, by liberating the Christ of faith from the vicissitudes of the historian's labors. It will also be clear where I must disagree – with any formulation that interprets Christ as a symbol of human existential predicaments and thus obscures the cosmic reality of his redeeming work.

I have repeatedly used the word "perception": The disciples "perceived" Christ as having risen from the dead, we can "perceive" the kenosis of Jesus' life and its being the prelude to the Resurrection, and so on. These "perceptions" are movements of human consciousness, occurring within human history. And, of course, in the act of faith these "perceptions" are deemed to be insights into truths that transcend human consciousness, that are, as it were, "out there" in the reality of the cosmos. But in the act of faith one can also speak here of *revelation*. I have touched on this point before in referring to the religious development recorded in the Hebrew Bible: As Eric Voegelin put it, Israel "discovered" God (or, one could say, Israel "perceived" God in a distinctive way). But, if God exists, then he had *to allow* this discovery, this perception to take place. We can then say that God revealed Himself to Israel. By the same token, we can say that God revealed Himself in Jesus Christ.

Chapter Six

"He was conceived by the power of the Holy Spirit and born of the virgin Mary"

The question discussed in the preceding chapter was how the historical Jesus relates to the Christ of faith. The question to be addressed now is, as it were, the other side of the coin:

How does the Christ of faith relate to the one God of the Biblical tradition?

In theological terminology, this is the question of Christology. It is arguably *the* central question of Christian theology, and it has troubled the Church from the beginning to our own time.

The sentence from the Apostles' Creed that serves as the title of this chapter, like other sentences of the Creed, contains within it an immense tension. On the one hand, Jesus Christ is defined as some sort of supernatural being. On the other hand, he is described as a human being born of a particular woman. Eternity and time collide in this sentence. God, who dwells in eternity infinitely removed from the vicissitudes of the human condition, breaks into that condition at a particular time and in a particular place. It was clear from the beginning of Christian thought that this paradoxical proposition reflects a mystery that cannot be grasped by finite human minds. As we talk about it, we can only babble. Yet, endowed with reason, we must reflect about it, even if what comes out is so much babbling. Christian thinkers have been babbling about it for centuries, and the results of their efforts are of continuing interest.

There are two items in the sentence that will not be dealt with here at any length. This chapter will not deal at all with the question of what is meant by the Holy Spirit. This will be discussed in a later chapter and, of course, it involves the peculiar Christian doctrine of the Trinity. But brief mention must be made of the question of the virginity of Mary, if only to suggest that it is not of great significance for the central concern of this chapter (though it is very much a concern to many Christians, especially in the Catholic and Orthodox traditions, for whom Mary is part and parcel of their faith).

The great majority of New Testament scholars agree that the stories dealing with the virgin birth of Jesus constitute a late insertion into Gospels and were not present in the original oral tradition that preceded the written texts. Probably there were two reasons for this insertion. For one, there was the intention to show that the events of the life of Jesus fulfilled certain prophecies of the Hebrew Bible. Specifically, the birth of Jesus was linked to the prophecy in the seventh chapter of the Book of Isaiah, which predicted that a young woman would give birth to a man of great salvific who would be called Immanuel (in Hebrew, "God with us"). Jesus is then to be understood as that Immanuel, in whom God indeed came to us. Very likely this proposition in the Greek text of the New Testament is the consequence of a mistranslation. The Hebrew word in the Isaiah prophecy is *almah*, which simply means a young woman, with no implication of virginity. The Septuagint, the great translation of the Hebrew Bible into Greek (which became the Bible of Greek-speaking Jews outside Palestine and which, of course, was known by the New Testament writers), translated *almah* as *parthenos*, which does mean virgin. This may well be the most important case in history of the carelessness of a translator having huge consequence! Be this as it may, the other reason for the appearance of the virgin birth in the Gospels may be the influence of Hellenistic culture on the young Greek-speaking Christian communities outside Palestine. Graeco-Roman religion was full of stories about divine or semi-divine figures whose birth was supposed to have a supernatural character. The virgin birth would certify that Jesus was not inferior to these figures in terms of his supernatural status. But all these matters, I would contend, can be left to the historians. As far as the question of the present chapter is concerned, the topic of the virgin birth can be safely bracketed.

The development of Christological doctrine engendered immense and often irritating complexities. At its core, however, there is an essentially simple concern: The first Christian community, after the event of the Resurrection if not earlier, perceived in Jesus a quality that transcended his human person and which had to be in some sense divine. If so, how was this to be understood without offending belief in the one God of the Hebrew Bible, which Christians continued to adhere to? Here was from the beginning the central paradox of Christian faith, the "scandal" of which the Apostle Paul spoke. As he well understood, both Jews and Greeks were "scandalized." Jews saw a blasphemous infringement of the monotheism at the core of their faith, and it was exactly for this reason that the Jewish religious authorities excommunicated Christianity. Greeks on the other hand had no problem with a divine being descending into the human world (after all, their gods did it all the time), but they could not swallow the historical location of the life and death of this allegedly divine being – born of a particular Jewish woman and crucified by a particular Roman governor.

As Christology developed in the early centuries of the Church, its increasingly complex formulations were couched in the language of Greek philosophical thought. This was unavoidable, as Christians had to explain their faith, to others as well as to themselves, within their cultural milieu. The terminology they used in this ongoing effort is quite alien to modern minds and difficult to translate so as to make sense to people in a very different milieu. There are such terms as *ousia, prosopon, hypostasis* – inadequately rendered by modern terms such as "being," "substance," "person." Sometimes the early Christological controversies seem densely obscure, and sometimes they give rise to the suspicion that they were carried on by academic types enamored of philosophical hair-splitting. What is more, historians are able to show how many of these theological positions served very hard political interests – power plays by emperors, patriarchs, and bishops, and rivalries between different Christian centers such as Constantinople, Alexandria, Antioch, and Rome. All of this can be stipulated. To be sure, some of these controversialists were probably individuals who (like academics ever since) had no interests but a passionate desire to shoot the theories of others out of the water, and of course there were Macchiavellian types who could not care less about theology but who embraced this or that position because it served their political interests. It is all the more important to understand that, at their core, the Christological controversies were *driven by soteriology* – that is, they were driven by the overriding need to affirm the redemptive significance of Jesus Christ. This concern meant that, somehow, the human and the supernatural aspects of Christ had to be balanced. Losing the balance in either direction endangered his redemptive significance. If the human aspect was overemphasized, Jesus would be simply one in a long line of prophets or great teachers, in which case the startling *novum* of Resurrection would have to be set aside. If on the other hand the supernatural aspect was overemphasized, Christ would be a divine being who only seemed to be human during the short episode of his life on earth, and this would set aside the central Christian belief that God Himself came to share the human condition in Jesus Christ. In either case, the redemption proclaimed by Christian faith would become implausible. Hence the long struggle to maintain the balance.

Historians of the early Church have as many disagreements as any other group of historians, but the probable sequence of events is as follows (in the main, I rely here on the classic work of Wilhelm Bousset, *Kyrios Christos*, which dates from 1913 but still seems to be a reliable source). As mentioned in the preceding chapter, there was no assumption of identity between, Jesus and God in the original Palestinian community of followers, both in Jesus' lifetime and immediately afterward. The earliest Christian community proclaimed Jesus as a human being revealed by the Resurrection to be the coming Messiah, though even then there was a perception that he had qualities that were more than human. In the early Christian communities among Hellenized Jews outside Palestine (notably in Damascus and Antioch) there developed a cultic worship in which Jesus Christ was invoked as Lord, *kyrios*, in ever-closer proximity to God. This worship was particularly centered in the celebrations of baptism and eucharist. Paul's so-called "Christ mysticism" reflects the beliefs of these communities – after all, it was in Damascus that Paul first made contact with a Christian community after his conversion. Yet Paul nowhere identifies the *kyrios* with God.

In the Johannine tradition (which, at least in its written texts, post-dates the writings of Paul) there is found a decided emphasis on the pre-existence of Christ as the *Logos*, the word of God – that is, Christ as existing before the earthly life of Jesus. This belief is, of course, eloquently expressed in the prologue to the Gospel of John. The belief in this pre-existing Christ is now quite divorced from Jewish Messianic expectations (the name "Christ" has now lost its original Hebrew connotations and has simply become part of the Lord's name – Jesus Christ). Jesus' earthly life is now seen as a sort of episode in the eternal being of the *Logos*/Christ, which implies an increasing proximity between Christ and God. It seems likely that John built on Paul, but with an important difference: Paul had no interest in Jesus "after the flesh" – that is, in the events of his life on earth – while the Gospel of John draws a detailed picture of this life, but now reinterpreted in terms of the beliefs pronounced in the prologue.

There is an almost inexorable logic to this development. If a divine presence is perceived in Jesus, this creates a push toward both pre- and post-existence – that is, the divine presence must have preceded Jesus' earthly life and must be continuing after his departure from this life. Again, this push is "soteriologically driven": If God was indeed in Jesus for the redemption of mankind, it could not be contained within one brief episode of human history. Rather, it must have been prepared long before and its culmination is yet in the future. The early Church Fathers (such as Clement and Ignatius) now speak of Jesus Christ as having a dual character, both divine and human. Inevitably, there now had to be reflection on how this duality was to be understood.

Obviously there is no possibility in this chapter of going in any detail into the labyrinthine complexities of the Christological controversies of the early Church. All that can be done here is to seek some grasp of the underlying logic. For reasons that probably have very non-theological roots, the Christian centers of Alexandria and Antioch (both seats of patriarchs from early on) were major antagonists in these debates. Alexandria tended toward emphasizing the divine aspects of Christ, Antioch the human. One can only speculate about the reasons for this – perhaps due to the very different cultural histories of these two cities. Both had a coating of Hellenistic culture and both sets of theologians wrote in Greek. But beneath this Hellenistic facade were very different indigenous cultures – in the case of Alexandria a non-Semitic culture going back many centuries of Egyptian history, in the case of Antioch a Semitic culture with an equally long history. Be this as it may, the two emphases were not geographically determined in an exclusive way – there were Alexandrian theologians who stressed the human character of Christ, and Antiochian ones with the opposite emphasis.

Gnosticism represented an extreme case of de-emphasizing, indeed denying the human character of Christ. A complex body of doctrines, some of which anteceded Christianity, it saw the world as fundamentally evil (thus rejecting the Biblical view of creation) and redemption as total deliverance from this world. Its major Christian proponent was Marcion, one of the early great heretics, who very logically rejected the entire Hebrew Bible (he identified the God of Israel with a satanic figure, the world being the latter's creation) and limited the New Testament to bowdlerized writings of Paul and the Gospel of Luke. Christ then appears as a divine savior coming from a remote God utterly beyond this world. Adolf von Harnack, who wrote the classic study of Marcion, caught this view very aptly in the title of his book *The Gospel of the Alien God*. The church decisively rejected the Marcionite heresy – *its* God was not "alien," but was the creator, who was also the God of Abraham, Isaac, and Jacob revealed in the Hebrew Bible. But, especially in Alexandria, there developed less extreme Christological doctrines, loosely labelled as Monophysite (Christ has only one nature, *physis*, and that a divine one) or Docetism (from the Greek *dokein* "to seem" – Christ only seemed to take human form and thus only seemed to die on the cross). There are various versions of this view, but they all understand Christ as a purely supernatural being, whose human appearance as Jesus is either radically devalued or denied altogether. At the other Christological pole are the so-called Ebionites (the name derives from an early group of Jewish Christians). Here Jesus, the son of Joseph and Mary (no virgin birth at all), so fully fulfilled the Jewish law that God *chose* him to be the Messiah. From this heresy derive various forms of what later came to be called Adoptionism. Here any pre-existence of Christ is denied. Jesus of Nazareth was a fully human being, who was *adopted* by God to be the bearer of redemption. Needless to say, this heresy too was rejected by the mainstream Church early on.

The great Christological debate of the fourth century revolved around Arianism. The major antagonist of this particular heresy was Athanasius, bishop of Alexandria. Its original proponent was Arius (confounding any idea of geographical determinism, he too was an Alexandrian priest). Arius strongly emphasized God's transcendence, which can never be contained in any finite being. Christ belongs to the created world, though he was *similar* (*homoiousion*) to God in his nature. Put simply, Christ was understood as a sort of intermediate being between God and man. Against this , Athanasius insisted that Christ's nature is *identical* (*homoousion*) with God's. Only one letter differentiates the two views, the Greek *iota*, and many jokes have been made about this ever since (the English phrase "not one iota of difference" derives from this ancient debate). Yet it is not too difficult to see that something much more serious than grammatical hairsplitting is involved here. It is not a simplification to say that Arius tried to veer away from the central paradox of Christian fait, while Athanasius was passionately concerned with maintaining it. (Athanasius was also, by all accounts, a thoroughly unattractive individual, intent not only on rejecting opposing views but on utterly liquidating them – but that is neither here not there.)

Athanasius' position was upheld, and Arianism rejected, by the Council of Nicaea, in 325 CE. Despite its glorification by church historians, it was not a particularly savory affair. It was convened by the emperor Constantine, newly converted to Christianity. Whether that conversion had motives other than political expediency is a matter of debate among historians, but it is clear that Constantine had no great interest in the nuances of theological controversy. In the best traditions of Roman statecraft, he believed that political unity required religious unity as well, and therefore these priestly squabbles had to be settled once and for all. As far as Arianism was concerned, the Council certainly did this. And whatever its murky origins, it gave us the Nicene Creed with its eloquent Christological language, affirming faith in "one Lord Jesus Christ, the only-begotten Son of God, begotten of his Father before all worlds. God of God, light of light, very God of very God, begotten, not made, being of one substance (*ousia*) with the Father, by whom all things were made" – after which formulation the Creed goes on to speak of the Incarnation. One may say that the central paradox was gloriously maintained. Needless to say, though, this was not the end of the story.

Different Christological positions continued to oscillate between the two poles and a number of councils sought to maintain the Nicaean balance. In the fifth century the so-called Nestorian controversy became the focus of attention. Nestorius, a priest from Antioch, became patriarch of Constantinople in 428 CE. He engaged in an escalating debate with Cyril, the patriarch of Alexandria. Once again, Alexandria was pitted against Antioch, though the latter was strengthened by its proponent having attained a key position at the center of imperial power. Some modern scholars have argued that Nestorius has been misunderstood and that he was actually closer to the orthodox position than either his critics or his followers believed. Be this as it may, Cyril understood Nestorius to over-emphasize Jesus' humanity and to hold the position that came to be called Adoptionist. Cyril, on the other hand, came very close to a Monophysite view: The only person (*hypostasis*) in Christ is the divine *Logos*, which "took flesh." In this view, Jesus was not really an individual man.

Again, of course, very un-theological political interests were entangled in this controversy. There was not only the old rivalry between Alexandria and Antioch, but also resentment in the former against the pretensions of Constantinople. These persisted for a long time. It is even possible that the same resentment was a factor in the ease with which Islam conquered Egypt a couple of centuries later, and it is also possible that the Monophysite inclinations in Egypt made for an affinity with the radical monotheism of Islam.

There was a curious focus to the Nestorian controversy – Mary, in terms not of her putative virginity but of her relationship to Jesus. It had become common (and not only in Alexandria) to refer to Mary as *theotokos* – "mother of God" – a paradoxical formula if there ever was one. The paradox was too much for Nestorius. He denounced it, instead referring to Mary simply as the "mother of Christ." Cyril waged a relentless campaign in favor of the term *theotokos* and against Nestorius. Appeals were made to the emperor in Constantinople and to the pope. The Council of Ephesus, in 431 CE, endorsed Cyril and Nestorius was banished to an uncomfortable exile in Upper Egypt. It is interesting to note that Nestorian missions continued to be successful in areas outside the Empire, as far east as India. Most of the Christological heresies constituted great simplifications, and these appealed to populations far removed from the sophisticated theological centers of the Mediterranean world (the success of Arianism among German tribes is another case in point).

Two powerful figures finally decided to put a definitive end to the whole matter, the Emperor Marcian and Pope Leo I. The Council of Chalcedon was convened in 451 CE. It attempted to find a middle ground between Alexandria and Antioch. It endorsed the term *theotokos* and it affirmed that there was a single reality (*hypostasis*) in Christ, but it also insisted that this reality was simultaneously that of the eternal *Logos* and of a singular human being. The key Chalcedonian "definition" sounds somewhat bizarre to modern ears, but behind the strained language one can once again perceive the passionate desire to preserve the central mystery of Christian faith:

> Wherefore, following the holy Fathers, we all with one voice confess our Lord Jesus Christ one and the same God, the same perfect in Godhead, the same perfect in manhood, truly God and truly man, the same consisting of a reasonable soul and a body, of one substance (*ousia*) with the Father as touching the Godhead, the same of one substance with us as touching the manhood, like us in all things except sin; begotten of the Father before the ages as touching the Godhead, the same in the last days, for us and for our salvation, born from the Virgin Mary, the Theotokos, as touching the manhood, one and the same Christ, Son, Lord only-begotten, to be acknowledged in two natures, without confusion, without change, without division, without separation; the distinction of natures being in no way abolished because of the union but rather the characteristic property of each nature being preserved, and concurring in one person (*prosopon*) and one hypostasis, not as if Christ were parted or divided into two persons, but one and the same Son and only-begotten God, Word (*Logos*), Lord, Jesus Christ; even as the prophets from the beginning spoke concerning him, and our Lord Jesus Christ instructed us, and the Creed of the Fathers was handed down to us.

I thinks it is fair to say that any modern person, who is unfamiliar with the nuances of Hellenistic philosophical discourse, will read this text with mixed feelings. On one level, it reads like gibberish. But on another level it is clear what the people assembled at Chalcedon tried to do – to preserve the redemptive status of Christ against two opposite positions that would, each in its way, diminish it.

Nobody was totally happy with the Chalcedonian resolution. Christological controversies, in ever new forms, continued throughout Byzantine history, at least through the twelfth century. Nor were the various political interests finally resolved. The pope played an important role in convening the Council and in influencing its course. But, at the insistence of the emperor, the Council also adopted a statement declaring that the ecclesiastical status of Constantinople was equal to that of Rome – a move that infuriated the pope.

What, then, is one to make of all this? It is a murky history. Yet it is also the history of the Church developing a consensus on how to understand the redemptive role of Christ. It seems to me that one can agree with this effort, even if much of the language and the conceptual machinery is grating on modern ears.

Most of modern theology has gravitated toward "Antioch" rather than "Alexandria." The liberal Protestant interpretation of Jesus, which was touched upon in the preceding chapter, could well be labelled "Ebionite" in tendency. For an example, we can turn once more to John Hick, an unusually prolific author, who has included Christology in his many intellectual concerns. In 1977 a book was published under his editorship, *The Myth of God Incarnate*, which gave rise to a prolonged controversy. The book was a collection of essays by a group of liberal Protestant theologians. The title of the book succinctly sums up their central thesis, as does the title of an essay by one of them, Maurice Wiles, "Christianity without Incarnation?" (the question mark is somewhat disingenuous). Frances Young summarizes the findings of New Testament scholarship that we have previously touched upon: There is no evidence that Jesus, or his immediate disciples, or even Paul, attributed divinity to him; all of this was a later development. However, as Hick says in the preface, there continues to be the belief of "honest and thoughtful people who are deeply attracted by the figure of Jesus and by the light which his teaching throws upon the meaning of human life" (p. ix). Therefore, in order to safeguard this belief, Christian thought must adapt itself to the cognitive presuppositions of the modern mind. As to what this modern mind can supposedly tolerate, Hick is in substantial agreement with Rudolf Bultmann. It is thus necessary to abandon the "mythological" elements from the New Testament, and to concentrate on the "figure of Jesus" and on "his teaching," so that "honest and thoughtful people" (many of them domiciled in academia) can go on regarding themselves as, in some sense, Christians. Here, once more, we have Jesus as an admirable exemplar and as a great teacher. There is no reason to repeat here what I have suggested earlier – that this Jesus is eminently uninteresting and that, "honestly and thoughtfully," we can do well without him.

Here is how one of the authors, Michael Goulder, describes this position: "I see the growth of a community of self-giving love as the basic thrust of the will of God in human history, and I see that community as exemplified primarily in the church founded by Jesus" (p. 57). And a little further on: "I understand Jesus to have been destined by God to establish the community of selfless love in the world" (p. 60). It seems to me that what we have here, all too common in liberal Protestantism, is a pallid moralism. I would contend that its maxims are utopian and that, in the real world, they are very likely to lead to catastrophic consequences. But that is another story. What is relevant to the present argument is that this understanding of Christianity must divorce itself from the portrayal of Jesus in the New Testament (Albert Schweitzer had this right) and that it leads to a religious position that is unable to answer the searing questions raised by the harsh realities of the human condition. Goulder himself describes his position as "a christology of agency rather than substance" – and the "agency" of his Jesus never transcends the parameters of this world.

However, there are more nuanced voices within the volume edited by Hick. Perhaps the most interesting contribution is by Frances Young, herself a New Testament scholar rather than a systematic theologian. She certainly shares the (so to speak) Bultmannian assumptions about that awesome creature "the modern mind":

> The Christians of the early church lived in a world in which supernatural causation was accepted without question, and divine or spiritual visitants were not unaccepted. Such assumptions, however, have become foreign to our situation. In the Western world, both popular culture and the culture of the intelligentsia has come to be dominated by the human and natural sciences to such an extent that supernatural causation or intervention in the affairs of this world has become, for the majority of people, simply incredible. (p. 31)

One wonders what kind of sociological research Young undertook outside the campus of the University of Birmingham (where she was then teaching) to arrive at this lapidary statement. "Simply incredible" – to whom? More importantly, it does not seem to have occurred to Young that the "majority of people" might conceivably be mistaken, and that all sorts of supernatural beings might be hovering around Birmingham, unseen by her colleagues gathered in the common room. Still, having delivered herself of this empirically dubious manifesto concerning credibility, she develops an argument considerably less pallid than the positions staked out by Hick and Goulder.

She becomes quite eloquent at this point: "Salvation and atonement are the core of the Christian message . . . Faith demands a doctrine of atonement, and atonement means a conviction that God has somehow dealt with evil, with sin, with rebellion; that on the cross, God in Christ entered into the suffering, the evil and the sin of this world – entered the darkness and transformed it into light, into blazing glory" (pp. 34f). Note the phrase "God in Christ" – it does not exactly fit into the modern epistemology which, just before, Young had declared to be mandatory. And note the word "somehow" – and here Young suddenly finds herself in the company of the people who tried to puzzle this out at Nicaea and Chalcedon.

To be sure, Young continues to insist that this faith must free itself from what she calls "mythological language." But then she says: "I find salvation in Christ, because in him God is disclosed to me as a 'suffering God'" (p. 38). I, for one, am quite comfortable with this sentence. It agrees very nicely with the nexus I tried to formulate in the chapter on the problem of theodicy. And I agree further with Young's statement that, in thinking about the status of Jesus Christ, one must acknowledge the "primacy of soteriology." In this acknowledgment both she and I find ourselves in (possibly uncomfortable) proximity to those who define themselves in more orthodox terms.

Let me introduce here a couple of such more orthodox types in recent theology. The first is Donald Baillie (*God Was in Christ*). Here is how he explains the reason for trying to formulate a Christology, whose purpose is to explicate our understanding, not just of Jesus, but of *God*: "A true Christology will tell us not simply that God is *like* Christ, but that God was *in* Christ. Thus it will tell us not only about the *nature* of God, but about His *activity*, about what He has done, coming the whole way for our salvation in Jesus Christ; and there is no other way in which the Christian truth about God can be expressed" (pp. 66f).

Baillie then explains what happened in the early Christian centuries in the developments discussed in the previous pages of this chapter. The Church, in its historic credal statements, insisted on the paradox of Christ being both fully man and fully God, rejecting both the depreciation of his humanity (as in Monophysitism and Docetism) and the depreciation of his divinity (as in Ebionite Christianity), as well as rejecting the (Arian) view of his being some sort of demi-god: "The question was: Is the redeeming purpose which we find in Jesus part of the very being and essence of God? Is it His very nature to create, and to reveal Himself, and to redeem His creation? Is it therefore not some subordinate of interme-diate being, but the Eternal God Himself, that reveals Himself to us and became incarnate in Jesus for our salvation?" (p. 70).

Let me bring out another reasonably orthodox spokesman, John Macquarrie (*Christology Revisited*, Harrisburg, PA: Trinity Press Interna-tional, 1998):

> If we say "God was in Christ", then we are claiming that there was or is something transcendent in Jesus Christ, something that goes beyond a his-torical human life, something that is eternal . . . It would be wrong to say that there is merely an eternal component in Jesus Christ, for that would seem to be splitting him in two, and in any case the eternal component would, so to speak, swallow up the temporal component, as indeed it was allowed to do in some idealist philosophies, with the result that Jesus Christ becomes simply and ideal or an archetype, deprived of his human and his-torical actuality and therefore of his significance for the human condition. (p. 99)

And further:

> If Christ lived on in the power of God after his death, must he not be, like God himself, without beginning as well as without end? . . . Jesus Christ is the expressive being of God, the Word in whom the Source of Godhead,

the Father, has come out of his hiddenness and silence to form a creation. In that creation, the Word had found fullest expression in a human life. We must not suppose that Christ pre-existed in the sense of waiting like an actor in the wings for the cue when he would step on to the stage of history "in the fullness of time". But it does mean that from the beginning Christ the incarnate Word was there in the counsels of God, and even his human-ity, like the humanity of us all, was taking shape in the long ages of cosmic evolution. There is nothing in all this that offends reason, though it cer-tainly goes beyond what reason can reach; and there is nothing in it either that would deny that the divine Word has manifested itself beyond the human life of Jesus, in nature, in history, in the non-Christian religions. But for the Christian, he remains, as Pascal claimed, the centre of every-thing. This is the absolute paradox – that this humble crucified man is also the eternal Word of God. (p. 114)

I have some difficulty ending this chapter. I would not really like to come out of the closet as an orthodox Chalcedonian. I can only return to the nexus I proposed earlier in this book – that God is only credible by way of the kenosis, wherein God is understood as participating in the suffer-ing of this world and as passing through this suffering into triumph. This process is decisively disclosed in Jesus Christ, specifically in his death and resurrection. If God is really in this process, it cannot be simply as a sym-bolic representation that Jesus discloses it. In other words, Jesus Christ cannot simply be a metaphor. What is more, the event of God's disclo-sure in Christ must be cosmic in scope, because it is not just the human condition that is in need of redemption. There is a great flaw in the cre-ation and that flaw must be repaired (in what Jewish mystics called the *tikkun olam*, the "repair of the world"). Therefore, God's presence in Christ must have a cosmic dimension. For these reasons, with all reservations, I can give assent to the Christological affirmations in the historic creeds, even if I wince at the Greek metaphysics. And at this point, perhaps sur-prisingly, I find myself in agreement with Bultmann. I refer to an inci-dent discussed in the preceding chapter. After Bultmann expressed his doubts about the insistence of the World Council of Churches that Jesus Christ be identified with God, he suggests that perhaps we should be "cheerfully content" with saying that Christ is the Word of God. And that Word, the Johannine *logos*, resounds throughout the cosmos and throughout human history.

Excursus: On Prayer in Christ's Name

If Christ is understood as the Word of God, this understanding is grounded at the very core of the Biblical view of God – the view of a God *who speaks*. That is, God is not some impersonal ground of being in which one can eventually immerse oneself, but a person who is obviously immensely different from human persons but who has in common with them, precisely, the quality of speech and thus the capacity of being spoken to. The Hebrew Bible is the testimony of God's speech to Israel and the New Testament of God's having spoken through the man Jesus who is also the cosmic Christ of redemption. As the Christological formulations were puzzled over in the development outlined in the preceding chapter, it became necessary to assume that this Christ pre-existed the earthly life of Jesus – in the Johannine formulation, as the *Logos* who was with God or in God from the beginning, and through whom the speech that brought forth the creation was uttered. And, most important, Christ is the Word that brings about the redemption of the world, the restoration of the damaged creation to its intended glory. It was consistent, then, that from quite early on Christians prayed not only in Christ's name but prayed *to Christ* – the beginnings of the "*kyrios* cult" that was also mentioned in the preceding chapter.

But the question remains for us, living many centuries after these developments:

What does it mean to pray in Christ's name?

First of all, this is clearly not an exercise in magic. In the Gospels Jesus is supposed to have said that, if two or three of his disciples are gathered together in his name, their prayers will be answered. In popular piety this has often been understood as a sort of magical credit card: A prayer issued in the name of Christ must be honored by God with a positive answer. And sometimes this notion was accompanied by the profoundly reprehensible implication that any other prayer (say, by Jews or Muslims or Hindus) would not be acknowledged by God. These ideas are nothing but superstition and can only be dismissed as irreconcilable with the Biblical understanding of God, who cannot be manipulated by magical means.

The most straightforward explanation of what it means to pray in Christ's name is that one should pray as Jesus prayed. New Testament scholars, as we have seen, disagree about virtually everything, but there is a high degree of consensus to the effect that the so-called Lord's Prayer reflects a credible tradition concerning Jesus' teaching on prayer. It has been at the very center of Christian piety over the centuries, magnificent in its simplicity, though that simplicity hides quite a few serious problems. In any case, the Lord's Prayer contains the pregnant phrase "thy will be done on earth as it is in heaven." If this means anything, it means that whatever is prayed for is subject to God's will and that the one who prays submits himself to this will. This phrase has been the most important traditional explanation of unanswered prayers (incidentally, by Jews and Muslims as much as by Christians): Even if God seemingly denies what I have prayed for, I trust that even this denial will ultimately be for my benefit, since God wills my salvation. It seems to me that this explanation accords with the essential character of faith, which is trust in the ultimate goodness of creation. Yet this leaves a lot of open questions. It is useful to make a number of distinctions.

A simple distinction, especially important today when there is a lot of so-called "spirituality" around: *Prayer is not meditation*. In most of its forms, meditation is an inward movement: The individual focuses his attention within himself, "centering" himself, presumably to find some salvific truth in the depths of his own consciousness. I'm not interested here in whether there is anything to be found in these alleged depths other than the murky debris allegedly disclosed by psychoanalysis, or indeed whether there are such depths within us in the first place (I tend to be skeptical on both counts). But even if these inner depths are stipulated as being real, there still remains the question of whether God is to be found there (I can only refer here to the previously mentioned agenda of a theology of mystical experience – an agenda which, I'm happy to say, is beyond the scope of my argument here). The point to be made is, quite simply, that prayer is something different: It turns attention *outward*, not inward, and it is an act of *speech*, not an immersion in a speechless reality. Perhaps a useful way of making this clear is to suggest a mental exercise: Imagine the prophet Isaiah, say, delivering his message while sitting in the lotus position. I would suggest that the exercise must fail. I would even suggest that it would be very difficult to utter the Lord's Prayer from the lotus position. This, of course, does not preclude the possibility that prayer and meditation might be engaged in at different times, perhaps ever sequentially, but this possibility need not be pursued here (I will say that I'm not terribly interested in this possibility).

A further distinction (a traditional one in Christian piety) is between doxological and petitionary prayer. Doxological prayer is prayer of praise, without this or that concrete benefit being asked for (*doxa* is the Greek word for praise). Petitionary prayer is prayer for something – that God may grant this or that, or that He may prevent this or that. In the context of faith, I think, doxological prayer is unproblematic. If one has faith, the impulse to praise is irresistible – presumably not all the time, but certainly in certain moments. In doxological prayer the believer joins, however feebly, in the angelic chorus of praise for (in Dante's words) the love that moves the stars. Petitionary prayer, however, raises many questions.

What should one pray for? Some would suggest that one should only pray for "spiritual" benefits – deeper faith, a greater sense of God's presence, deliverance from the more odious aspects of one's own character. To be sure, such benefits are fit topics for petition. But the Lord's Prayer also includes the petition that God may give us "this day our daily bread." This phrase too has been interpreted in a "spiritual" way – the petition is supposed to be for "spiritual bread," perhaps even for the eucharist (singularly implausible if put in the mouth of Jesus). I rather think that the phrase "daily bread" includes the full range of our mundane, mostly very un-"spiritual" concerns. We pray here that God may sustain our wellbeing and avert the misfortunes that may befall us. This understanding is most fully in accord with Biblical piety, which is not "spiritual" at all, but rather is concerned with the material fate of God's people and with the fate of individual human beings. One only has to read the Psalms, which are the prayer book of ancient Israel.

There is then the argument that petitionary prayer is selfish and therefore to be eschewed. I think that this argument is completely fallacious. Not that there is anything wrong with my praying for myself – after all, if I address God as "Father," I must place before him my own hopes and fears. But petitionary prayer need not be for myself at all. To put it concretely: I may pray to be delivered from an illness that is afflicting me, but I may also pray for the recovery of my neighbor's sick child. And there is nothing selfish about that. Rather, such prayer must flow naturally from my faith in God's love and His care for suffering creation.

Let us say, then, that I pray for my neighbor's sick child. What am I asking for? Am I asking for a miracle – that is, for God's intervention in the causal sequences of this world? I would not dismiss this possibility out of hand. Miracles are not easily imagined within a worldview greatly influenced by modern science, but it seems to me that, if one believes in God's omnipotence, one cannot exclude at least the possibility of His intervening in the causal dynamics of the world. But am I then asking that God should save *this* child, and by implication that He need not save the child down the block? Of course not. My praying for this child is not invidious, and in principle (though hardly in practice) I may pray with equal fervor for all sick children. The empirical fact is that some children recover from illness, while other children do not. This, of course, raises once more the question of theodicy. But this question will be raised regardless of my praying or not praying. And while, as I argued earlier in this book, no neat answer is possible to this question, the act of faith includes the trust that, ultimately, "all will be well."

All the questions about prayer touch upon mystery. No theological for-mulations can liquidate the mystery. But there is one additional consid-eration that might be useful here. My prayer takes place *in time*. The child has been sick since yesterday, I pray for his recovery today, and tomor-row will show whether he recovers or not – a sequence from point A through point B to point C. But God, to whom I pray, is *beyond time*. In Biblical language, He dwells in eternity. Thus what to me appears as a temporal sequence, under the aspect of eternity (*sub specie aeternitatis*) is somehow *simultaneous*. It is possible to speculate that in this eternal per-spective my prayer has, so to speak, been already "figured in," the outcome (point C) affected by the seemingly antecedent event (point B). Charles Williams (the British writer who might be called a metaphysical novelist) has an episode in one of his novels where a prayer uttered today has an effect on a man facing martyrdom many centuries ago – prayer somehow participating in the simultaneity of an eternal reality. I don't think that this line of thinking can penetrate very far into the mystery which envelops God's work of salvation.

If I have faith, I cannot *not* pray. Whatever else my prayer may do, it is my reaching out to the redemptive power that is embodied in Christ. And this, probably, is the most important thing to say about my praying "in Christ's name."

Chapter Seven

"He suffered under Pontius Pilate, was crucified, died and was buried"

There are two rather obvious points to be made about this sentence in the Apostles' Creed. The reference to Pontius Pilate is certainly not intended to bestow a special honor on the sleazy Roman governor who ordered Jesus' crucifixion. Rather, it underlines the historicity of Jesus: He is not to be understood as the ahistorical avatar of some divinity, but as the particular Jewish individual who lived and died in Palestine when Pilate was in charge of that territory. Also, the threefold reiteration of Jesus' end – crucified, died, and buried – is clearly intended as an anti-Docetic statement: Jesus did not *seem* to die on the cross, as various Gnostic and other heretics maintained, but he *really* died as a fully human being. There is no need to say any more here about either of these two points.

There is, however, a pressing question that arises here:

Why did Jesus die?

This question could, of course, be understood as one of empirical history. As such, it has been exhaustively discussed by New Testament scholars. It particularly concerns the question (very relevant in the discussion about the roots of Christian anti-Semitism) of the respective role of Roman and Jewish authorities in the execution of Jesus. While this is an important topic, it is not the one that concerns us here. The question here is not a historical but a theological one: What was accomplished by the death of Jesus Christ? Or, to put it differently: Could Christ's redemptive action not have been accomplished without his death on the cross? Or again: What is the place of the cross in the drama of redemption? In theological parlance, this is the question about the nature of the *atonement* brought about by Christ.

The English word is suggestive: "at-one-ment." Literally, it describes a process of making one what was not one – that is, making whole what was not whole. And it clearly refers to a particular un-wholesome rift, that between God and mankind. Behind this reference stands the Biblical account of mankind's fall from the place God intended for it at its creation, that fall which in the Book of Genesis is symbolized by the story of Adam and Eve, their primeval rebellion against God and their expulsion from paradise. And the terrible consequence of the fall is the loss of immortality: Mankind was created to be immortal, but it now stands under the curse of death. Sin and death are thus linked in the Biblical account of the fall, and they remain linked in the New Testament statements about the atonement: What the atonement is all about is the liberation of mankind from both sin and death.

It may be useful to reiterate here a point made earlier in this book: Evil and suffering, and death itself, are only "natural" in the sense that they mark the human condition as it is now. But to say that this condition is "natural" in no way implies an acceptance of it. This is particularly important with regard to death. It implies a rejection of the facile consolation that death is "natural" and should therefore be accepted. No! Death is not to be accepted; it is an offence against the core "nature" of mankind – that is, the human nature as it was intended in God's creation. An atheist can passionately refuse to accept death; the believer can endorse this refusal by placing it in the context of God's original creation.

Key New Testament texts are clear about one thing: Christ died for us and for our sins, and the purpose of this action is to overcome death and to restore mankind to the immortal state that was lost in the fall. This is stated succinctly in what is probably the most frequently quoted New Testament passage, from the Gospel of John: "For God so loved the world that he gave his only Son, that whoever believes in him should not perish but have eternal life" (John 3:16). Put most simply: The purpose of the atonement is the abolition of death. Other New Testament texts link this action with human sin. Thus a Pauline text: "Jesus our Lord, who was put to death for our trespasses and raised for our justification" (Romans 4:25). And a text from the Johannine tradition: "We have an advocate with the Father, Jesus Christ the righteous, and he is the expiation for our sins, and not for ours only but also for the sins of the whole world" (1 John 2:1–2). To be sure, there are different emphases in different traditions within the New Testament. Thus, I think it is fair to say that the Pauline tradition emphasizes mankind's guilt for its fallen condition, while the Johannine tradition presents that condition as a fate not to be directly or exclusively ascribed to human guilt. Be this as it may, there is a general anthropological presupposition: Mankind is caught, imprisoned, in a condition marked by sin and death. Sin is the state of being separated from God and death is the consequence of this separation. Looming behind the separation from God are what Paul describes as "principalities and powers," meta-human forces of evil personified in the figure of Satan. The latter amplification, if nothing else, implies that the fallen condition of mankind is not simply the result of human guilt. Put differently, sin is not just a moral but an ontological category.

These anthropological assumptions in the New Testament, of course, are the basis of the doctrine of "original sin" – original both in the sense of deriving from the sin of Adam and in the sense of being prior to any particular sinning by individual human beings. Leaving aside the myth of Adam and Eve (which, I daresay, was taken literally by most if not all New Testament writers), the anthropological point that can be made apart from any mythology is that mankind is caught in its rift with God and thus in its "unnatural" subjection to death, and that men cannot overcome the rift by their own efforts, no matter how morally admirable such efforts may be. Only an act of God Himself can repair the damage. What is more, the damage goes beyond the human condition, affecting the entire creation. Thus the work of atonement must have a cosmic scope.

Later on we will have to come back to the various meanings of the term "sin," but one additional comment may be appropriate here. As I try to apply this term to myself, it clearly has a double meaning. First, it applies to particular acts of mine, which are deemed evil and of which I should feel guilty, acts of cruelty or degradation against others. But secondly the term also applies to the very structure of my condition as a human being, which includes a propensity toward evil and which subjects me to the unacceptable fact of death. A Roman Catholic theologian of my acquaintance once remarked that there is one Christian doctrine which requires no faith at all but which can be verified empirically, namely the doctrine of original sin. Well put. Clearly, though, I cannot be held responsible for a condition that antecedes any deliberate act of mine, and I can thus legitimately refuse to feel guilty about it. Saying this, I'm well aware, puts me at odds with a long tradition of Christian piety and thought, probably originating with Paul and proceeding in western Christianity from Augustine to the Protestant Reformation. With all due respect for this tradition, it seems to me that it represents a sort of metaphysical masochism which, I think, is not a necessary component of Christian faith.

In the history of Christian thought, at least in the West, there has been a predominance of the so-called "objective" view of the atonement. It is very rational, indeed juridical in character. The atonement is understood as a sort of legal transaction. The sacrifice of Jesus, his crucifixion and death, is undertaken by him as the representative man (the "new Adam", as it were) as a payment for human sin to God the Father (or, in some versions, to Satan, who is somehow entitled to it).

The classical and immensely influential elaboration of this idea was made by Anselm of Canterbury (1033–1109 CE) in his work *Cur Deus homo?* ("Why did God become man?"). Anselm was an Italian by birth, who became a monk at the monastery of Bec, in Normandy. He achieved considerable renown as a theologian and became archbishop of Canterbury in 1093 (note that this was less than a generation after the Norman conquest of England). He had various disputes with the English/ Norman royal authorities over matters of ecclesiastical jurisdiction, and went to Rome to obtain papal rulings on these disputes. He finished the aforementioned work in 1098, while staying in a village near Benevento. By all accounts Anselm was a man of admirable moral probity and of a very astute mind. I would venture the opinion that the latter quality was not an unmixed blessing, as it led him into an argument of great logical consistency and by the same token to a theory of the atonement imply- ing a rather repulsive view of the nature of God.

The basic Anselmian argument is as follows: The atonement consists of a remission by God of the punishment due to Him for human sin. The question then becomes why God cannot grant the remission by compas- sion alone. He cannot do so because His will cannot be arbitrary, but must be in conformity with the moral order of the universe established by Him. This order cannot be violated and God cannot be inconsistent. Sin must be punished. The debt must be paid. And this is where Christ comes in. This is how a commentator describes the core of Anselm's argument: "God will not pay the debt, because he has no debt to pay; man, because he cannot – he has made himself impotent by his fall. One being alone could do this, one who is perfect God and perfect Man" (Arnold Whately in his essay on Anselm, in L. W. Grensted, ed., *The Atonement in History and in Life*, p. 205).

But let Anselm speak for himself: "The just treatment of unatoned sin is to punish it; if it be not punished, it is unjustly forgiven. . . . Therefore it beseemeth not God thus to forgive unpunished sin. . . . And there is somewhat else which follows, if sin be thus forgiven unpunished: since the same treatment would at God's hands be dealt to sinful and sinless; which is not consistent with God" (St Anselm, *Cur Deus homo*, p. 25). (Incidentally, the term 'sinless" refers to the angels – no men are deemed to be sinless.)

One may observe in passing here that Anselm's argument runs counter to Jesus' teachings, as reported in the New Testament – for example, as stated in the parable of the prodigal son. Jesus, it appears, had a more ample view of the scope of God's compassion. Be this as it may, Anselm insists that man is unable to escape punishment on his own: "Look at the matter in the light of strict justice, and judge according to that, whether man can make unto God an adequate satisfaction for sin, unless he restores by vanquishing the devil, that very same thing which he took from God by allowing the devil to conquer himself" (in other words, man is deemed guilty of his own captivity to the "powers and principalities" that govern his condition). The title of the next section of Anselm's book sums up what I would call the masochistic strain of the argument: "That so long as man repays not to God that which he owes, he cannot be made blessed; nor is he excused by his want of ability" (ibid., pp. 53f).

Since man cannot make reparation on his own, it must be done for him: "If, then, it be necessary that the celestial citizenship is to be completed from among men [in Anselm's view, this is to make up for the fallen angels who, as it were, reduced the necessary quorum of "celestial citizens"], and that this cannot be made unless there be made that beforementioned satisfaction, which God only can, and man should, make, it is needful that it should be made by one who is both God and man" (ibid., p. 67).

Anselm did not develop his view all by himself. It can validly be traced back to certain portions of the New Testament, especially to the Pauline texts and the Letter to the Hebrews. But Anselm pushed these strains to a logical extreme which, arguably, was not present there. In that he is a good representative of the Latin mind, both very rational and very moralistic. His view of God, then, is also very moralistic, indeed legalistic. In that, one could perhaps say, he violates the core concern of Paul, despite those elements in Pauline thought that adumbrate Anselm's argument. For Paul, Christ's sacrifice frees man from the burden of the Law (understood by Paul as the Law given to the Jews). For Anselm, it appears that God Himself cannot be freed from the burden of His own Law (understood now not in the sense of Torah, but of the moral order of the universe). That, I would propose, is a great distortion. Yet Anselm has cast a long shadow over the development of Christian thought in the West, both in Roman Catholicism and in Protestant orthodoxy (Lutheran as well as Calvinist).

Against this "objective" conception of the atonement there has been the so-called "subjective" one. Actually, neither of these two adjectives are very helpful. The conception of which Anselm is emblematic had best be called the juridical one. And the conception labelled "subjective" is best described as humanistic. It was a product of the Enlightenment and became characteristic of Protestant liberalism in the nineteenth century (although there are earlier versions of this, as in the thought of the early medieval theologian Abelard). Here Jesus Christ is understood as an exemplary man, who as such has induced God to forgive mankind its sins. One could say that God is still understood here as the universal judge and man as culpable from the beginning, but, compared to Anselm's divine judge, this one has a more flexible notion of justice. That, rather obviously, leaves open the question of why God could not forgive without Jesus having to die on the cross. After all, this form of liberal Christianity has always thought that Jesus was exemplary throughout his ministry, so surely God could have spared him the ultimate sacrifice. In an even weaker version of this humanistic approach Jesus is understood as a moral model to be emulated, up to and including his self-sacrifice. In that case the atonement is seen as a process of perfection for human beings. It is not so much a matter of man's relation to God as one of man's relation to himself – that is, atonement means that human beings come ever closer to moral perfection. In that sense, perhaps, the adjective "subjective" does apply.

I suspect that in all likelihood this humanistic understanding of the atonement is still the prevailing view in mainline Protestantism today, even if it is not explicitly articulated. I also suspect that many liberal Catholics have more or less similar ideas. And, of course, it is this view of Jesus that often evokes admiration among people who do nor consider themselves Christians at all. Gandhi, for example, comes to mind here. While the humanistic view of the atonement is sharply different from the juridical one, it shares important characteristics with it: It too is very rational and very moralistic.

Let me just give one textual example of this. It is from an essay written in 1906 by the Swedish archbishop Ekman:

> Let us imagine a nation which is universally despised, but among it is a noble hero, who exercises a mighty influence on the nation; then we become reconciled in our thought towards this nation. There radiates from the hero a reconciling light over the nation . . . So, in the midst of mankind God sees Jesus Christ. He sees a human radiance which scatters its beams over the human race. He sees streaks of truth, purity, and righteousness spreading among men. He sees in the body of mankind a new heart, whose strong pulse is spreading new life through the veins of the body. . . . He has then no further displeasure with mankind seen as a whole, He no longer despairs of mankind, He reconciles Himself with mankind. (quoted in Gustav Aulen, *Christus Victor: An Historical Study of Three Main Types of the Idea of Atonement*, p. 157)

What can one say about this? Jesus as a "noble hero," and as such either softening God's heart toward mankind or/and softening all the harsher possibilities of human existence toward an ideal of moral perfection. The first version of this humanistic vision implies a strangely sentimental God, vastly different from the God disclosed in the Biblical tradition. The second version is purely secular, in that God becomes quite irrelevant in this alleged process of moral improvement. Either way, this is a Jesus who has virtually nothing to do with the Jesus portrayed in the New Testament, who can only be squeezed into the image of a "noble hero" by doing violence to all the sources. Needless to say, this view of Jesus' mission must dismiss all the Christological efforts discussed in the preceding chapter. Jesus here is a purely human figure, his life and death are purely human events, and to speak of his resurrection is at most a metaphor. I, for one, would not be greatly troubled by this break with both the scriptures and the tradition of the Christian religion, if that break led to some great new insights. What it does lead to is an enormously trivial view of both God and man. Let me put it this way: If this is Christianity, it is not very interesting. And if we are interested in the moral ideal suggested here, we can do without the ancient metaphor. I may add that the ideal – let us call it a Gandhian ideal – does not appeal to me at all. It is a sentimental view of human nature, it does not take seriously the reality of evil, and in its practical application is quite irresponsible. Most importantly, this reduction of religion to a moral project provides no answer to the most searing question about the human condition, which is the question of death.

The Swedish theologian Gustav Aulen, in his influential book *Christus Victor* (originally published in 1931), argued persuasively that the two aforementioned types of atonement theories, the "objective" and the "subjective," are not the only ones in the development of Christian thought. There is also a third type, which he calls the "dramatic" one. He proposes that this type is actually older than the other two, already found in the New Testament (especially but not only in the Johannine texts) and in the early Church, and then developed most fully by the Greek Church Fathers and generally in eastern Orthodoxy. It is a dualistic view, understanding atonement as a gigantic struggle between God and the evil powers holding the creation captive. It is also a cosmic view, in that the atonement far exceeds human reality in its scope. Christ is then seen as being in mortal combat with the forces of evil, triumphing over them through his death and Resurrection.

Here there is less emphasis on individual sin than in the Latin view. Sin is, as it were, part and parcel of the human situation, bound up with death and the dominance of the devil. One might say that in this view man is victim rather than perpetrator (though, of course, it is understood that man commits sins that call for forgiveness). Thus, in the eastern church, one does not find the Latin fixation on penance and on the passion of Jesus (though, again of course, Jesus' passion is understood as an important part of his redemptive action). The emphasis is less on Good

Friday, emphatically more on Easter. Aulen also argues (though, I suspect, this is more controversial) that this note of combat and triumph is also central to Luther's understanding of the atonement, and that Luther's insights were then bent toward the Anselmian theory in the development of Lutheran orthodoxy (Melanchthon is seen by Aulen as the original villain in this development). I have some doubts about this (despite my strong bias in favor of Lutheranism), given Luther's early obsession with guilt. But then Luther freed himself from this obsession in what he thought was his rediscovery of Paul's understanding of justification by faith alone and by grace alone – *sola fide/sola gratia*. Certainly Luther's view of salvation is neither rationalist nor moralistic. Perhaps Aulen's opinion on the Lutheran understanding of the atonement is supported most strongly, not so much by Lutheran theology, but by Lutheran hymnody – beginning with Luther's own compositions ("A Mighty Fortress" and other hymns) and reaching a culmination in the music of Johann Sebastian Bach. But be this as it may, the "dramatic" view of the atonement is most fully represented by both the piety and the thought of eastern Christianity.

Here is how Aulen describes this view of the atonement, which he already finds in the early Fathers: "According to Anselm, Christ became man in order that He might die, but this isolation of the death of Christ is impossible for the patristic view. Death is, indeed, the way by which the victory is won, but the emphasis lies on the victory. Therefore *the note of triumph sounds like a trumpet-call through the teaching of the early church*" (*Christus Victor*, p. 59, my italics). Of course, Easter was not neglected in the western tradition. But it was in the east that it became the pivotal point for liturgy, piety, and theological reflection.

I will turn here to John Meyendorff, who was instrumental on the revival of Orthodox theology in western Europe and in America in the twentieth century (I refer particularly to his book *The Orthodox Church*). Meyendorff makes a clear distinction between east and west in the doctrine of original sin: The west has had a more *moral* understanding of this, the east a more *ontological* one. As observed before, this is a significant difference. The east emphasizes *mortality* rather than sin as the consequence of Adam's fall. Man was created to be immortal and to have a loving relationship with God. The fall, an event both primeval and cosmic, mysteriously linked to the evil powers of this world, deprived man of the condition intended by his creation. Redemption means that the evil powers are overcome and that man is restored to this original condition – not, of course, immediately, but in the process initiated by Christ's action. Orthodox thought refers to this process as *theosis*, a term usually translated as "deification." I think that this translation is misleading, as it suggests that man will become God. This is not the intention of Orthodox thought. Rather, "deification" means that man will, again, participate in the divine being, thus returning to his true nature, which is to be "in the image of God."

Here is how Meyendorff describes the "anti-Anselmian" approach of eastern Orthodoxy:

> Western theologians have always insisted on the *joint guilt* of all men for the sin of Adam: punishment for sin could not affect all humanity unless all men sinned "in Adam" and had therefore merited the divine wrath. . . . The Eastern Fathers . . . never attempted to prove the *joint guilt* of all the descendants of Adam for the sin of their ancestor: they merely observed that all men have inherited corruption and death by a process of inheritance and that all have committed sins. They preferred to interpret the state of affairs inherited from Adam as a slavery to the Devil, who exercises a usurped, unjust, and deadly tyranny over mankind since the sin of man's Progenitor. (*The Orthodox Church*, p. 198)

And further: "Thus, the Christian East has remained a stranger to the juridical conceptions of salvation which have been dominant in the West since medieval times (the doctrines of the 'merits' of Jesus Christ and indulgences) and which have so profoundly affected Western spirituality" (ibid., p. 199).

Again, one must not exaggerate the differences. Theologians in ecumenical dialogues have had no difficulty finding theoretical formulations that both sides could agree with. Thus the idea of "ransom" (that is, Christ paying a debt incurred by mankind) can also be found in the east, for example in the works of Gregory of Nyssa. But, as so often, these ecumenical exercises, which always focus on doctrine and theory, tend to obscure the real differences in the piety of ordinary believers. And very important in this connection are the liturgical differences: The core of Orthodoxy is in its liturgy, not in its theoretical formulations (the west has been much better with the latter for a very long time).

Meyendorff makes clear that it is mortality, rather than sin, which the east perceives as the essence of man's unredeemed condition. The atonement is not a juridical transaction, but the victory of the resurrected Christ over all the flaws in creation brought about by the fall and especially over death. I think that one can understand this best, not primarily by poring over the difficult writings of the Greek Church Fathers, but by paying attention to the Orthodox liturgy. And that liturgy reaches its absolute climax in the celebration of Easter. I quote from the Easter liturgy: "Today are all things filled with light, heaven and earth and the places under the earth. All creation does celebrate the Resurrection of Christ on whom it is founded." And then the repeated proclamation (the

Paschal Triparion): "Christ is risen from the dead, trampling down death by death, and upon those in the tombs bestowing life."

One is reminded here of what supposedly happened with the conversion of Russia to Christianity. According to one version of this, the rulers of Kiev (the original center of Russia) were uncertain as to whether they should affiliate with the western or the eastern version of the faith. Thus emissaries were sent both to Rome and to Constantinople to bring back information to help with the decision. The emissaries to Constantinople attended the liturgy in the great basilica of Hagia Sophia. They came back to Kiev and reported: "We have seen heaven on earth!" *Theosis* indeed. And that report decided the issue.

There is also this story from the period of persecution of the Church in the Soviet Union. In one of the campaigns to promote atheism a Communist official was sent into a village. The villagers were forced to attend a meeting. The official made an hour-long speech, explaining how religion was nothing but superstition, designed to divert people from the task of building a better society. At the end of the speech he said, magnanimously, that the village priest would be allowed to make a rebuttal, but that he would be given just five minutes to do so. The priest, a very simple man, came forward. He said that he did not need five minutes. He turned to the assembly and said: "Brothers and sisters, Christ is risen!" The villagers responded with the words of the Easter greeting: "He is risen indeed!" The story does not tell what the Communist official did after that.

What is one to make of all this? I, for one, have no difficulty making a choice between the three types of atonement theory enumerated by Gustav Aulen. The "objective" theory is utterly repulsive, presupposing a divinity that acts like a rigid and vindictive jurist. The "subjective" theory is completely uninteresting: If *that* is Christianity, one may politely decline the offer. Only the "dramatic" theory can be relevant to the nexus between experience and faith outlined in the preceding chapters.

Here it is clear that the redemption can only occur if God Himself suffers with His creation. Put differently, the kenosis is a necessity. The cross – Jesus Christ's *real* humiliation, suffering, and death as a human being – is the extreme point of the kenosis. This very extremity, in ways that must remain a mystery, makes possible the triumph of the Resurrection, and with it Christ's victory over evil, suffering, and, above all, death – "trampling down death by death."

It may be mentioned in passing that in the third century CE there was an interesting controversy that bears on this point, namely the controversy over the heresy of the so-called Patripassiani – that is, those who asserted that God the Father, not just the Son, suffered on the cross.

Against these people, who were condemned as heretics, the mainstream Church affirmed the "impassibility" of God the Father – that is, the impossibility of His suffering. The argument was that suffering was not compatible with the idea of the Godhead. I tend to think that the mainstream Church was mistaken on this. For one thing, both the Hebrew Bible and the New Testament are full of examples of God's suffering because of the sins of men. But more importantly, if God the Father remained unaffected by Christ's suffering, then in a curious way Christ is once again understood in an essentially Arian mode – that is, as some sort of semi-divine, semi-human being. On this the mainstream Church had the correct instinct: Such an understanding undermines the core mystery of the Incarnation and atonement.

I have argued that the kenosis is a necessary aspect of the God affirmed by Christian faith. This necessity is grounded in the issue of theodicy. This leads to a possible aspect of atonement that may seem startling and even blasphemous. The atonement is defined in virtually all strands of Christian thought as the process by which God forgives mankind: But the atonement can also be understood as the process by which *mankind can forgive God*. Is such an understanding blasphemous? I don't think so. A God who "impassibly" presides over the endless pain of His creatures, whom He then judges for their misdeeds (paltry as compared with the totality of horror within creation), is a being whom one would repudiate morally if He were a human individual. In an ironic way, He would be a sort of cosmic Pontius Pilate. One could hardly worship Him with love; at most, one could submit to Him in a masochistic posture (a cosmization, perhaps, of the so-called "Stockholm syndrome"). Such a God would be morally inferior to many human individuals. *That*, however, is unthinkable. God's goodness is a necessary aspect of His nature, as the Biblical witness insists. However God's nature can be described in the babbling conceptualizations of human thought, He cannot be understood as morally inferior to the best of us.

The kenosis is overcome in the Resurrection (the Hegelian term *aufgehoben* would be appropriate here. The German word has a double meaning – "abrogated" and "lifted up." Both meanings apply here). The Resurrection, as we have seen in an earlier chapter, was clearly pivotal in the days after Jesus' death, as the frightened remnant of his disciples was suddenly transformed into a community proclaiming his triumph. The Resurrection remains pivotal for Christian faith ever since: Without it, this faith would not be worth considering. Hence, in Aulen's term, Christ must essentially be understood as victorious – *Christus Victor*.

Furthermore, while the events of Jesus, life and death occurred within human history, "under Pontius Pilate," the redemption must be cosmic in scope, because the flaw in the creation which is being repaired is more ample than this history. Thus, as will be discussed further on, the risen and triumphant Christ is also understood as the ruler of all. In eastern iconography he is typically represented as such, as the *pantocrator* – literally, the ruler of all (usually in icons placed in the ceiling above the nave of churches). And it is as *pantocrator* that he will return at the end of history "to judge the living and the dead."

The New Testament presents the redemptive action of Jesus Christ as a unique, never to be repeated event, and it has been so understood by the Church ever since. The Letter to the Hebrews, in referring to the sacrifice of Christ, repeatedly uses the Greek word *ephapax*, "once and for all" – for example: "We have been consecrated through the offering of the body of Jesus Christ once and for all" (Hebrews 10:10). This, of course, signifies that we are redeemed through Christ and therefore need not look elsewhere for redemption. This was a message of liberation for people surrounded by the luxurious religious pluralism of the Hellenistic world, where competing soteriologies were on offer on every street corner. And, of course, for those still living in proximity to these events it was inconceivable that similar events, and similar redemptive actions, might have existed elsewhere. Today we are centuries removed from what occurred in Palestine at the beginning of Christian history, and we live in a world that is at least as religiously pluralistic as the one in which the early Cristians lived. Consequently, the question of the uniqueness of Jesus Christ arises for us in a rather different context.

Could it be that the same constellation of kenosis and triumph may have occurred elsewhere? Perhaps bearing names other than that of Jesus Christ? In the actions of this or that *Bodhisattva*? In a long-forgotten episode somewhere in pre-Columbian America (say, in the life of a "Christ of the Andes," whose records have been lost)? Or, let us assume for a moment that the absurdly small planet on which human evolution and history has taken place is not the only place in the universe in which the original design of creation has been flawed by suffering and evil. Could there be, somewhere in the ocean of galaxies, another race of "sentient beings" (to use the Buddhist term), whose fallen condition was or will be in need of redemption? If so, I think, such an eventuality would not undermine our faith in the redemption that has come *to us* in Jesus Christ (*Christus pro me*). If we want to engage in such speculation, it seems to me that the previously mentioned idea of the *Logos spermatikos* would be helpful: The *Logos*, who is Christ the Word of God, knows no limits in time or space, but is capable of sowing his "seed" anywhere in creation.

Is this thinkable? Yes, it is. But we do not know. We cannot know. We need not know.

Excursus: On the Empty Tomb and Other Miracles

Earlier on I took the position that the empty tomb was not a necessary presupposition for faith in the Resurrection of Jesus. Rather, that faith is based on the conviction that Jesus' death on the cross, the ultimate step in the divine kenosis, was not and could not be the end of the story. Given that conviction, the empirical events subsequent to that death are, *theologically speaking*, of only peripheral significance. Put differently, faith in the Resurrection (which Rudolf Bultmann discussed under the heading of the "Easter faith") is not dependent on the particular supernatural event asserted in the story of the empty tomb – the miraculous disappearance and transformation of Jesus' corpse. Nevertheless, it is of obvious interest to ask which elements of the Resurrection stories are historically credible. And this raises the larger question of how one is to think of the other miracles reported in the New Testament, and indeed of miracles in general.

What *can* we know historically about those long-ago days and weeks in Jerusalem? The historian must note that the New Testament is the only available source; there are no corroborations from outside the New Testament texts, and these are obviously highly biased and were not intended to be exercises in objective journalism. What is more, there are somewhat different accounts in Paul, in the Gospels, and in the Book of Acts. But there is one fact that we do know: There occurred a sudden reversal in the mood of the surviving disciples of Jesus, from understandable despair to a triumphant affirmation that Jesus had returned to life and was present among them. *Something*, clearly, must have happened to account for this dramatic shift. Just what that something was, empirically speaking, we cannot know. Nor can we give a historically adequate explanation of the disciples' conviction that the resurrected Jesus had appeared to several of them on various occasions, both in and around Jerusalem and in Galilee. These appearance stories also make clear that their subject was not a revived corpse (say, like Lazarus awakened from death), but some sort of spiritual body not subject to the constraints of ordinary bodies. This becomes especially clear in Paul's view of this, when he puts the appearance of Christ to him on the road to Damascus, years later, into a sequence of appearances going back to the first days after Easter. The appearances ceased not long afterward, by which time the Resurrection had become absolutely central to the Christian message. The cessation of the appearances was, as it were, ratified in the story of Jesus' ascension to heaven, one further event that the historian cannot deal with in terms of his craft. All he can say is that by then, very early in Christian history, Jesus had been certified as *kyrios*, and thus as victor over death. Here is how one New Testament scholar describes this matter: "Liberal criticism explains the appearances as psychological effects of the Easter enthusiasm. But according to all the accounts it was the other way around; the appearances caused the Easter faith. That alone corresponds to the situation of the disciples after the collapse of their messianic hopes. It would also be inexplicable that the appearances ceased when belief in the resurrection had triumphed in the Church" (essay on the Resurrection by Werner Bulst, in Karl Rahner, ed., *Encyclopedia of Theology*, p. 1437). In other words, *something* happened, and it must have been very powerful.

Of course this argument is not conclusively convincing. A skeptic could come up with alternative interpretations that would allow more scope to the psychopathology of religious enthusiasms. Still , in the perspective of faith God disclosed Himself in these events, no matter whether they involved supernatural interventions or not. But one must further ask: Are such interventions to be excluded *a priori*? Put simply, this is the question: *Can one believe in miracles?*

A common-sense definition will do here: A miracle is a supernatural intervention in the causal sequences of the empirical world. In the Biblical texts, and indeed in religion generally, such interventions have been credited to God, but also to angels and other supernatural beings, and indeed to the devil.

Supposedly, belief in the possibility of miracles is no longer credible to modern people. Any student of contemporary religion must have serious doubts about this presupposition. There is massive evidence for the continued belief in all sorts of miraculous happenings, even in the most modern societies. This has always been so, but it has become more visible in the luxurious flowering of different supernaturalisms since the emergence of the counter-culture in the mid-twentieth century in America and Europe. Just think in this connection of the vast phenomenon of

New Age spirituality, with millions of certifiably modern people seeking contact, in one way or another, with realities beyond the empirical world. The worldwide explosion of Pentecostalism (arguably the most dynamic religious movement today) is replete with supernaturalist beliefs. Indeed, one could say that right here, in modern Western societies, there are million of people whose worldview is as full of magic, miracles, and omens as was the worldview of the New Testament – witness the vast numbers who swear by their horoscopes! Needless to say, this is even more the case outside the West. As I have argued at length in other places, the pervasiveness of secularization has been greatly exaggerated. What *can* be said is that modernity (for reasons that I cannot go into here) has undermined the taken-for-granted certainty regarding supernatural beings and events. In other words, supernaturalist beliefs are, precisely, "counter-cultural" in that they come up against a secular worldview, which is allegedly based on science and which is culturally established through the agency of powerful institutions, notably the educational system and the media of mass communication. The loss of the taken-for-granted quality of the supernatural does indeed differentiate modern from less modern societies.

Some years ago I was in Nepal, enjoying a short time as a tourist after a series of conferences in India. If anywhere there is a place in which the supernatural seems to be taken for granted, Nepal is that place. I had hired a car with an English-speaking guide, evidently a man of some education. We visited an elaborate temple complex on a hilltop, not far from Katmandu. As we walked around the grounds we noticed a group of people who were staring and pointing at the sky. My guide was curious and walked over to find out what was gong on. He came back with a puzzled look in his face: "Earlier this morning a girl who works in the temple says that she saw Garuda flying by in the sky." (Garuda is the mythological bird who, in the Hindu epic, carries Rama to the island of Sri Lanka to rescue his beloved Sita from the clutches of the demon king.) After a moment's thought my guide shook his head and said: "I don't think she saw Garuda." I did not pay much attention to this at that moment, but I reflected about it later. What struck me then was the tone in which my guide had been speaking about this alleged supernatural event: He did not question the possibility that someone might see Garuda in the sky; he just doubted that this particular girl had seen Garuda on that particular morning. When he said that he did not think that she saw Garuda, he said it in the tone that one might say: "I don't think the train we just saw is the 10.30 train to Chicago; I think it was the 10.25 train to Milwaukee." Could a person in, say, Milwaukee claim to have seen a supernatural being in the sky? Absolutely yes. In the minds of some contemporary Americans the sky over Milwaukee contains every sort of mythological creature. However, an American Garuda-watcher would not have spoken of his vision in an ordinary tone, implying that such an event could be taken for granted as, at any rate, a real possibility. More likely, he would have whispered secretively, conscious of the fact that his mythological assumptions conflict with the "official" definitions of reality in a modern society.

Miracles, both those recounted in the Bible and those reported to have occurred in more recent times, were assumed through much of Christian history. The Protestant Reformation put this assumption in doubt, and since then there has been a big difference between Catholics and Protestants in the attitude toward miracles. It is not that the early Reformers were any more skeptical than their Roman adversaries as to the possibility of supernatural occurrences; certainly not Luther, who on one occasion supposedly threw an inkpot at the devil. The Protestant attitude toward the miraculous was rather shaped by opposition to specific Catholic practices which were opposed, not because they implied supernatural realities, but because they contradicted the Protestant understanding of salvation – including the miraculous Catholic understanding of the eucharist and such Catholic practices as indulgences, veneration of saints and their relics, and the like. But as Protestantism developed in later times, its critical attitude toward these specific allegations of supernatural interventions came to extend to the miraculous in general. This development was particularly strong in Calvinism and its various offshoots. One need only compare, say, a baroque Spanish basilica, full of images purporting the presence and continuing activity of miraculous entities, with the plain, white-washed churches of Puritan New England. As we saw earlier, Max Weber coined the perfect description of this Protestant development – "the disenchantment of the world" (the German word is *Entzauberung* – literally, a world deprived of magic). This Protestant attitude to miracles was termed "cessationism": This means that the miracles reported in the Bible, especially in the New Testament, were accepted, but it was further proposed that since then miracles have *ceased*; they are no longer necessary in God's plan of salvation. Later on, under the influence of modern scientific thinking, a distinction was made between miracles of healing (such as Jesus making a lame man get up and walk) and so-called "nature miracles" (such as Jesus walking on water): The latter were rejected, the former at least tentatively accepted as reconcilable with such modern notions as psychosomatic illnesses. (An excellent account of this matter can be found in Robert Mullin, *Miracles and the Modern Religious Imagination* – a fascinating piece of intellectual history.)

What is one to make of all this? A fundamental insight of all religion is that there is a reality that transcends the ordinary world of human experience. Christian faith necessarily assumes an intrusion of transcendence into the empirical world, most importantly the one that took place "under Pontius Pilate." I have argued that faith in the Resurrection of Jesus does not depend on a miraculously emptied tomb. The other miracle stories of the New Testament are even less essential for faith. But this by no means implies that one must axiomatically disbelieve these miracles or, beyond that, other miracles since then. There is a Christian fundamentalism, which insists that every Biblical text is inerrant and must be accepted as written. I think that this is a perversion of faith, indeed a rejection of it (as it substitutes an alleged certainty that takes the place of faith). But there is also a modernist fundamentalism, which is just as dogmatic. I think it was G. K. Chesterton who described this worldview as assuming that reality is what is experienced by a slightly drowsy businessman after a three-course lunch, and that no other reality is conceivable. It seems to me that this worldview is just as narrowly dogmatic as the traditional one it feels so superior to.

There is a thin line between the notions of miracles and of answered prayers. The latter, though, does not necessarily imply a suspension or interruption of empirical causality: In answering prayer, God could act *through* natural causes. Nevertheless, the discussion of petitionary prayer in an earlier excursus is also relevant to the issue of miracles. If God is omnipotent, there can be no limits to His possible agency. What we consider to be the "natural" universe is His creation, including all its sequences of cause and effect, and it is sustained from moment to moment by His creative power. There is no law that stands above Him and that limits the exercise of His power, and thus no *a priori* reason for the denial of miracles.

While Catholicism has retained a robust supernaturalism, it has also developed rather skeptical procedures in dealing with allegations that a particular supernatural event has occurred. And while the miraculous character of its sacramental apparatus is insisted upon, Catholic authorities are not greatly enamored of, as it were, extracurricular manifestations of the supernatural. Sociologically speaking, this hesitancy is grounded in the suspicion of bureaucrats regarding any activity of free enterprise. Thus commissions are appointed, extensive investigations are initiated, and the prevailing attitude is one of skepticism. Eventually, perhaps, this or that miracle will be formally accepted. In cases of proposed beatification or sanctification, this process of skeptical inquiry can go on for a very long time indeed, sometimes for several centuries. This always involves the issue of miracles, since the capacity to perform them is supposed to be one of the marks of sainthood. (John Paul II has been criticized for moving much faster on some of these cases. One recalls that he was fond of skiing as a young man – perhaps this is a sport that encourages speed!) I have little admiration for the procedures of Vatican bureaucracy, but the attitude underlying them has a certain appeal: Openness to the possibility of miracles in principle, but skepticism toward any particular alleged miracle in practice.

Some years ago I came upon a rather bizarre movement in my native Austria – an organization calling itself the Emperor Charles Prayer League, whose purpose was the beatification and eventually sanctification of the last Habsburg ruler, who was deposed at the end of World War I and died in exile on the island of Madeira. The organization published a yearbook, in which Charles was called "the peace emperor" (he made some rather feeble attempts to secure a separate peace for Austria-Hungary toward the end of the war) and "the martyr emperor" (he was forced into exile by the victorious allies, and the climate on Madeira has been blamed by some, not very plausibly, for his premature death). I obtained several years' worth of the organization's rather remarkable publication. It contained essays about Emperor Charles, his life, and his character, some by apparently reputable historians. But the real payoff came toward the end of each volume: Accounts of occasions on which prayers addressed to the dead emperor were allegedly answered. Most of them came from the more bucolic regions of Austria and Bavaria, and reported on the alleged miracles in a dry bureaucratic style: "It is respectfully reported that I prayed to the Martyr Emperor for the healing of my prized cow, after the veterinarian had pronounced her incurable, and the prayer was answered"; "I herewith report that prayers to Emperor Charles were efficacious in the successful outcome of my lawsuit with envious relatives" – and so on. One imagines an obscure office in some corner of the vast Vatican complex, where a monsignor of sour temperament (his can hardly be a sought-after assignment in the Curia) spends his days poring over these documents, perhaps classifying them in accordance with a system formalized two hundred years ago, getting them ready for the day (perhaps two hundred years in the future) when, if all goes well, the case of Charles of Habsburg may be formally opened . . .

Chesterton's drowsy businessman exists within what Alfred Schutz called the "paramount reality" – the world of ordinary, everyday life, the parameters of which are well known and shared with most if not all one's fellow-men, a world which contains few surprises. Yet this reality is vulnerable, breached by events that suggest other realities, by dreams and ecstasies that are indeed surprising. Not all of these are religious, but at the very core of the religious attitude is the sense (sometimes the conviction) that there is an ultimate transcendence of the ordinary world and that this transcendence is benign. Put differently: The world contains mystery. It seems to me that, even before one gets to an act of religious faith, it is important that one is open to the mystery.

Chapter Eight

"He descended into hell. On the third day he rose again. He ascended into heaven, and is seated on the right hand of the Father. He will come again to judge the living and the dead"

These sentences of the Creed span the entire Christological drama, from the agony of Jesus' death, through his Resurrection, to his status as cosmic ruler and coming judge. As I have argued before, the Resurrection is the pivotal event of this drama, without which it makes no sense. Obviously, this chapter cannot deal with every issue raised by the passage. Some parts of this I will not deal with at all. There is the descent into hell. Very likely the word "hell" is misleading, as far as the original intent of the Creed is concerned. The sentence probably intends to say no more than that Jesus actually died, against all Docetic views of the matter, and the word rendered as "hell" here then simply refers to the realm of the dead (German Protestant liturgies indeed render the sentence as "descended into the realm of the dead"). It is later that there developed the idea that Jesus, in a sort of hiatus between his death on the cross and his Resurrection, went into the netherworld to proclaim salvation to the dead. We will have occasion later to ask some questions about the links between the living and the dead in the economy of salvation. Nor do I intend to discuss here the matter of Jesus' ascension into heaven – an episode that may or not refer to an actual event, but that clearly expresses the fact that, after a while, there were no more appearances of the risen

Jesus, and that the disciples had to acknowledge that Jesus was no longer with them. The end of the passage, about the Parousia, the second coming of Christ, will be discussed later in the book. As to the metaphor of his being seated on the right hand of the Father, it eloquently expresses what was discussed in the previous chapter – that the risen Christ, now manifested as *kyrios*, is the victor over evil, suffering, and death. The kenotic Jesus has become the Pantocrator, the ruler over all things.

All of this, however, leads to an essentially simple question:

If Christ is victorious over evil, suffering, and death, why do these realities still dominate the human condition in this world?

This is the question that must be addressed now.

There is an immense tension between what faith affirms as having *already* happened and what experience shows, that the full effect of this has *not yet* happened. All the events in the life of Jesus up to and including the Resurrection are believed to constitute the inauguration of the Kingdom of God, but the latter is not yet visible in human experience of life in this world. Put simply, the world is as miserable a place as it has ever been. The victory, while it has already been achieved, is yet to be realized. In Christian thought, the tension between the "already" and the "not yet" has led, from the beginning, to reflections about *eschatology* – that is, about the "last things" or "last days," when Christ's victory will be, as it were, visible to the naked eye. Only then will the victory be fully manifest and the human condition, and indeed the entire cosmos, will be utterly transformed. The Parousia will then bring about, visibly, "a new heaven and a new earth."

The tension is already evident in the New Testament. Jesus' message was emphatically eschatological. He announced the coming of the Kingdom of God, expected to be imminent and crucially linked to his person. This message had its roots in Jewish eschatological thinking, which almost certainly influenced Jesus. New Testament scholars disagree as to whether Jesus conceived of the Kingdom in *historical* terms (that is, in essentially Jewish terms as the establishment of a righteous Messianic regime) or whether he already thought of it in *cosmic* terms (that is, as transforming not only history but the entire universe). It is clear that in the early Church, possibly from the very beginnings in Jerusalem and Galilee, the coming transformation was conceived in cosmic terms. The Parousia would transform *everything*.

There is strong evidence in the New Testament that Jesus himself expected the coming of the Kingdom to be imminent, within the lifetimes of his disciples. The early Church expected the Parousia to be imminent. As long as such an expectation could be maintained, the tension between the "already" and the "not yet" was obviously lessened. One only had to hold one's breath for a short time, as it were, and then all would be well. But there is also evidence in the New Testament that, as the first generation of disciples died away, there came the realization that there might be a long period before the final culmination. The Parousia failed to come about imminently, and it became rather difficult to hold one's breath. Biblical scholars coined a heavy Germanic term for this putatively distressing fact – *Parousieverzoegerung*, "Parousia-delay." It is as if people are waiting in a railway station for a train to arrive, standing on the edge of the platform, looking eagerly in the direction from which the train is supposed to come. But the train doesn't come. More and more delays are announced. Then people step away from the platform, sit down on benches or in the coffee shop, and settle in for what may be a very long wait. If people have invested hope in the imminent arrival of the train, trusting the published timetable of the railway company, there will be a lot of disappointment. There may even be doubts about the reliability, not only of the timetable, but of the company that had published it. There will be, as it were, a crisis of faith and with it a cognitive problem: How is one to explain the delay? Christian eschatological reflection has been a sustained attempt to confront this problem.

There are, of course, different versions of eschatology in the history of Christian thought, and there is no possible way in which these could be dealt with here. There is, though, one version that has been dominant. It could perhaps be called the unilinear version: Visible, empirical history is understood as moving in a straight line toward a cataclysmic conclusion, with each stage on this line being marked by specific divine actions. This is precisely the eschatological scheme developed within Judaism, though, of course, with a crucial difference: The Jewish Messianic expectation faces the future; it is, as it were, dominated by the "not yet." Christian eschatology also looks toward the future, the Parousia, but the latter is the final realization of something that has "already" happened in the past, namely the events around the life of Jesus. This means, among other things, that the tension between the "already" and the "not yet" has a sharpness in Christianity which is much less, if not absent, in Judaism. Abraham Heschel, a Jewish thinker who was much concerned with a dialogue between Judaism and Christianity, once observed that, in contrast to Jews, Christians do not take seriously enough the unredeemed character of the world. This is a bit of an exaggeration, but there is an important element of truth in the observation. In any case, the dominant Christian view has been that history moves in a straight line from the creation through the revelatory events of the Old Testament and the Christ event to the final establishment of the Kingdom of God, which final event is to be preceded by catastrophes most graphically depicted in the last book of the New Testament. Quite apart from what theologians think, this is very probably the prevailing view among ordinary Christians even today. The flurry of bestselling novels around the millenium, about the so-called "rapture," provides evidence for this (the "rapture," mentioned in the Book of Revelation, is supposed to be a miraculous event when believing Christians will be suddenly whisked away from the earth before the final catastrophe – thereby, among other things, causing a lot of traffic accidents).

Fundamentalists of various stripes like to dwell on the apocalyptic events forecast for the "last days," such as the doings of the Antichrist, and they often try to find cues by which to predict the date when these events may be expected to begin. But a unilinear view of the history of salvation can also be found in the thought of highly sophisticated theologians. An influential modern example of this is a book by the Swiss Protestant theologian Oscar Cullmann, *Christ and Time* (the French original, *Christ et le temps*, was published in 1947). Cullmann stresses the unique linearity in the Biblical view of history, which sharply differentiates Judaism and Christianity (he could have added Islam) from the Greek view of cyclical time. In reference to the work of Christ the New Testament (especially in the Letter to the Hebrews) repeatedly uses the word *ephapax*, meaning "once and for all." But the word can also be applied to the divine actions reported on in the Hebrew Bible – the "mighty deeds of Yahweh," from the calling of Abraham through the Exodus and the giving of the law on Sinai, to the taking of the land of Israel. *God acts in history*, and from these acts all history derives its salvific meaning. Against this stands the view that everything repeats itself, the "return of all things," which implies that any salvific meaning must be sought *outside* history. Cullmann is quite right in contrasting this with the Greek understanding of time and history. But the non-linear, cyclical view is characteristic of other worldviews as well, notably that of Indian civilization.

There is a Hindu legend, concerning a dialogue between a holy man and Ishvara, the creator of the world, one of the mightiest gods in the Hindu pantheon. It is a philosophical conversation, much of it dealing with the idea of reincarnation. Then, suddenly, the holy man laughs. When asked why he is laughing, he says "the ants, the ants," pointing to a train of ants marching across the marble floor of Ishvara's heavenly palace. And when asked why the ants are making him laugh, he replies: *"Because every one of these ants was once Ishvara, and will be Ishvara again."* It is a sentence that one should ponder slowly, letting its full significance sink in. One will then begin to understand why the endless wheel of reincarnations, *samsara*, produced such horror in the Indian religious imagination, so that salvation meant release from that wheel. But one can then also see the contrast with the Biblical view, from the first sentence of the Hebrew Bible, "In the beginning God created the heavens and the earth," to the penultimate sentence of the New Testament – "Come, Lord Jesus!" (*maranatha*, an Aramaic phrase that was probably one of the earliest Christian liturgical formulas).

Cullmann puts it thus:

> The unique element in the Christian conception of time as the scene of redemptive history is of a twofold character . . . In the first place, salvation is bound to a *continuous time process* which embraces past, present, and future. Revelation and salvation take place along the course of an ascending line. Here the strictly straight-line conception of time in the New Testament must be defined as over against the Greek cyclical conception and over against all metaphysics in which salvation is always available in the "beyond" . . . In the second place, it is characteristic of this estimate of time as the scene of redemptive history that all points of this redemptive line are related to the *one historical fact* at the mid-point, a fact which precisely in its unrepeatable character, which marks all historical facts, is decisive for salvation. This fact is the death and resurrection of Jesus Christ. (*Christ and Time*, pp. 32f)

Cullmann, in his polemical stance against all "metaphysics," claims that the New Testament does not have a notion of eternity as being timeless; rather, eternity means time without end, so that salvation either now or after the final culmination never means an exodus from time.

The present stage, which is our own existence AD, is the period between the central Christ event and the Parousia. Cullmann, who wrote his book during World War II, uses an eloquent analogy to describe this stage – it is the period between D-Day and V-Day: The final "invasion" has already occurred, but the manifest victory is yet to come. This is so regardless of the expected timing of the Parousia, that is, regardless of whether the victorious second coming of Christ is expected imminently (as was the case with the early Christians and still is with all sorts of "Adventists") or is expected in an undetermined future (as has been the case with most Christians since the time of the Apostles). Thus the present time is the "last days"; thus the Kingdom is always "near." Its presence is already manifest in the church, which since the event of Pentecost is under the aegis of the Holy Spirit. Thus, although it lies in the future, the Parousia is "available" here and now, especially in the sacraments of the church (Cullmann here emphasizes the eucharist). And thus the tension between the "already" and the "not yet" is substantially mitigated.

It is not surprising that there have always been people who found intolerable the classical Christian stance of waiting patiently for God to bring about the final culmination. Some people are unwilling to settle down in the coffee shop of the railway station; they want *to force* the arrival of the expected train. Thus, throughout Christian history (and indeed throughout Jewish and Muslim history) there have been repeated attempts to bring about the *eschaton* through human efforts. There is a long list of Messianic and utopian movements who set out to inaugurate the Kingdom of God, often by means of armed force, sometimes by means of fervent prayer and piety. In the sixteenth century, amid the spiritual turmoil of the Reformation, there arose armed insurrections intended to set up the promised Kingdom – for an important example, the utopian movement that set up a supposedly holy city in Muenster in northern Germany (Luther vehemently denounced such movements under the rubric of *Schwaermerei*, a derogatory term usually translated as "enthusiasm"). But there have been similar attempts to storm heaven, as it were, both before and after the sixteenth century. One can generalize by saying that any religious tradition with a linear conception of time is prone to generate Messianic movements seeking to force history toward a salvific culmination. And, of course, the modern age has seen a number of examples of secularized eschatology. Marxism is a prime case in point, with its linear redemption-history stretching from a putative original state of human equality though the "fall" of private property and the expected apocalyptic collapse of capitalism to the inevitable revolution, which is to be followed by the "paradise" of the classless communist society. It has often been pointed out that Marxism could not have been conceived without the cognitive presuppositions of a Biblical view of time and history, its own "line" of redemption bearing an uncanny resemblance to its Judaeo-Christian antecedents.

But there are alternative views of eschatology, opposed to any notion of the redemptive culmination occurring *within* history and *within* the empirical parameters of human existence in this world. Here there is not only a rejection of any attempt to bring about the *eschaton* by human efforts, but also the belief that history itself must come to an end in a culmination that must necessarily be cosmic in scope, since the entire cosmos awaits redemption. Most importantly, the *eschaton* must include the overcoming of death – a feat that cannot conceivably be accomplished within the empirical realities of both history and nature. This was the view of Emil Brunner, yet another Swiss Protestant theologian (best known for his differences with Karl Barth within the broad school of Protestant neo-orthodoxy):

> Is the ideal [i.e. the realization of the Kingdom of God] never to be realized? That it will ultimately become a reality is the plain witness of the Gospel. But in order that this may happen things must not only happen

within history but historical existence itself, "the body of this death", must itself be done away. It is precisely this that is meant by the message of resurrection and eternal life – and with this the message of the Gospel is identical. (*Eternal Hope*, p. 81)

We shall presently return to this point.

Brunner here points to the major way in which the tension between the "already" and the "not yet" has been resolved in the history of Christian thought. This has taken many different forms, many of them incompatible with each other, but they all have one common characteristic: The drama of redemption is *dehistoricized*. That is exactly what Brunner means when he rejects "metaphysics" and talks about the "beyond." The expectation of redemption is shifted from the future to the present, from a world to come to an other world that is accessible here and now. This shift is reflected in an interesting way in which Biblical terms are made to refer to space rather than time – the term *olam* in the Hebrew Bible and the term *aion* in the New Testament, which originally referred to an age ("this age" as against the "age to come"), is now referred to a space ("this world" as against the "other world," the "beyond"). The eschatological culmination, even if its future manifestation is not denied altogether (sometimes it is), is now conceived of as being accessible, indeed as taking place here and now. The contrast between time and eternity is then interpreted as eternity breaking into time here and now, with time (including all the miseries of history and nature) becoming, so to speak, soteriologically irrelevant.

Some historians have interpreted this shift as an accommodation of the Biblical worldview to Hellenism. Be this as it may, the shift was there from early on in Christian history. Probably its first important expression was in Gnosticism, which radically denied the historicity of salvation and reinterpreted it as the attainment of a state of perfection that could begin here and now. But an ahistorical view of salvation is implicit in just about every form of mysticism, Jewish and Muslim as well as Christian. The mystic does not wait for a great event to come in the future. Rather, the great event is the mystical experience, an encounter or perhaps even a union with the divine reality that transcends time. Thus Meister Eckhart, arguably the greatest mystic of the Christian Middle Ages, speaks of the eternal "now" (*das Nun*) which is the goal of the mystical quest.

The relativization of history can also be undertaken by means of a "high" concept of the Church. As we have seen, even in the unilinear understanding of eschatology, already in the New Testament, the Church is seen as an anticipation of the Parousia: Christ will come again in the "last days," but he is already present in his glorified status here and now in the sacraments of the Church. We have previously mentioned the eastern Orthodox notion of "heaven on earth" in the liturgy. In the western church a similar idea was developed in Augustine's *City of God*. While other traditions have operated with such a "high" ecclesiology, it is fair to say that the Roman Catholic Church has developed it in its most magnificent version. Its understanding of the miracle of the mass as repeating the sacrifice of Christ eloquently expresses this idea, provoking the Reformers to insist on the "once and for all" of Christ's original sacrifice, as in the words of the Anglican Book of Common Prayer in one of the prayers preceding communion – thanking God for Christ's death on the cross, "who made there (by his one oblation of himself once offered), a full, perfect, and sufficient sacrifice, oblation, and satisfaction, for the sins of the whole world." Of course, neither the Orthodox nor the Catholic traditions gave up the expectation of the Parousia to come, but the heavy emphasis on the sacramental apparatus of the Church, which is available here and now, softens the expectation considerably.

Karl Barth in his early writings emphasized the "here and now" of the encounter between an individual and the *kerygma*, the proclamation of the Gospel (he modified this radical position in his later work). One could say that the early Barth replaced the mystical or the sacramental "now" with a kerygmatic "now." This comes out nicely in his commentary on Paul's Letter to the Romans (the original publication, in 1918, was the opening salvo of the movement that became known as "dialectical theology" or "neo-orthodoxy"). Barth comments on the passage in Romans 13:11–12, where Paul says: "Salvation is nearer to us now than when we first believed; the night is far gone, the day is at hand." Other commentators interpret this passage as indicating that Paul still shared the expectation that the second coming of the risen Christ was imminent. Not so Barth: He proposes that the Kingdom is *always* "at hand" as we confront the Word of God. Thus there is no real "Parousia delay." The tension is not between present and future, between the "already" and the "not yet," but between the Word and our sinful condition. Barth refers to Kierkegaard's comment that the "nineteen hundred years of church history" (that is, the great delay) makes faith difficult. Not so, according to Barth: Those nineteen hundred years are as irrelevant to faith as the time it took the messenger Phoebe to carry Paul's letter from Corinth Rome, or the time it took Paul to dictate the letter! In other words, history itself becomes irrelevant and the *eschaton* is *now*.

Rudolf Bultmann, whom we have met before in this book, is commonly seen as representing a liberal antithesis to neo-orthodoxy (Barth himself vehemently rejected Bultmann's program of "demythologizing" the New Testament). Yet Bultmann's thought was formed in the milieu of Barthian theology, and it shows. Bultmann's "demythologized" Gospel is encountered as an existential event, here and now. For example, in the original essay *New Testament and Mythology* (written during World War II and published shortly afterward), Bultmann discusses the Resurrection at some length. As we have seen, he brushes aside all questions about historicity. The Resurrection, he argues, is not a "mythic event" in the past. Rather, the risen Christ meets us in the Word of proclamation, here and now, and *nowhere else*. The truth of the Easter faith is faith in this Word. Here is a particularly sharp expression of the kerygmatic "now." And, once again, albeit in a very idiosyncratic way, the tension between "already" and "not yet" is resolved.

The possibilities of eschatology, however, are not exhausted by the alternatives of a unilinear and an ahistorical approach. There is also what might be called a multilinear, or perhaps more accurately a dualistic approach. Put simply, this is to propose that there is not just one line of history but at least two lines: There is the visible history that historians can study and within which, indeed, there are salvific events, such as the death of Jesus "under Pontius Pilate." But there is also an invisible, a hidden history, which is the unfolding of the world's redemption. It is completely inaccessible to the historian or to any other empirically oriented observer, although there are moments where one might catch glimpses of it within the visible stream of history. This means that it is futile to ascribe an empirically available purpose to history. There is no rationally discernible *telos* or meaning to history. James Joyce, in *Ulysses*, wrote that "history is a nightmare from which I am trying to awake," and the observation is apt. Empires and civilizations come and go, and they do so amid an immeasurable accumulation of human suffering. It is only by relating this sorry record with the hidden history of salvation that one can ascribe purpose or meaning to it, and that only by way of faith. Those who do ascribe a teleology to history, who claim to know what it is, and who then proceed to help it along by their own actions typically only add to the endless accumulation of suffering, as the great Marxist experiments have shown with horrible clarity.

I cannot offer a ready-made exposition of how this hidden history of salvation is to be conceived. But I find a hint of it in the concept of the invisible Church as it emerged from the Protestant Reformation. Luther was fighting a two-front battle as he developed his understanding of the Church. On the one hand he came to reject the Roman Catholic understanding, which made the visible Church a central object of faith and the locale of salvation here and now. On the other hand he rejected the utopian understanding of the *Schwaermer*, such as the "prophets of Muenster," who wanted a charismatic Church to bring about a visible Kingdom of God, also here and now. Against Rome, he rejected the idea of the Church as a hierarchical succession of bishops, and instead spoke of a "succession of the faithful" (*successio fidelium*) – the Church is the community of the faithful. But we can never know with any assurance who the faithful are – not necessarily those who announce their faith in the noisiest tones. Thus there is an invisible Church, hidden from sight within the visible Church and possibly also outside the latter's boundaries. Luther, as far as I know, did not use the phrase "invisible Church"; it was developed later in Lutheran doctrine; but the idea is there in Luther's own thought. It should be said that this idea by not means rejects the importance of the visible Church as the place where the Gospel is preached and where the sacraments are administered. If he had done so, he would not have bothered to try and reform it! But the visible Church is not the whole story, and this reservation is important.

I think one can say that we have here a dualistic vision of the Church. The far-reaching ecclesiological implications of this need not concern us at the moment. But it seems to me that we have here a suggestion of how the relation of the "two histories" is to be understood. Thus, in trying to come to terms with the present age between the Resurrection and the Parousia, and with its tension between the "already" and the "not yet," we need not restrict ourselves to the visible course of history. There is another stream of history, mostly hidden, in which God's plan to redeem the world is slowly coming to fruition.

The progress of redemption is hidden. It is not given to us to know its workings or its stages. We can only have faith that it is talking place as Christ's victory moves toward its final culmination. Nietzsche (very pejoratively) said that Christianity brought about a "transvaluation of all values." What he had in mind (and rejected violently) was the elevation of the weak over the strong, the promise that the last will be the first. He was dreadfully wrong about much of this, but there is a genuine insight here nonetheless: *Christian faith puts in question what we ordinarily regard as important or unimportant.* This "transvaluation" is already very clear in the entire Biblical account of God' interventions in the course of human affairs. The ancient Near East saw a succession of enormously self-important empires, but what really mattered would have been barely visible to observers at the important centers of this world – an encounter between a radically different God and a completely marginal band of nomads at the fringes of these empires. The entire course of Jesus' life occurred in a provincial corner of the Roman world, so much so that we do not have a single contemporary report of it. Let me put it this way: If CNN had existed in ancient times, most of the history of Israel and all of Jesus' life would have been invisible on its radar screen. As to the Reformation, Paul Goodman described its beginnings as a conspiracy of junior faculty in a provincial university. To be sure, these hidden events later became "important" on the stage of visible history, but in becoming so they risked losing precisely what was important in terms of their salvific

significance. Thus Christianity was "victorious" as Constantine established it as the religion of the Roman state, making it very "important"
indeed. But, as became amply clear, this victory was very problematic
indeed in the perspective of faith and is certainly not to be identified with
the victory of Christ proclaimed in the Gospel.

A Russian legend has it that there were three holy men who lived on
an island, engaged in constant prayer and works of compassion. The
bishop under whose jurisdiction the island fell was informed that these
men were completely ignorant of the doctrines and rituals of the Church.
He found this fact scandalous. He visited the island and spent some time
teaching these men the basic creeds and prayers of the Church. He then
left the island. As his boat was getting away from the island he noticed,
to his amazement, that the three holy men were following the boat,
walking on the water. They reached the boat and explained that they followed the bishop because, after he had left, they realized that they had
forgotten the words of the Lord's Prayer. The bishop told them that they
should not worry about this – they did not need these words. "Transvaluation": In the economy of redemption, a lonely island, and not the
(let us imagine) splendid palace in which the bishop resided, was an
important place.

Oscar Cullmann was almost certainly correct in proposing that the unilinear version is closest to the Biblical account. But I don't believe that
we must accept that account in a literalistic way: The Bible is the account
of events in which we can invest faith; it is not itself the object of this
faith. Thus we can have faith in the redemption of which the Bible is the
principal witness, without necessarily accepting the cognitive structure
within which this witness is communicated, including its much-vaunted
linearity (Rudolf Bultmann was right about this, despite the dubious
assumptions of his "demythologization" program). Against Cullmann I
would say – linearity, yes; unilinearity, probably not. As to all utopian
attempts to take control of the "line" by political or any other means,
I think that Cullmann is in agreement with a rejection of those as being
a distortion of Christian hope.

As against all the versions of eschatology which deny or deprecate its
futurity in terms of a "here and now," it is necessary to insist, I think,
that history cannot simply be irrelevant and that the historicity of the
Biblical worldview cannot simply be abandoned. Biblical faith affirms that
the world of human experience is the arena of God's redemptive actions
and that it derives ultimate meaning from these actions, even if we
cannot perceive this meaning "with the naked eye." Reducing the hope
of redemptive culmination to a mystical or an existential event trivializes
that hope. Thus the Parousia cannot be an event within my own

consciousness or existence. It must be *objectively real*, as a future event, otherwise it would not constitute the final awakening from the nightmare of history. Furthermore, the Parousia must be *cosmic in scope*, because (as I tried to argue in the discussion of theodicy) it is not only history but nature, and probably the entire universe, which is in need of redemption. As the Apostle Paul put it (in Romans 8:22): "We know that the whole creation has been groaning in travail together [with us] until now."

And I am constrained to insist that eschatology too must be included in a nexus that relates faith to the questions raised by the human condition. Thus eschatology, in confronting the tension between the "already" and the "not yet," must also contain a theodicy. Therefore, it must have the Resurrection as its foundation, and with this must embody the hope for an overcoming of evil, suffering, and death. Anything less is, in the most serious way, "not interesting." Put differently, if Christianity promises anything less, we can well do without it. I would once again particularly emphasize the centrality of the overcoming of death. Ivan Karamazov was right: A God who accepts the death of innocent children is not acceptable. Death is not acceptable. Eschatology must insist that *death is not acceptable to God*, and that the final manifestation of redemption will ratify this unacceptability. Thus faith affirms that we were made for eternity – whether understood as being outside time or in an endless time (both are strictly unimaginable, given our limited cognitive abilities) – but in either case being without death. It is in this faith that we can, however hesitantly, join in the prayer with which the New Testament ends: *Maranatha* – "Come, Lord Jesus!"

Chapter Nine

"I believe in the Holy Spirit"

It is probably fair to say that the average Christian in contemporary Western societies has a more or less coherent notion of the meanings of "God" and "Christ," but would be at a loss if asked to specify what is meant by the "Holy Spirit." (The exception would be Pentecostals, who talk about the Spirit all the time. More about them later.) A similar embarrassment, even more so, would occur if the subject of the "Trinity" were brought up (a subject, of course, intimately linked to the question about the Spirit). In the argument of this book, then, the time has come to address this question:

What, or who, is the Holy Spirit?

As with earlier questions discussed in the book, it is very helpful to get some understanding of the historical process which gave rise to this idea and to the body of doctrine that was developed from it. The New Testament term for the Spirit (Greek *pneuma*) stands in continuity with the use of a cognate term in the Hebrew Bible (*ruach*), referring to the "Spirit of God," the divine power as it is active in the world, both in the events of the history of Israel and in empowering individuals, such as the prophets, to carry out some special God-given mission. All the authors of the New Testament were, of course, fully familiar with the antecedent Hebrew usage.

In the New Testament the "discovery" (if that is the right word) of the Spirit is closely linked to the experience of Jesus' continuing presence after his disappearance from this world – that is, with the cessation of appearances of the risen Christ to the disciples left alone in Jerusalem and in Galilee. The second chapter of the Book of Acts tells of a gathering of the disciples in Jerusalem for the Jewish feast of Pentecost (Shevuot), when a miraculous event occurred: "And suddenly a sound came from heaven like the rush of a mighty wind, and it filled all the house where they were sitting. And there appeared to them tongues of fire, distributed and resting on each of them. And they were all filled with the Holy Spirit and began to speak in other tongues, as the Spirit gave them utterance." This "speaking in tongues" meant that the crowd of pilgrims drawn to the gathering heard the disciples speaking in their several languages, were understandably perplexed, and became a receptive audience when the Apostle Peter preached to them about Jesus, the crucified Messiah, having risen from the dead.

There is no way by which a historian could reconstruct "what really happened" in those days in Jerusalem. One fact, however, is quite clear: Even when there were no more accounts of the resurrected Christ appearing here and there to the disciples, they had a vivid sense of his continuing presence and of his power being active in the world. And this sense may well have been reinforced, by whatever means, when a large number of the disciples were gathered together on the occasion of the first Jewish feast to follow Passover/Easter. It is also likely that the sense of spiritual presence would be expressed through ecstatic language ("speaking in tongues," the not uncommon phenomenon called "glossolalia" by scholars of religion). Be this as it may, Christian tradition has viewed the event at Pentecost to be the founding of the Church as a creation of the Spirit.

In continuity with the Hebrew Bible, the Spirit is understood as being active both in the unfolding history of the community, the Church, and in the lives of individual believers. There are the "gifts of the Spirit," some of them miraculous (especially in miracles of healing). In the New Testament the conception of the Spirit is developed most fully in the Pauline texts. Paul sharply differentiates between life "in the Spirit" and life "in the flesh" (*sarx*), the latter term referring to the human condition before its transformation by the Spirit.

Here as elsewhere in the history of a religious tradition, it is important to differentiate between religious experience and the development of theoretical reflection about this experience. The history of religion is not a multi-semester theological seminar. The experience of the disciples (none of whom were theologians) following the disappearance of Jesus was raw, immediate, just beginning to be reflected upon. Within the New Testament, both the Pauline and the Johannine texts provide evidence of an intense process of reflection, which soon led to a body of intellectually articulated doctrine. As reflection about the Spirit developed, there is an interesting parallel with the development of Christological thought. As was discussed in an earlier chapter, there was pressure to understand

Christ as being both pre-existing and post-existing the earthly life of Jesus. This pressure was "soteriologically driven" – that is, it was driven by the concern to understand the redemptive significance of Jesus Christ. Similarly, there was pressure to understand the Holy Spirit as pre-existing the Pentecost event – not only in the life of Jesus ("conceived by the Holy Spirit"), but in all the mighty acts of God recounted in the Hebrew Bible (it was the Spirit who "spoke by the prophets"), and was even present from the very beginning of creation – in the words of the first chapter of Genesis, when even before the creation of light "the Spirit of God was moving over the face of the waters." What is more, if the Spirit was to be understood as the active presence of God, then the Spirit could not be understood as some sort of impersonal force or energy. Just as God was understood in personal terms, so the Spirit had to be understood *as a person*. And here, of course, is the nascent idea of the Trinity – Father, Son, and Holy Spirit as manifestations of the same personal God. I would argue that this development of ideas about the Holy Spirit and, subsequently, the Trinity was also "soteriologically driven." Not surprisingly, though, as these ideas were developed in the context of Hellenistic philosophical thought, they led to bodies of doctrine characterized by staggering metaphysical complexity. I would further suggest that, if we keep in mind why this development came about in the first place, we will be less put off by the metaphysics (and, I may add, those of us in liturgical churches will wince less when reciting the metaphysical formulas of the Nicene Creed).

There is a direct line from reflection about the Spirit to the doctrine of the Trinity. (I'm following here, more or less, the account by Adolf von Harnack in his classic history of Christian dogma. It was first published in 1909. Obviously there have been developments in scholarship since then, but, as far as I can tell, the main outline remains valid.) From early on, the baptismal formula implied the Trinity – people were baptized in the name of the Father, the Son, and the Holy Spirit. Yet in the early history of Christian theology there was great uncertainty about the mutual relation of these three entities. Thus there was a notion of the Spirit as a force only released after Christ's ascension. Then, as just mentioned, there was the notion of the Spirit as the power of God in the creation of the world and existing even before that. There was further the understanding of the Spirit as a personal entity, the Paraclete (the "comforter", promised by Jesus to remain with the disciples after his disappearance from this world), a being subordinate to both the Father and the Son. Some conceived of the Spirit as a created heavenly being, the highest of the angels. Some thought of the Spirit as identical with Christ (another term for the Logos), others yet as Sophia, the wisdom of God, a feminine presence within God (an idea which, unsurprisingly, has found favor among current feminist theologians). It took a few centuries for all of this to be sorted out.

Tertullian first spoke of the Spirit *as* God. The orthodox doctrine of the Trinity developed fully in the fourth century – three persons within the divinity, distinct from each other yet being of the same "substance" (the *homoousion* of the Nicene formulation being applied to all the three persons). But while the second person of the Trinity was stated as being "begotten" by the first person, the third person, the Spirit, was stated to have "proceeded." Inevitably, there ensued a debate about the nature of this "procession." Later theology distinguished between the "economic" and the "immanent" Trinity. The first term is emphatically soteriological; it refers to the role of the Spirit in the "economy" of salvation. The second term is metaphysical; it refers to the place of the Spirit in the inner life of the divinity. Theologians have always stated that the latter reality is a mystery that cannot be penetrated by human minds. This, one must rather regret, has not stopped many of them from speculating about it at length and in enormous detail.

While there is ample language about the Spirit in the New Testament, it is difficult to find a New Testament warrant for the doctrine of the Trinity as formulated by the time of the Council of Nicaea. In the so-called "Great Commission" (Matthew 28:19), Jesus is supposed to have instructed his disciples to "go . . . and make disciples of all nations, baptizing them in the name of the Father, and of the Son and of the Holy Spirit." It is very unlikely that Jesus said anything like this, much more likely that the baptismal formula developed in the early Church was retroactively put into the mouth of Jesus. But even that formula does not as yet imply the full-blown doctrine of the Trinity. Rather, it emphasizes the continuing presence of Christ's redeeming power mediated by the Spirit. In other words, the concern here is emphatically soteriological. The edifice of metaphysical concepts was built on top of this concern. Unless we are professional theologians, most of us today find it difficult to identify with these conceptualizations. Yet they do contain an important intuition: If God is love (and *that* idea is central for the "economy" of salvation), that love must already be present *within* God prior to His love for the creation. Once again one may recall Dante's wonderful sentence about "the love that moves the stars." This eternal love is then understood as the "immanent" relation between the three persons of the Trinity.

Are these doctrinal conceptualizations important for faith? I rather doubt it. I have great difficulty following those who maintain that Christian faith must inevitably be Trinitarian. But this does not make me a "Unitarian." If one grasps the motives that originally gave birth to the development of Trinitarian thought, one will be able to assent to it, though without absolutizing it – if you will, with a grain of salt.

What is the place of the Spirit in the drama of redemption?

There is an episode in Church history that had extraordinarily important consequences and that today seems close to incomprehensible to anyone who is not a professional theologian. This is the so-called *"filioque* controversy," which was a key issue in the great schism between the eastern and western branches of Christendom, and which has remained a bone of contention between the two. It seems to me that, in a curious way (and, I'm sure, in a way not intended by the original protagonists in the controversy), it serves to throw some light on the above question.

While both the east and the west adhered to the Nicene formulation of the *homoousion"* – that is, that all three persons of the Trinity are of the same "substance" – the east insisted much more strongly on the priority of the Father. It then seemed to eastern theologians debating the relationship between the three persons that, if the Spirit is thought of as proceeding not only from the Father but also from the Son, the Spirit would become a sort of "grandson" of the Father – a truly offensive notion. Therefore, the east insisted that the Spirit "proceeds" from the Father only, and fervently adhered to the original formulation of the matter in the Nicene Creed – "the Holy Spirit, who proceeds from the Father, and who with the Father and the Son is worshipped and glorified." (The Council of Nicaea met in 325 CE and officially settled the Arian controversy. The so-called Nicene Creed was not composed until 381 CE at the First Council of Constantinople. But that, I suppose, is neither here nor there.)

A different view developed in the west. Augustine already spoke about a procession of the Spirit from both the Father and the Son, but he did not make this into a big issue. It became a big issue through the usual coincidence of theological and political interests. In 589 CE a western assembly held in Toledo defined the "double procession" as official orthodoxy (already offensive to the east) and changed the wording of the Nicene Creed to read that the Spirit "proceeds from the Father *and the Son"* – in Latin, *filioque* (in the eastern view, an intolerable messing of a by-now sacrosanct text and thus an official endorsement of heresy). Harnack was of the opinion that this was not done in order to oppose the east (an opinion shared by more recent historians), but may have been motivated by a concern to combat remnants of Arianism in the west – that is, by emphasizing the full divinity of Christ. Be this as it may, in 809 CE a synod held in Aachen confirmed the *filioque,* and the changed text of the Nicene Creed was now enforced by the Emperor Charlemagne. We may safely assume that Charlemagne at Aachen had interests that were as little theological as those held by Constantine at Nicaea. It was just nine years since Charlemagne had himself crowned as emperor, and in this role he had a strong interest in enforcing religious uniformity in his realm – and indeed had an interest in underlining his imperial status against the competition in Constantinople. The *filioque* thus became a political football between the western and eastern empires. The issue is a good example of a generalization made by Harnack about the history of theology – a movement from affirmations of faith to theological systems to legally binding criteria of Church discipline, the last of these frequently arrived at in collusion with secular authorities.

But the *filioque* became most visibly an issue of ecclesiastical politics in the struggle for primacy between Rome and Constantinople. The eastern position was most vehemently propagated by Photius, who was patriarch of Constantinople from 858 to 867 and again from 878 to 886. He accused the west of a medley of heresies, the *filioque* being the foremost one. The pope of Rome was formally condemned as a heretic by a synod held in Constantinople in 876. Mutual edicts of excommunication were issued between Rome and Constantinople. The final break came in 1054, in quite a theatrical scene: Papal legates marched into the great basilica of Hagia Sophia in Constantinople and deposited a bull of excommunication on the high altar.

Eastern polemics on the issue interestingly combine the aforementioned metaphysical concerns with concerns of ecclesial authority. There has been the argument that, if the Spirit proceeds from Christ as well as from the Father, then the individual claiming to be the "vicar of Christ" would be, so to speak, in charge of the Spirit. This strikes me as rather far-fetched. But it is clear that both popes and patriarchs felt that they were in a position to rule on the matter, and then to read each other out of the true Church because of this disagreement. It is probably safe to say that, ever since 1054, the east has had stronger feelings about this than the west. These feelings were not assuaged by such incidents as the sack of Constantinople by the Fourth Crusade in 1204 (an event craftily managed by the Republic of Venice, which wanted to eliminate a rival in its trade with the east) and by the failure of the west to save Constantinople from the Ottoman Turks.

There have been various attempts to find a compromise on the *filioque* issue. In the nineteenth century a number of Anglo-Catholic theologians urged the Church of England to eliminate the *filioque* from the Creed (since Rome wouldn't accept them, maybe Constantinople might). Similar moves were made by the Old Catholics (the community formed by Catholics who left the Roman Church over the proclamation of papal infallibility by the First Vatican Council). In 1978 the Lambeth Conference (the periodic international meeting of bishops of the Anglican communion) actually recommended the deletion of the *filioque*, but as anyone attending an Episcopal service will be able to ascertain, the offending clause is still there. As recently as 1981 a commission of Orthodox, Catholic, and Protestant theologians, convened under the auspices of the World Council of Churches, also recommended the deletion (while expressing respectful understanding of the western position). Ordinary Christians in all these communities are blissfully ignorant of these negotiations. This is probably a good thing. Still. I would argue that, despite the murky history of this controversy, it raises some interesting points. Let me so argue.

The eastern position clearly envisages a broader efficacy of the Spirit, as being in an immediate relationship with God the Father not dependent on the mediation of the Son. *Potentially*, this could have far-reaching implications for an understanding of non-Christian religions. The Spirit could be present in places where even the name of Christ is unknown. I find this, at the least, an intriguing speculation. Let me hasten to say that I'm not imputing this idea to eastern theology. (I tried out the idea on an Orthodox theologian of my acquaintance. He firmly rejected it, saying that he knew of no one in Orthodoxy who had proposed it. I take his word for this. But this does not stop me from speculating along this line.) The western position is obviously more emphatically christocentric. It is for this reason that Karl Barth, arguably the most important Protestant theologian of the twentieth century, embraced the *filioque*. As was pointed out in an earlier chapter, the west, much more so than the east, has been focused on human depravity and thus on the need of a savior from sin, which may partially account for the christocentric emphasis. By contrast, the east has had a less sin-centered anthropology, and the Spirit could be seen as an agent of *theosis* – the journey toward union with God which is supposed to be the destiny of man. Yet again on the other hand, the western *filioque* could serve as a barrier against free-floating "spirituality" – an arbitrary, idiosyncratic, and frequently destructive reliance on emotional experiences, divorced from the corrections provided by scripture and tradition.

It seems to me, then, that both the western and the eastern positions have useful points. I, for one, do not feel constrained to decide between them (I'd happily recite the Nicene Creed in either version). It also seems to me that the controversy illuminates a specific tension in the Christian understanding of the drama of redemption. It could be called the tension between *here* and *everywhere*. Christian faith has insisted that God revealed Himself *here* – in the history of Israel, in the Incarnation, death, and Resurrection of Jesus Christ, and in the continuing proclamation of the Gospel. But Christian faith has also insisted that God is omnipresent, that He is *everywhere* – in every place and time of the created world in which we live, and in all other possible worlds. The Spirit of God, then, is both *here* and *everywhere*. The tension of this "both . . . and" cannot be resolved by means of theological formulations, however sophisticated, and certainly not by committees of professional theologians. The tension can be sustained and (perhaps paradoxically) overcome in the act of faith.

How does one gain access to the Spirit?

This is a question that has been around since the beginnings of Christianity, and indeed before that – as in the issue, repeatedly addressed in the Hebrew Bible, on how to distinguish between true and false prophecy. The question is very timely today. One of the most important phenomena on the religious scene today is the explosive growth of Pentecostalism throughout wide regions of the world (the British sociologist David Martin, who has studied the phenomenon for many years, estimates that there are at least 250 million Pentecostals in the world today). Pentecostalism is a complex and variegated phenomenon, but it is everywhere characterized by the claim that, in order to be a fully accredited Christian, one must undergo a "baptism of the Spirit" – that is, an experience similar to the one reported in the Book of Acts (hence, of course, the name "Pentecostal"). Out of this experience are supposed to flow the "gifts of the Spirit," notable among these the power to heal the sick (and Pentecostals have none of the bureaucratic caution that characterizes the Roman Catholic handling of alleged miracles) and the ability to "speak in tongues" (glossolalia is the most distinctive feature of Pentecostal worship). There are also sizeable charismatic movements within mainstream denominations, so that the issue is broader than just the churches that call themselves Pentecostal. How is one to assess these claims? But quite apart from the massive presence of Pentecostalism in contemporary Christianity, there is the widespread phenomenon of so-called "spirituality," especially in North America and in Europe. There are numerous people who will tell you that they are "not religious," but "spiritual." Not much probing is needed to clarify what they mean by this: They mean that they don't feel an allegiance to any particular religious tradition (especially not the one out of which they come), but that they have had or seek experiences that put them in direct contact with transcendent realities defined in one way or another. Frequently, as in the so-called New Age versions of "spirituality," this enterprise is marked by borrowings from Asian religious traditions, especially in various contemplative techniques employed to produce the "spiritual" experience. But these latter-day "spiritualists" also stand in a long tradition of popular Christian mysticism – not in the footsteps of the great Christian mystics, such as Meister Eckhart or Teresa of Avila, but of ordinary people who (as John Wesley put it) had their hearts "strangely warmed." And how are *those* claims to be assessed? Thus, in asking the question heading this passage, we are not just engaging in an exercise of trying to understand Church history, but are confronting the beliefs and practices of many people in the contemporary (allegedly "modern") world. (As far as Church history is concerned, I have found useful a recent book on this topic – Stanley Burgess, *The Holy Spirit: Medieval Roman Catholic and Reformation Traditions*.)

Jeffrey Russell, a Church historian, has written of an ongoing tension between two Christian traditions, which he calls the "spirit of order" and the "spirit of prophecy." In the first case, the Holy Spirit and all his gifts are understood to be confined within the institutions of the Church, which is assumed to be itself a creation of the Spirit. Thus the Spirit can be accessed only via the Church and its sacraments. As we have seen in the Roman Catholic case, some churches will allow for some exceptions, but they are dealt with cautiously and in any case are not allowed to threaten the institutionalized means of grace. The churches coming out of the mainstream Protestant Reformation (Lutheran, Calvinist, and Anglican) have been the most radical in frowning on the exceptions: Miracles of any sort are rarely welcomed in those austere Protestant territories. In the second case, the Spirit is deemed to erupt freely, within or outside the institutional structures, and often in direct opposition to them. That is, the Spirit can be accessed directly, without institutional mediation. Sociologically, the tension between these two views of the Spirit can be, respectively, attributed to priests and to prophets – two types of religious figures whose conflicts can be traced very far back indeed.

Since sociology has been mentioned, I might also point out that this tension was discussed in great detail by Max Weber in his theory of the "routinization of charisma" (the phrase is used repeatedly in his writings both on religion and on politics – charisma is an important phenomenon in both areas). What he meant by this is the following: "Charisma" (the term itself derives from the New Testament, where it denotes, precisely, the "gifts of the Spirit") is the claim to authority by institutionally unaccredited individuals. It is a claim based on an allegedly direct divine mandate given to the individual in question – as when Jesus repeatedly says "you have heard it said [by the official guardians of the tradition, "scribes and Pharisees"], . . . but I say unto you." In the "but I" lies the claim to charismatic authority, over against the authority of the institution. Charismatic authority is highly individualized, immediate, and extraordinary. But Weber also proposed that such authority is, just about inevitably, of limited duration. Typically, it wanes as the first generation of those who were followers of the charismatic leader pass from the scene. There are both psychological and sociological reasons for this vulnerability to time of charismatic authority. Psychologically, the second generation can no longer replicate the amazing experience of its elders – to the children of the first disciples, the extraordinary has become ordinary – typically, they have lived with it as far back as they can remember. Sociologically, if the insights or beliefs of the charismatic experience are to survive over time, they must be given institutional forms – precisely because the original experience is no longer available. What happens then, according to Weber, is that "charisma of person" ("I say unto you") is transformed into "charisma of office" ("the Church says unto you"). Priests replace prophets. Or, to put it differently, the charisma becomes "routinized" – the extraordinary has become ordinary. (The German term used by Weber is more graphic – *Veralltaeglichung*, literally "everydayization" – what was once an astounding interruption of ordinary life now becomes a routine of everyday life.) Weber had little use for a notion of sociological laws, but his "routinization of charisma" comes close to being one – minimally, a widely recurring process in the history of religion (and indeed of charismatic movements in other areas of human life, notably in politics). It is a sociological parallel to the theological process traced by Adolf von Harnack, from affirmations of faith to bodies of ecclesiastical dogma and discipline. Put simply, after a while the priests always win – though they can never be sure that some inconvenient prophet will not suddenly appear and challenge their authority.

Put differently again, the "spirit of order" ever faces the danger of lapsing into calcification, while the "spirit of prophecy" always moves on the brink of chaos. The ecclesiastical institution understands itself, quite reasonably, as the guardian and administrator of the Spirit. A freely flowing Spirit is a potentially revolutionary force, not only against the Church, but against all the institutions of society. But even short of its revolutionary potential, the "spirit of prophecy" is marked by an anti-institutional animus, stressing "inwardness" against the allegedly superficial forms of organized religion. For contemporary examples of this, one only has to look at the Pentecostal polemics against the mainstream churches or the disdain expressed by "spiritualists" for the allegedly empty religiosity of those churches.

There have been eruptions of "spiritualist" radicalism throughout Christian history (and, needless to say, in the history of other religious traditions). The radicalism can be either revolutionary, in the sense of rebelling against social institutions, or in terms of withdrawing from institutional religion into some form of "inwardness." The latter form of "spiritualism" is characteristic of all mystical movements. It provided a formal challenge to the early Church in the form of Gnosticism, which rejected all the institutions of this world, as not having been created by God but rather captive to demonic powers, and which insisted that "spiritual" reality alone came from God. Throughout the Middle Ages there were radical movements claiming direct access to the Spirit.

A very important figure in the development of Christian "spiritualism" was Joachim of Fiore (ca. 1130–1202), a Cistercian monk from southern Italy, who became abbot of a monastery and then founder of his own order at San Giovanni in Fiore. The order was approved by the pope and Joachim became famous in his lifetime, though his orthodoxy was questioned after his death (he was a *lucky* prophet!). He taught that the world would be going through three ages, dominated respectively by the Father, the Son, and the Spirit. The third age was just beginning in Joachim's own time (we need not concern ourselves here with the obscure calculations which led to Joachim's datings). This new age would be marked by progressive eruptions of the power of the Spirit. When the age of the Spirit reaches its fullness, all people on earth (including, importantly, the Jews) would be converted to the true faith. The Church would remain (a concession which, we may assume, gratified the pope), but it would be "spiritually" transformed, along with all other institutions. The whole world will then be filled with the Spirit, and heaven will descend upon earth. This culmination is to be anticipated and brought closer, not by revolution (again, the pope must have been pleased – not to mention the emperor), but by rigorous contemplative disciplines.

Joachim's influence has been profound and long-lasting. One could even say that, even for people who have never heard of him, the Joachimite scheme has provided a template for their thinking – from various heretical movements in the Middle Ages all the way to the Marxist notion of the stages leading to the Communist fulfillment. Again, one can distinguish between two possibilities of Joachimite thinking, the quietistic and the revolutionary one – respectively, quietly preparing for the coming of the new age of the Spirit by turning inward, or bringing about the new age by forceful action in the outside world. It is important to note that *both* constitute challenges to the authority of the Church and its claim to control access to the Spirit.

The most radical "spiritualist" challenge in the Middle Ages came from the Albigensian heresy, which flourished in the twelfth century in Languedoc (what is now southern France), and which was defeated in a bloody crusade and finally extinguished by the Inquisition. It was a latter-day eruption of Gnosticism. It taught that all matter is evil, denied both the creation and the Incarnation, and most importantly denied the legitimacy of the Church and its sacraments. Within the Albigensian movement (named after the town of Albi, where it was centered) a sharp distinction was made between ordinary followers (in its heyday this included a substantial proportion of the population of Languedoc) and those, called *perfecti*, who had achieved spiritual perfection. The only sacrament recognized in the movement was the so-called *consolamentum*, which either brought about or symbolized "baptism in the Holy Spirit." Curiously, this extremist religion co-existed with an exuberantly sensual culture (Languedoc was the birthplace of the cult of love propounded by the Troubadours). Those receiving the *consolamentum* had to abjure all the comforts and pleasures of this world. It is not surprising, then, that this sacrament was very frequently sought by individuals on their deathbed! Albigensianism (and along with it the distinctive culture of Languedoc) was annihilated in an ocean of blood. But this did not spell the end of quasi-Joachimite radicalism in Christian history.

There were intermittent explosions throughout the Middle Ages. A particularly violent one occurred in the sixteenth century, stimulated at least in part by the upheaval caused by the Protestant Reformation. (On this episode I am indebted to a book by a colleague – Carter Lindberg, *The Third Reformation?*) The radicals of this period can be loosely subsumed under the name of Anabaptists (literally "re-baptizers," because they rejected infant baptism), sometimes also called the "left wing" of the Reformation ("left" referring to their radical social and political agendas). Groups of Anabaptists were involved in violent rebellions, notably in the establishment by armed force of the "heavenly Jerusalem" in Muenster (mentioned in the preceding chapter), a utopian experiment which was brutally destroyed by a joint force of Lutherans and Catholics in 1535.

In the sixteenth century one can again observe the two directions typically taken by "spiritualism." There is the revolutionary direction, whose protagonists are not content to wait for the coming age of the Spirit, but try instead to bring it on by violent actions of their own. A key figure here is Thomas Muenzer, a contemporary of Luther, whom he first followed and then turned against in vitriolic controversy. In 1525 he took part in a widespread uprising of peasants, and was then captured, tortured, and executed. Muenzer taught that all Christians can experience the "baptism of the Spirit" and the gifts presumed to flow from it. The God-given mission of these "spiritualized" Christians is to bring about a true Reformation (as against the false one of the Lutherans) and thus bring about a new creation. But then the Anabaptists also had a quietist wing. Key in that was the Dutch preacher and theologian Menno Simon (ca. 1469–1561). He opposed Muenzer's revolutionary program. He too believed in the "baptism of the Spirit," but it was meant to result in pacifism and withdrawal from the world. The Mennonites, to this day, continue this tradition. It also continues with the Quakers and other adherents of Christian pacifism. (The oscillation between violence and pacific withdrawal has also been extensively discussed in the work of the British sociologist David Martin.)

If the "spirit of order" can lead to calcification and the "spirit of prophecy" to chaos, there must also be the search for a reasonable course that avoids both dangers. Such a search, in the Christian context, must involve an understanding of the Spirit that allows for prophecy without undermining all order. In the sixteenth century, such was eminently the position of Martin Luther. (On Luther's understanding of the Spirit, see Regin Prenter, *Spiritus Creator*.)

(*A personal interjection:* In accordance with the ethics of honest labelling, I should mention here once again that I am a Lutheran – more or less, and certainly not in the sense of Lutheran orthodoxy. I continue to believe that the Protestant Reformation rediscovered certain central elements of Christianity and that Lutheran theology succeeded in considerable measure in formulating these discoveries. Luther himself deserves great credit for this achievement. But this does not mean that one must follow him in every respect, even less make him into an icon. I, for one, cannot identify with the overwhelming sense of sin and unworthiness which was the root of his religious experience and which colored much of his subsequent thought. And I am repelled by the savagery with which he endorsed the campaign to eradicate the rebellious peasants, and even more so by the vicious anti-Semitism of some of his late writings. These reservations do not preclude assent to a number of his positions – including the position under consideration here.)

In much of his public career, Luther found himself fighting on two fronts – on the one hand, against the calcification of the Spirit in the institutional Church, and on the other hand, against the "spiritualism" of the Anabaptists, whom he called *Schwaermer*, "enthusiasts." In other words, Luther positioned himself in the middle between Rome and Muenster. He rejected the Roman exaltation of the Church, developing an ecclesiology that provided an elaborate counter-interpretation. But he also insisted that the Spirit was only active for redemption in the Word of God, both as written in the scriptures and as proclaimed in the preaching ministry and the sacraments of the Church (he finally allowed only two sacraments, baptism and eucharist, which he believed to have been instituted by Jesus). The Lutheran motto *sola Scriptura* embodies this double opposition: The Spirit is to be found in the Biblical witness, which cannot be superseded either by the authority of the Church or by this or that personal experience. Now, one must recognize that Luther's understanding of the Bible is difficult to accept fully in the wake of modern historical scholarship. Also, Luther's views on these matters were subsequently calcified (yes, one might say "petrified" – that is, moving in a

Roman direction) in Lutheran orthodoxy. It is still remarkable how he managed to stake out a reasoned middle position.

Luther's understanding of the Spirit is thoroughly christocentric – that is, focused on the Spirit's place in the drama of redemption centered in Christ. For this reason, Luther had no difficulty accepting the western position on the *filioque*. The Spirit mediates the experience of Christ, making Christ *present* – that is, transforming an event of the past into an event occurring today. Scripture, preaching, and sacraments become means of grace only by way of the Spirit. Without the Spirit, the Bible is a dead text, sermons are nothing but human concoctions, and the sacraments are empty rituals. This view of the role of the Spirit differentiates Luther both from the arid Biblicism that has characterized so much of later Protestantism and from the Catholic understanding of the sacraments operating mechanically regardless of the circumstances. The "real presence" of Christ, the Word of God, in the *kerygma* and in the sacraments is always the work of the Spirit. At the same time, the Spirit can only be accessed through these means. Luther differentiated between the "outward" and the "inner" Word – the outward performances taking place in the Church and the inner life which is the work of the Spirit. But this does not imply a form of "spiritualism" (it became that, later, in Pietism and other quietist Protestant movements): The Spirit is always dependent on the "outward" Word.

Luther's opposition to the "enthusiasts" is succinctly summarized by Regin Prenter:

> In all Luther's difference with the enthusiasts we are concerned with only one thing: the exclusive understanding of the Spirit as the Spirit of God. Over against this is the idea of the enthusiasts about spirit and spirituality, which is orientated from the point of view of a spiritualistic, metaphysical dualism between the body and the soul, between the visible and the invisible, between matter and thought. – To Luther the Spirit is not "something spiritual". The Spirit is the Triune God himself in his real presence as our sphere of life. (*Spiritus Creator*, pp. 288f)

Luther himself summarized his view in simple language in his *Small Catechism*, the little book intended for the instruction of the young, in the explanation of the Third Article of the Creed:

> I believe that I cannot believe and come to Jesus Christ, my Lord, out of my own reason or strength. Rather, the Holy Spirit has called me through the Gospel, has enlightened me by his gifts, and has sanctified and preserved me in the true faith. Moreover he calls together, enlightens, and sanctifies all the Christian community on earth, and keeps it in Jesus Christ in the one true faith. And in this community he daily and richly forgives

me and all the faithful all our sins. And on the last day he will resurrect me and all the dead, and will give me and all the faithful in Christ an eternal life. – This is surely true. (my translation)

This chapter has been a, possibly bewildering, rapid tour through Church history. It is important to be clear about the central issue, which provides the nexus between faith and the tradition as it developed in that history. The issue is the tension between the tradition and the experience of God's presence now, as well as the tension between the intuition that God is everywhere but that He is here, in the tradition, in a special way. God revealed Himself *then*, and I seek him *now*: The Spirit mediates between the *then* and the *now*, and also mediates between the *everywhere* and the *here*. It is not necessary that one agrees with everything said by Luther on these matters, but one can be impressed by the balanced position he arrived at after much struggling. Such a balance is very important. If one emphasizes the *then* without taking into account the *now*, faith becomes an antiquarian exercise that can only end in a great disappointment – the tradition becomes irrelevant. If one neglects the *then* in favor of the *now*, religion (or "spirituality") becomes a night in which all cats are gray – anything goes. Similarly, if one insists on God's omnipresence without taking into account His self-disclosure as the "God of Abraham, Isaac, and Jacob, and of our Lord Jesus Christ," one arrives at a religious position in which all questions of truth are dissolved (as I have tried to show in my criticism of John Hick's "pluralism"). But if, on the other hand, one focuses on the *here* to the exclusion of the *everywhere*, one sets impermissible limits on how God chooses to disclose Himself to human beings.

The example of Luther shows that it is not easy to achieve such a balance. It also shows that it is not impossible, even if one cannot go along with every aspect of Luther's thought. One can stake out such a balanced position, faithful to the tradition and yet free in one's approach to it. It seems to me that this has great contemporary relevance – as one faces the absolutist claims of "petrified" churches (notably the claims of Rome as the "rock of Peter"), the rigid approach to the scriptures of Protestant fundamentalism (which is far removed from Luther's principle of *sola Scriptura*), and, last but not least, the free-floating "spirituality" that is so fashionable today. I continue to think that Lutheran theology provides some concepts that are useful in the achievement of such a balanced position. I also think that other concepts are possible. In other words, it is not necessary to be a Lutheran if one strives for the needed balance.

Chapter Ten

"... the holy catholic church, the communion of saints"

Unlike other matters defined as objects of faith in the Creed, the Church is not only an empirical phenomenon, but a sociologically researchable entity in our contemporary world. And in all societies in which religious liberty has been established, especially in America, there exists an exuberant plurality of institutions which claim the label of "church" or can be so described by a non-theological observer. For reasons that I have not been able to discover, there is a locale in Washington which can convey an almost mystical experience of religious pluralism. Get in a car and drive north on Sixteenth Street from the White House toward Walter Reed Hospital. After a few minutes from the start of this trip there is a religious building on just about every block. Since we are concerned here with the notion of "church," let us just leave aside the various non-Christian occupants (there are several synagogues as well as Buddhist, Hindu, and Bahai shrines). There are churches of every major Protestant denomination (including African-American ones), a large Roman Catholic church, and two Orthodox churches (Greek and Serbian). Just which one of these is the "Church" intended by the Creed? Could it be all of them? Or perhaps none? The tension between theological affirmation and sociological reality becomes very tangible here.

What does it mean to say that the Church is an object of faith?

Clearly, it does not mean faith in the empirical fact of institutions that call themselves "churches." No faith is required to establish that fact – a half-hour drive in Washington will do it. But faith is very much required if one looks at the terms ascribed to the Church in the wording of the Creed. The Church is called "holy" (and then associated with "saints") and it is called "catholic" (which here, of course, does not refer to the Roman Catholic Church, but is simply the Greek synonym for "universal"). We will discuss presently what "holiness" and "universality" might mean theologically. For now, just let it be emphasized that neither of these characteristics is empirically ascertainable. On the contrary, the empirical reality is one of emphatically non-holy activities and of all sorts of sometimes vicious tribalism. Upon closer inspection (and sometimes even upon a cursory one), churches have the all-too-human characteristics of secular institutions. Their clergy can be fanatical, greedy, power-hungry, and exploitative. Their members can be narrow, petty, and prejudiced. And often enough (though, happily, not often in America) churches have blessed and encouraged the most murderous atrocities. To be sure, now and then one comes across individuals whom one might call saintly, but they are few and far between. A holy institution? Not likely. As to universality, the recommended excursion into the heartland of American pluralism will make this term pressingly implausible. It is not only that there is this multiplicity of churches. There is the further fact that many of them do not recognize each other as legitimate churches at all, or at best as imperfect substitutes for the one true Church (whichever it may be deemed to be). The empirical picture, most of the time, is devastatingly uninspiring. To perceive holiness and universality in this picture indeed requires an act of faith!

Did Jesus intend to found an institutional "church"? Christian tradition has generally made this claim. It is very likely mistaken. Two New Testament passages are usually cited to buttress the claim. There is the so-called "Great Commission" (Matthew 28:19), as we saw in the preceding chapter, where Jesus is supposed to have instructed his followers to go and "make disciples of all nations," and baptize them in the words of the standard Trinitarian formula. Most Biblical scholars would regard it as very unlikely that Jesus said anything like this. And then there is the other, the so-called "Petrine Commission," supposedly uttered by Jesus after Simon (thereafter called Peter) confessed Jesus to be "the Christ, the Son of the living God" (Matthew 16:18): "You are Peter, and on this rock I will build my church, and the powers of death shall not prevail against it" (the older translation says "the gates of hell shall not prevail" – as usual, a much more awesome formulation). This passage, of course, has been strategically central in the Roman Catholic self-understanding as the true Church, based on the alleged facts that Peter became the first bishop of Rome and that all the popes since then have been successors of Peter. The passage contains a pun – in Greek, the name Petros linked to the word for rock, *petra*; the pun also worked in Aramaic, which Jesus would have spoken – the name Kephas linked to the word for rock, *kepha*. Protestant exegetes have argued that the "rock" refers, not to the person of Peter, but to his confession of faith – an unconvincing argument, precisely because of the pun. More importantly, the assertion that Peter became the first Roman bishop (whatever that title may have meant in this first period of Christian history) is historically very shaky at best. One might be intrigued by the possibility that this may be the only case in history of an institution founded on a pun. Be this as it may, I would propose that the likelihood of Jesus having made this statement is about the same as the likelihood of his having recited the Gettysburg Address.

Less subject to historical falsification is the other tradition, by which the Church was founded by the Holy Spirit at Pentecost, in the event discussed in the preceding chapter. It is very likely that such an event occurred, even if we cannot be certain as to just what transpired there, and it makes sense to think that as of this event the followers of Jesus conceived of themselves as a Spirit-filled community, though the term "church" may not as yet have been used. It is clear that there was an early experience of Christ's continuing presence in the community of believers, to the point where this community could be understood as "the body of Christ" in the world from which the human body of Jesus had departed.

In the beginning, we can be sure, this community had few if any organizational forms. It was free-flowing, spontaneous, with the principal disciples, the Apostles, exercising a very personal, "charismatic" authority (the New Testament term for it is *exousia* – the authority to speak in the name of Christ). Increasingly, as time went on, the community developed firm institutional forms – a hierarchy, chains of command, legal criteria for authority and membership, and, last but not least, obligatory adherence to specific ceremonies and doctrines. As discussed earlier, the necessity for such a development was expressed in Max Weber's theory of the "routinization of charisma." If the religious message carried by the first community is to survive over time, it must be transmitted through institutional forms that are less effervescent than the charismatic authority of the early days. "Charisma of person" is transmuted to "charisma of office": The divine authority (*exousia*) is now no longer dependent on the personal qualities of the individual exercising it, but is now inherent in the official role occupied by an individual.

Historians differ as to the stages and the speed of this change. At the latest, the implications of this change were ratified in the early fourth century, in the so-called Donatist controversy. In one of the last great persecutions of the Church by the Roman government, a number of clergy in North Africa had recanted their Christian faith in order to save themselves. When the persecution was over, some of them repented and wanted to resume their ministry. The question arose whether, as a result of their apostasy, they had lost their priestly status and therefore would have to be re-ordained. The Donatists (a rigorous party within the North African Church, named after a bishop Donatus) answered the question in the affirmative. The contrary view, however, prevailed in the Church. This had implications far beyond the immediate procedural question. It established the notion of the "indelible character" of priesthood – that is, a priest remained a priest, regardless of personal foibles and wickedness, and therefore the sacraments (notably baptism and eucharist) administered by even the most flawed priest were "valid." In both western and eastern Christianity this notion has been firmly established in the legal definition of the status of priests and bishops. It reached a certain epitome in the Roman Catholic doctrine of the papacy. Thus, when the First Vatican Council proclaimed the infallibility of the pope, it made clear that this quality did not pertain to any pope as an individual and to his personal opinions, but only to statements on faith and morals proclaimed by a pope explicitly in his office as pope (*ex cathedra*, "from the throne"). This, of course, raises an interesting question: What if the Borgia pope, Alexander VI (1492–1503), had made a statement *ex cathedra* on some matter of faith or morals: Would that too have been infallible? Recall that this gentleman obtained the papacy through bribery, fostered the political careers of his bastard children Cesare and Lucrezia, was famous for his unbridled lechery, in pursuit of which he established a harem of concubines in a wing of the Vatican, and at one point tried to poison the entire college of cardinals. Roman Catholic doctrine will have to maintain that Alexander's disreputable personal qualities could not affect the "validity" of his papal office or of any acts performed on the basis of this office, but would then add the belief that the Holy Spirit would surely prevent his misusing that office in proclamations *ex cathedra*. Fortunately, faith and morals were matters of no concern whatever to Alexander Borgia, so the question remains moot.

The emergence of an institutional Church is fully understandable in terms of the sociology of religion. It is useful to understand that religious institutions must necessarily perform two functions, which are often in tension with each other. On the one hand, they have the function of preserving and transmitting from one generation to another the core of the religious experience in which they originated. On the other hand, in doing this they function to domesticate that experience, by ensuring that it can be inserted into ordinary social life without completely disrupting the latter. Take, for example, the collection of Jesus' sayings constituting what we know as the Sermon on the Mount. We have here a set of moral imperatives that have been inspiring over the centuries, yet any human society that would organize itself on the basis of the Sermon's unrealistic demands would promptly lapse into chaos. The Church was compelled to transmit this moral vision, but also to domesticate it by interpreting it in such a way that it does not explode the normal business of social life. (The different forms taken by such interpretation – for example, by setting up a double standard for ordinary Christians and the more saintly types among them – need not concern us here.) Be this as it may, the institutional development just described is almost certainly very far from anything intended or commanded by Jesus.

I would not be misunderstood: I do not propose an antithesis between Christianity and the Church, as some radical thinkers and agitators have repeatedly done in the course of Christian history. Faith in Christ is certainly compatible with faith in the Church as the vehicle (or perhaps, more cautiously, as *a* vehicle) of Christ's continuing presence in the world. In other words, one can look at the Church as a means, indeed a necessary means, to the end of maintaining that presence. But I also want to point to the far from infrequent shift from the end to the means, so that it is the means that now becomes the principal object of faith. In that case, at least potentially, faith in the Church replaces faith in Christ. And that indeed can be described as a deformation or even a loss of Christian faith. Such a shift has been repeatedly denounced by prophetic voices in Christian history. A radical case in point was the vehement attack, in the nineteenth century, by Søren Kierkegaard against "Christendom," by which he meant the Lutheran Church of Denmark. I would differentiate between what is exaggerated and what is valid in Kierkegaard's attack. He had a heroic vision of Christian faith, an extreme version of the "imitation of Christ." He insisted that the believer must make himself "contemporaneous" with Jesus. This, I think, is an impossible suggestion. But I would agree with Kierkegaard's view that Christian faith could not mean a comfortable and undemanding membership in a socially (and, in the Danish case, legally) established religious institution.

I will tell a personal anecdote here. Soon after I came to America I attended a college in the Midwest. I had a Finnish girlfriend, who had also arrived in America recently. Since, then as now, I was interested in religion, I dragged her along to various religious events, most of which were new to both of us. One such event was an old-fashioned Protestant revival meeting. When the preacher invited people to come to the altar and to confess Jesus as their lord and savior, ushers fanned out around the church and encouraged individuals to heed this call. As one such usher approached the pew in which we were sitting, my companion visibly tightened up. When the usher came to us, he turned to her and asked, "Sister, are you saved?" She replied, in strongly accented English, "I am a member of the Lutheran Church of Finland." The usher was taken aback, but he apparently took her answer as a "yes," because he moved on to the next pew. (He didn't ask me; I suppose that he took her answer to include me as well.) I thought at the time that this answer was both correct, in rejecting the revivalist assumption about the nature of "salvation," and incorrect, in identifying "salvation" with a legally defined church membership. I suppose that the argument of this chapter may be taken as an elaboration of this youthful reflection of mine.

Throughout Christian history there was the question of what constitutes the authentic community of believers, or differently put, the question of where to locate the true Church. The New Testament suggests that the oldest answer was to the effect that the authentic community, the true Church, was wherever the "gifts of the Spirit" could be discerned. But this is a very volatile criterion. However these gifts are defined, they can be found in more than one community – be it the gift of prophecy or of healing, "speaking in tongues," or more mundane gifts such as eloquent preaching, wise counseling, or the devoted care of those in need. In other words, antagonistic communities, which failed to recognize each other as belonging to the same true Church, all could provide evidence of the "gifts of the Spirit." Almost inevitably, then, the authenticity of a community came to be defined by institutionally established criteria, such as orthodox doctrine, correct forms of worship, or alleged "succession" of the hierarchy from the founding generation. The "marks of the Church" (*notae ecclesiae*) could then be formulated in juridically precise terms. This was done in both western and eastern Christianity, and could then be utilized in mutual excommunication between them. The western church, presumably because of the heritage of the Roman legal genius, did the more thorough job in this matter.

The Protestant Reformation, at least in its early stages, constituted a rebellion against this elaborate juridical structure. This rebellion was classically stated in Article 7 of the Augsburg Confession, the founding document of the Lutheran church: "It is enough for the true unity of the Christian Church that the Gospel be purely preached and that the sacraments be administered in accordance with God's Word" (my translation). And it goes on: "It is not necessary for the true unity of the Church that there be everywhere the same humanly instituted ceremonies." The phrase "true unity" is to be understood as the unity of those who belong to the true Church. And the phrase "humanly instituted ceremonies," while referring directly to forms of whoship, also implies everything else that was "humanly instituted" in the course of history – including the various institutional structures of the Church, eventually (as the Lutheran movement distanced itself more and more from Rome) including the papacy. There is a great weight to the lapidary sentence at the opening of this passage – "it is enough" (*satis est*).

The subsequent history of Protestantism shows that the fixation on institutional forms is not that easily done away with. Indeed, the Augsburg Confession, in the aforementioned article, already contained two loopholes through which the old institutionalism could creep back in. After all, how is one to determine whether the Gospel is "purely" preached? Or whether the sacraments are administered "in accordance with God's Word"? Lutheran orthodoxy then developed its own more or less juridical formulation of the "marks of the church," as did the Calvinist and Anglican branches of the Reformation. Lutherans and Calvinists did this largely in terms of doctrine. Anglicans, who have been more relaxed as to doctrine, did it by the assertion of the alleged "apostolic succession" of their bishops – a historically very dubious assertion indeed. (Leaving aside what happened between the age of the Apostles and the decision of Henry VIII to declare the independence of the Church of England because Rome would not allow him to divorce his wife and marry his mistress, his successor Queen Mary wiped out those bishops who went along with that declaration of independence, and her successor Queen Elizabeth did in the bishops who would *not* go along. It is rather doubtful how many were left to ensure the alleged "succession." It is ironic that the Evangelical Lutheran Church in America, in its agreement with the Episcopal Church in the late 1990s, promised that in future all its bishops would be consecrated with the help of Anglican ones deemed to have the proper "succession" credentials. The Lutheran church officials who pushed through this agreement suggested – one surmises, with a wink – that one need not necessarily share the Anglican understanding of such a ceremony in order to play along with it. Not exactly in the succession of the Augsburg Confession!)

But I am digressing (disguising this, unsuccessfully, by means of parentheses). Let me return to the *"satis est."* The mindset and the language of the sixteenth century are quite removed from our own. Let me try and formulate the core proposition here in more ordinary language (without claiming that the authors of the Augsburg Confession would have agreed with my formulation – unlike the leaders of the Evangelical Lutheran Church in America, I have not signed off on this document).

Let me suggest that the Church essentially is two things. First, the church is a big box, placed on a street corner. Every once in a while, usually on Sundays, someone climbs up on the box and says in a loud voice "Christ is risen!" And second, the Church is a gathering of people around the big box, also usually on Sundays, who sing, pray, and engage in rituals, intended however feebly to join the choir of angels who eternally praise God throughout all the galaxies and beyond. *Satis est.* Put differently, the Church is constituted by preaching and worship in the name of Christ, by *kerygma* and *leiturgia*. And while there are ways of trying to discern whether these activities are "in accordance with the Word of God" – that is, whether they accord with the witness to Christ that has come down to us in the New Testament – such discernment cannot be encapsulated in precise criteria of institutional or juridical correctness. Put differently again, all assertions of orthodoxy (correct doctrine) and orthopraxis (correct practice) should be treated with robust skepticism.

Let me concede that what I have said here expresses a very Protestant view, indeed a *liberal* Protestant view. I make no apology for this. But I would propose, with some hesitation, that Christians adhering to other traditions might find ways of agreeing – perhaps even some Catholics, though they would find themselves in considerable difficulties with the Roman authorities.

If the Church is considered to be an object of faith, then this must refer to two alleged qualities mentioned in the Creed – holiness and catholicity. Before reflecting on this possibility, a brief comment is in order concerning the phrase "communion of saints." Apparently it was not in the original text of the Apostles' Creed, but was introduced into it in the western Church sometime in the fifth century. The phrase had been used in the east, but not in the context of the Creed. The original intention of this expansion of the text is unclear. Probably it was intended to stress the holiness of the Church, to emphasize that all its members share in that holiness. In that case, "communion of saints" is to be taken as a subsidiary clause. The term "saints" was used by Paul to refer to all believers, and that usage continued in later times. However, both western and eastern Christianity developed much more restrictive understandings of sainthood, and the intention may have been to declare the unity between the saints in heaven and the Church on earth, and more broadly the community in Christ of the living and the dead. In Roman Catholic doctrine, the presence of saintliness is defined as one of the "marks of the Church" and, as we remarked in an earlier chapter, the attribution of this quality to an individual is subject to formal juridical procedures. For our purposes here, it is sufficient to regard the phrase as an amplification of the affirmation that the Church is holy.

What does it mean to say that the Church is holy?

The meaning of "holy" is pretty clear. It means a quality of moral perfection. Is the Church, then, a community of morally perfect individuals? Even the most cursory look at the history and present condition of the Church will produce mountains of counter-evidence. Throughout that history, though, there have been recurrent demands that the Church *should be* a gathering of moral paragons. The aforementioned Donatists are a good example, but the notion continues to more recent times. For example, in the late nineteenth century the American denomination of the Disciples of Christ split off from the Methodist parent body by insisting that sanctification, precisely in the sense of moral perfection, must be the aim of the Christian life (the term "Disciples" refers to this ambitious aim). The Methodists, in line with most churches all the way back to the rejection of Donatism, maintained on the contrary that the Church, while it may occasionally contain some saintly individuals, is essentially a gathering of sinners. The radical perfectionists, of course, agree with this characterization, which is why they attack the existing Church as hypocritical and as betraying true discipleship. Again, one can point to Kierkegaard as a case in point. The agenda of the moral radicals is, therefore, either separation from that hypocritical body or, somewhat less ambitiously, the creation of small groups of superior types within the large body of the morally unwashed (the Protestant Pietists called this option the *ecclesiola in ecclesia*, "the little church in the church"). I think that one can simply say, on empirical grounds, that this agenda is illusionary. Almost invariably, as one looks at these separationist groups, one finds all the moral flaws that exist in the larger churches from which they separated. In other words, the *ecclesiola* looks much like the *ecclesia*.

Different Christian traditions have dealt differently with this tension between believed holiness and observable unholiness. The Catholic option has been to say that the Church produces saints, here and there, while the bulk of its members continue to be morally imperfect. The saints are, as it were, the moral and spiritual vanguard of the Church. The majority Protestant option has been different. Here the Church is "holy" in the sense in which all believers are "holy" – that is, the holiness is an *imputed* one: In the act of justification God considers the sinful believer *as if* he were holy. Indeed, this imputation is at the center of the gift of justification. The Lutheran formulation of this option is to the effect that the believer, justified by faith, is "simultaneously just and sinful" (*simul iustus et peccator*). I have my doubts about many assumptions of this view, particularly the assumptions about the nature of sin (a topic to be taken up in the next chapter). All the same, it seems to me more plausible than the Catholic view. Few of the individuals declared to be saints by the Catholic Church (or, for that matter, the eastern Church) come out as moral or spiritual paragons under closer scrutiny. In other words, the Catholic version of the *ecclesiola* differs from the Protestant one in that most of its constituency is in the next world rather than this one, but it is just as shaky if one applies the criterion of moral or spiritual perfection.

One could usefully employ a concept here that the contemporary Protestant theologian Wolfhart Pannenberg has given currency: The church is holy in a *proleptic* way. This means that the holiness is anticipatory. What is anticipated is the coming culmination of the history of redemption, the *parousia* of Christ, when holiness will indeed be established on earth (presumably in an observable way). Be this as it may, the simplest way of summing up these reflections is that the Church is holy because of Christ's presence in it – in the box from which his Resurrection is proclaimed and in the worship that reaches out to the angels – despite the palpable failings of the empirical Church.

And what does it mean to say that the Church is universal?

Its most obvious meaning is that the Church must be open to all people, regardless of their nationality, race, class, gender, or any other collective identity. This universality, of course, was a key element in the separation from Judaism of the early Christian community – the insistence, most dramatically by the Apostle Paul, that the Church recognizes no distinction between Jews and Gentiles. But, of course, the insistence on universality came to mean much more, as membership on an equal footing in the Church was insisted upon for slaves as well as the free, for women as well as men, and for people of every race or nationality. And it must be said that, much more than in the matter of the affirmed holiness of the Church, its universality can indeed be observed on many occasions. And not only at ceremonial ecumenical gatherings. Thus on an average Sunday in many American churches, Protestant as well as Catholic, one can observe a remarkable variety of people from different racial or ethnic backgrounds. On such occasions the "proleptic" character of the Church's universality is tangible: The universality of the Church anticipates a redeemed humanity, made whole after its long history of murderous divisions. This anticipation is there, despite the miscellaneous tribalisms that still afflict the Church in many places.

There are cases where, for legitimate reasons, churches kept a "tribal" character. Examples would be the Orthodox churches under Islamic rule, or the African-American churches under conditions of slavery, segregation, or discrimination. In such cases the Church served as a refuge for persecuted or marginalized people, sometimes the one place where their full humanity was recognized. Yet even there, the universality of the Church was generally maintained *in principle*, even if circumstances did not allow this principle to be realized. The principle is, quite simply, that membership in the Church must not be restricted on the basis of any social or biological category.

In the final analysis the notion of the Church's universality is grounded in the belief that the risen Christ is Lord – Lord over all of humanity and over creation. I recall a rather fugitive but all the same memorable incident during a visit to Iran in the 1970s, a few years before the Islamic revolution. I was riding in a taxi in Tehran. The taxi driver turned on the radio to an American station, presumably for my benefit. It must have been some Evangelical broadcasting service that at that time could be heard in Iran. It was a short ride. All I heard was part of a worship service, the singing of a well-known Protestant hymn: "Go tell it on the mountain, go tell it everywhere: Jesus Christ is Lord." It was a powerful message, as I looked up to the impressive mountains that can be seen from the city of Tehran.

The approach that I try to convey here could, I suppose, be called a certain relativization of the concept of the Church. It refuses to absolutize any historical form of the Church. It considers the Church as authentic only insofar as it continues to bear witness to the central core of the Christian message. And I have already conceded that this is a distinctively Protestant approach, though I think that in this Protestantism returned very dramatically to the experiences and thought of the New Testament, especially of the Pauline tradition. There is a striking parallel between the Protestant relativization of the Church and the Pauline relativization of the Jewish law. In both cases the historically constructed forms of a religious tradition are exploded from within, and what emerges from this explosion is an immensely dynamic and by the same token immensely vulnerable faith.

I would make use here of a concept coined by Paul Tillich, arguably the foremost representative of liberal Protestant theology in the twentieth century. In an early essay (it dates from 1931) he coined the phrase "the Protestant principle." The main body of this essay is of no interest here. In this period of his life Tillich considered himself to be a "Christian socialist," and in the essay he was concerned with the relation of the Protestant church to what he believed to be the situation of the German working class. But here is the paragraph which describes "the Protestant principle"; it is worth quoting in full:

> Protestantism has a principle that stands beyond all its realizations. It is the critical and dynamic source of all Protestant realizations, but it is not identical with any of them. It cannot be confined by a definition. It is not exhausted by any historical religion; it is not identical with the structure of the Reformation or of early Christianity or even with a religious form at all. It transcends them as it transcends any cultural form. On the other hand, it can appear in all of them; it is a living, moving, restless power in them; and this is what it is supposed to be in a special way in historical Protestantism. The Protestant principle, in name derived from the protest of the "protestants" against decisions of the Catholic majority, contains the divine and human protest against any absolute claim made for a relative reality, even if this claim is made by a Protestant church. The Protestant principle is the judge of every religious and cultural reality, including the religion and culture which calls itself "Protestant". (Paul Tillich, *The Protestant Era*, p. 163)

The Protestant principle is *ipso facto* a principle of freedom. It is the freedom from every historically constructed form of religion and culture. Let me quote from a much more recent text by a liberal Protestant theologian, Friedrich Wilhelm Graf. Serving as an introduction to a volume of essays dealing with the question of what Protestant identity may mean today, it is actually entitled "Protestant Freedom": "Protestants do not allow their identity to be defined by institutions. Neither can books provide Protestants with an unambiguous, ready-made identity. They [institutions and books] can at best be of help in the acquistition of identity, an identity which can be accepted or refused in freedom" (Graf, "Einleitung: Protestantische Freiheit," p. 23; my translation). Freedom, in religion as in politics, is dangerous – dangerous to the institutions which it relativizes, but also dangerous to the individual who gives up the comfort of being safely embedded in an institution. Such an individual need not be left alone; there are, after all, communities of such individuals – such as the church communities that emerged from the Reformation. But in the final analysis such an individual has nothing to cling to except the fragile reed of faith. Here is the link between "Protestant freedom" and the Protestant understanding of salvation "by faith alone" (*sola fide*). It is no wonder that miscellaneous Protestant orthodoxies stepped back from this dangerous precipice and sought to return the individual to the alleged safety of institutional embeddedness.

These considerations take us back to the very beginning of this book when, in the first chapter, faith was described as a wager (Pascal's term; Kierkegaard described the same move as a leap). There can be no certainty in this. Yet the condition of uncertainty is very uncomfortable in the long run, and for some it is unbearable. There is then a longing for certainty. Where there is demand, there will be supply. Our pluralistic situation is full of offers to supply old or new certainties, many of them non-religious. I like to call these suppliers the certainty-wallahs; they carry on some very successful businesses in our bazaar of worldviews and value-systems.

This is not the place for a sociological or psychological analysis of the contemporary certainty market. In the, so to speak, Christian niche of this market there are three major types of certainty purveyors, each of them with a long lineage in Church history. There are those who offer certainty through the Bible, understood as literally inspired by God and therefore without errors ("inerrant"). This offer of certainty is, of course, a Protestant specialty, notably in the large Evangelical community. As the old hymn has it, "Jesus loves me, this I know, for the Bible tells me so." Since the literal and "inerrant" understanding of the Bible is very implausible as a result of modern historical scholarship, this offer of certainty tends to be taken up by people relatively distanced from contact with the results of this scholarship – that is, people who are relatively less edu-cated. Then there is the offer of certainty by way of an inner, "spiritual" experience. This path to certainty has taken many forms in the course of Christian history, most impressively in the great figures of Christian mys-ticism, less impressively in the many popular expressions of "spiritual" enthusiasm – within Protestantism in the powerful movements of conti-nental Pietism and Anglo-American Methodism, through all the waves of American revivalism, to the contemporary worldwide ascendancy of Pentecostalism. What all of these have in common, despite their many differences, is the insistence of a certainty-providing inner experience. As another hymn has it, "I know that my redeemer liveth." And how do I know this? Because I have had this particular experience – of conver-sion, of being "born again," of having been "filled with the Spirit." As this approach can take place on many levels of sophistication (say, from Teresa of Avila to a barely literate American revivalist), it is more immune to higher education than the Biblicist approach. But it is undermined, not by modern historical scholarship, but by modern psychology and soci-ology of religion. We now have a pretty good understanding of how these experiences of certainty can be induced, and this understanding invites, minimally, a robust skepticism about them.

The third type of certainty-wallah is the one that directly concerns us here. They offer certainty by embracing the institution – or perhaps more accurately, by being embraced by the institution. Quite different institu-tions can perform this function, including many secular ones. But in a Christian context, of course, the institution in question is the Church. The formula here is to give oneself up to the institution and thereby attain a conviction of certainty. Theoretically, just about any church can serve, even the little Baptist church down the road (it also holds revival ser-vices). In practice, it is those with a "high church" understanding of them-selves that do this best – that is, an understanding that gives the Church a key place in the economy of salvation. Eastern Orthodox and Anglo-Catholics are quite good at this, but there can be little doubt that the Roman Catholic Church can offer the most impressive version, as the offer includes a theological heritage of great sophistication and the accu-mulated treasure of an aesthetically attractive culture. At least for a con-temporary Western person, the attractions of Byzantium or Canterbury tend to pale in comparison with the splendors of Rome. I think enough has been said before about the corroding effects of modern scholarship in history and the social sciences to indicate why these offers of certainty can also be subsumed under the heading of illusions.

I would sum up the considerations of this chapter by proposing that Church adherence is a matter of vocation. Not all vocations are the same. It may be one's vocation to remain in the church in which one was raised, despite this or that reservation. (Despite the unfriendly things I have said in this chapter about the Roman Catholic Church, I am not at all sure that, had I been born into that church, I might not decide to remain within it and say, as many do today, that "I am Catholic in my own way" – however much Cardinal Ratzinger and the Roman authorities might question the validity of this position.) It may also be one's vocation to change one's church affiliation from a less congenial to a more congenial one. It may even be a vocation to remain without any formal church affiliation; this was Simone Weil's choice, and the data show that many people today make the same choice. As I have argued, though, Christian faith, like any other religious or moral commitment, requires institutional anchorage. It seems to me that the preferred choice for Christians should be to gather around a box from which the Gospel is preached and around which one tries, feebly, to reach out to the cosmic liturgy. But one should not absolutize the choice of any particular box.

If one believes that Christ is risen and that Christ is Lord, one can encounter him in the most different circumstances, some quite unlikely. I have had a sense of this encounter in a few Lutheran services (not very many), once in a pathetically empty Anglican service in London, at least once in a mosque. And even in a taxi as I looked up to the Elburz mountains of Iran.

Chapter Eleven

"... the forgiveness of sins"

It is a deceptively simple phrase. Yet it raises vast and difficult questions. Notably two:

What is sin? And who is supposed to forgive whom?

"Sin" is a word that does not fall easily from modern lips. Its most commonsensical synonym would be "evil," and "to sin" would then mean "to do evil." But even that translation is widely problematic today, at least among people who have had the benefit of higher education and fancy themselves to be progressive. It is perhaps enough to recall the unease when Ronald Reagan called the Soviet Union an "evil empire" and when more recently George W. Bush referred to states sponsoring terrorism as an "axis of evil." The unease, of course, was hardly ever caused by the belief that the governments of those countries were morally admirable. But the word "evil" evokes an attitude that a progressive worldview proscribes – being intolerant, "moralistic," 'judgmental." Some of the reactions to the terrorist events of September 11, 2001, especially in pronouncements of progressive clergy, sharply illustrate this: Instead of condemning the perpetrators of the massacre, one is supposed to understand "the root causes" of their actions, to recall the injustices of one's own society, and even "to look for the terrorist within every one of us." This is not the place to discuss the intellectual confusions and the political consequences of the worldview sustaining the aforementioned assertions. Suffice it to reiterate that the topics of sin and evil are not easily addressed in our contemporary cultural milieu.

Philosophers have distinguished between "moral evil" and "natural evil." The first refers to the acts of human beings, the second to the imperfections of the world quite apart from human actions – say, an act of murder as against the death of an innocent person (or, for that matter, of an animal) by "natural causes." Both raise the issue of theodicy, which has been discussed in an earlier chapter and which we will not resume here. Rather, we will focus on "moral evil" – acts of which human beings are guilty and for which they are culpable.

There is also a long philosophical tradition which holds that evil is not to be taken as a reality in its own right, but rather is simply the absence of good. Greek philosophers thought that evil, in this sense, is the result of ignorance – true knowledge, or wisdom, would eradicate evil. More recent philosophers, such as Spinoza, held that what we call evil is a necessary constituent of the universe; if one understands this, the notion of evil evaporates and whatever we used to call evil will presumably be more bearable. Mary Baker Eddy based her Christian Science on similar ideas (though hardly on Spinoza's level of philosophical sophistication). In contemporary culture, especially in America, explaining away the reality of evil commonly uses the conceptual tools of modern psychology: Acts called evil (not least by the criminal justice system) are the result of various unresolved problems in the biography of the actor: the agenda, then, is not to judge but rather to understand, and presumably to treat therapeutically (of course, this way of thinking has also made deep inroads in the criminal justice system itself, which is based on very different notions of culpability, and this has led to a good deal of confusion). Perhaps this approach can be summarized by saying "Hitler had a very bad childhood."

It seems to me that the entire tradition of denying the reality *sui generis* of evil, from the Greeks on down to contemporary social workers, constitutes a massive trivialization of the phenomenon. Reference to Hitler was not accidental. The Holocaust has been called an "icon of evil" for our time; correctly so, I think. It thus serves as a measuring device for any theory of evil.

I will only pick out one episode from the mind-numbing horrors of this period; it has been cited by various historians of the Holocaust (I first read about it in Hannah Arendt's book on the Eichmann trial, *Eichmann in Jerusalem*). It is about a speech made by Heinrich Himmler, the head of the SS and thus the chief executive of the Holocaust machinery, to officers of the *Einsatzgruppen*. These were units of the SS and the military police which, in the wake of the invasion of Russia, killed large numbers of Jews before the installation of the more efficient gas chambers in the death camps (apparently installed, among other reasons, to make the mass killings less stressful emotionally for the killers). Himmler described in considerable detail how the *Einsatzgruppen* went about their work, often for many hours, often killing entire families, including the children.

He said that he fully understood how difficult this work was for those who had to do it, especially how difficult it was when, after a day spent on these activities, they returned to their own families, perhaps played with their own children. He expressed his appreciation for those who, despite these difficulties, stayed faithful to their duty. And then he uttered a sentence that is almost unbearable to read: He said that "we" (including himself in solidarity with the murderers he was addressing) should be especially proud that, in spite of all this, "we have remained decent people" (the German adjective *anstaendig* adumbrates the cozy morality of bourgeois life).

It seems to me that all the trivializations of evil collapse in the face of this episode. Is genocide the absence of good? Is it the result of ignorance or of some unresolved Oedipal conflict? Did Himmler have a bad childhood too? Even if one gives credence to this or that empirical explanation of Nazi mentality and actions (and, *qua* social scientist, I will readily agree that such explanations are possible and can be useful), one must not allow such explanations to obfuscate the basic fact – that here one confronts moral monstrosity that is utterly *sui generis* and that calls out, not only for judgment, but for damnation. Put simply: To be "nonjudgmental" in the face of the Holocaust is to deny our very humanity.

Another matter comes to the fore here: There are not only evil actions; there are also *structures of evil*. This was affirmed by the war crimes tribunals which defined the SS as a "criminal organization," membership in which made an individual culpable (albeit to a lesser degree) even if he had not himself engaged in criminal acts. Put differently: We not only become guilty by our own actions, but we are also enmeshed by the actions of others to whom we are related in a historical community. This was a troublesome issue in the postwar debates in Germany over the question of guilt for the crimes of Nazism. The prevailing view, reflecting a long tradition of ethical thought, reaffirmed that an individual is *guilty* only for actions that he himself performed – the sons should not be condemned for the sins of their fathers. However, as members of a community we are *responsible* for the acts of others in the name of that community. It is this understanding that served to legitimate the large reparations to Jewish and other victims of Nazism by the postwar democratic government of West Germany (some of whose leaders had themselves been victims). Admittedly, the distinction between guilt and responsibility is not without difficulties. But it points to a basic fact – that, whatever we do or fail to do, we are enmeshed in history.

The Catholic theologian Karl Rahner (in the discussion of sin in his major work, *Foundations of Christian Faith*) has used an interesting term relating to the fact of "enmeshment": He speaks of the "objectification" of the sins of individuals. The example he uses to illustrate this point is far removed from the horrors of the Holocaust, but it also refers to the phenomenon of "enmeshment." I eat a banana – undoubtedly a morally inoffensive action. But there are all sorts of morally dubious events in the journey of the banana to me – such as the degrading conditions under which the banana workers are compelled to live in some far-away country, the tyrannical regime which imposes these conditions, the unfair trade relations between their country and mine, and so on. It follows that, while my eating the banana does not make me guilty of the actions of all these others, yet (at least when I become aware of the chain of events that brought the banana to me) I cannot disclaim all responsibility for the actions of these others – I have become *enmeshed* with them and with their sins. Rahner uses this example to introduce the notion of "original sin" (of which more shortly). I'm not quite persuaded by this analogy, but Rahner does make his point that we are always in history and that this fact has moral implications.

The Biblical view of sin is multi-layered. In the Hebrew Bible sin is any action that goes against God's commandments. In the history of ancient Israel there was very probably an evolution from very primitive notions of tabu (for example, the notion that touching the Ark of the Covenant, however inadvertently, would result in death) to much more differentiated understandings of morality (as in the lofty ideas of social justice in the prophetic literature). And the two tablets of the Decalogue make very clear that there are sins against God as well as sins against other human beings. While the Bible rejected any form of dualism as was typical of Iranian religion – an evil god engaged in an endless struggle with the good god, Ahriman against Ahura Mazda – there is also the enduring idea of supernatural beings opposed to God and tempting men to do evil. It is very possible that the Biblical figure of Satan is itself of Iranian origin, but the Bible, as it were, downgraded him to a status far below that of God and occupying that status only because of God's sufferance. But there is also the kernel of another idea which was to have far-reaching consequences in the development of Christian piety and thought – the idea that there are not only sinful acts but a sinful *condition* in which the human race is fatally enclosed. This, of course, is what led to the doctrine of "original sin."

The Hebrew Bible contains the idea of a "fall" – the fall from an original condition of innocence through the sin of Adam and Eve, and also some sort of fall by rebellious angels. But this idea is quite marginal to the moral teachings of the Hebrew Bible, and rabbinical Judaism was never very interested in it either. It was the New Testament which pushed this idea toward the center of its message, not in all its books but most importantly in the Pauline ones: There are not only individual acts of sinning, but the human condition as such is marked by sin. In other words, "original sin" became an important Christian doctrine, though, as we shall see, there were quite different interpretations of this, especially between the eastern and western traditions.

I think it is fair to say that the western tradition is more directly rooted in Paul. The *locus classicus* of Paul's understanding can be found in his Letter to the Romans (chapter 5:12ff):

> Therefore as sin came into the world through one man and death through sin, and so death spread to all men because all men sinned – sin indeed was in the world before the law was given, but sin is not counted where there is no law. Yet death reigned from Adam to Moses, even over those whose sins were not like the transgressions of Adam, who was a type of the one who was to come ... If, because of one man's trespass, death reigned through that one man, much more will those who receive the abundance of grace and the free gift of righteousness reign in life through the one man Jesus Christ ... Law came in, to increase the trespass; but where sin increased, grace abounded all the more, so that, as sin reigned in death, grace also might reign through righteousness to eternal life through Jesus Christ our Lord.

In looking at this passage, one should keep a few things in mind. First, it comes from a letter, possibly written in haste and under difficult circumstances; that is, Paul was not writing a theological treatise. Then, the whole context of the passage is a great thanksgiving for the redemptive grace to be found in Christ, not a thesis on sin for its own sake. Also, one should not be detracted from the evident fact that Paul took the Biblical accounts of Adam and Moses literally as historical facts – which, for us, is impossible with Adam and almost impossible with Moses. Still, the basic assumptions made by Paul here are quite clear: Human sinfulness is a condition into which we are born, which is sharply accentuated by a divinely given law whose commandments we are unable to fulfill, and for which we are culpable over and beyond any individual acts of sinning; and furthermore, death is intrinsically linked to this congenital condition of sinfulness.

To repeat, these are not assumptions to be found throughout the different traditions contained in the New Testament. The Johannine tradition in particular has a quite different picture of the human condition. Yet the Pauline understanding of sin has had an immense influence on the history of Christianity. In an earlier chapter we looked at this in terms of Anselm's view of the atonement. There is a clear line of development of this issue from Paul through Augustine to the Protestant Reformation (which, among other things, can be seen as a resurgence of Pauline thought after its mellowing in medieval Catholicism). The major theme is utter human depravity, of which every human individual is guilty and from which the individual cannot free himself. Luther's lonely struggle with his overly relentless conscience was very clearly a replication of Paul's struggle with the Jewish law, in both cases to the accompaniment of feelings of utter unworthiness. It was only logical, then, that it was another Pauline assertion – that we are saved by faith and not by the works of the law (Luther added that it was by faith *alone*) – which showed Luther the way out of his crisis of conscience. I have previously described this religious stance as masochistic, and (with all due respect for both Paul and Luther on other grounds) I see no reason to change my mind. The masochism reaches a certain climax in Calvinism, with its doctrine of "double predestination": Man is utterly depraved and justly merits eternal damnation; only gratuitous grace can save man from this well-deserved fate; and (the most distinctively Calvinist angle) God has decided from the beginning of time who will be saved and who will be relegated to damnation. To get a flavor of this view of the human condition, one need only read Jonathan Edwards' famous sermon "Sinners in the Hands of an Angry God," in which this New England disciple of Calvin describes how the saved denizens in heaven may look with satisfaction on the sufferings of the damned in hell.

However reluctantly, I will concede a certain grandeur to this religious stance. It attaches, for example, to the promise made by an individual upon being received into the early Protestant community in France (at a time, to boot, when this community faced severe persecution): The individual promised to obey all God's commandments and to live a faithful Christian life, *even if he knew that he was among those predestined to eternal damnation*. In other words, God was to be worshipped for His own sake, and not out of a hope of salvation. This is (even if in a perverse way) an impressive form of religion; as Max Weber demonstrated in his discussion of the unintended consequences of Calvinism (in *The Protestant Ethic and the Spirit of Capitalism* – the German original was published in 1901, and there have been several English translations since 1930), it was also a form of religion increasingly intolerable for those who adhered to it – in one way or another, they wanted *to know* whether they were among those "elected" for salvation. While Calvinism expresses this kind of religious masochism in, as it were, crystalline purity, it is not the only case in point. There are various mystics who insisted that one should love God absolutely, neither in hope of heaven nor in fear of hell, but for His own sake alone.

All the same, I think that it is essential to affirm that the loving God encountered in Christ's work of redemption is not recognizable in these versions of religion. This God does not ask us to grovel in the dust, and especially not in guilt for circumstances not of our own doing. Within the New Testament, the Johannine tradition serves as a useful antidote.

As in the classic text in the fourth chapter of the First Letter of John: "God is love, and he who abides in love abides in God, and God abides in him."

It has been a longstanding Christian view that the sacrament of baptism washes away the stain of original sin (though, of course, the baptized individual is still capable of sinning). A particularly repulsive episode in the history of Christian theology is the long debate over the fate of unbaptized infants. The scholastics endlessly argued over this, generally agreeing that these infants could not go to heaven, but disagreeing over whether they suffered pain in the "limbo" (an intermediary state between heaven and hell) to which they were relegated. Thus even Bonaventure, the disciple of the kindly Francis of Assisi whom we have favorably mentioned in an earlier chapter, argued that these infants, while spared the torments of hell, yet really suffered because of their deprivation. Thomas Aquinas rejected this view, arguing that the souls in limbo could be content with their lot because they remained ignorant of the bliss of heaven. The Augustinians generally insisted on the contrary view, that the unbaptized children in limbo suffered real pain, and they evidently felt that this view was compatible with the Christian Gospel. Thus Gregory of Rimini, who headed the Augustinian order at one point, earned the title "torturer of infants" because of his adherence to this rigorous view. (My source on all this is a scholarly work by a French Jesuit – Henri Rondet, *Original Sin: The Patristic and Theological Background*, pp. 176ff.) These debates are so odious that I, for one, in reading them am sorely tempted to join in Voltaire's famous dictum about the church – "destroy the infamy!" Put more moderately: If *this* is the God worshipped by Christians, I will turn my attention elsewhere.

It would probably be an exaggeration to describe the eastern Church as Johannine and the western Church as Pauline – the differences are more complicated. Yet the western tradition is undoubtedly more legalistic and indeed moralistic, presumably reflecting a prototypical Latin mindset (Calvin might be taken as the epitome of this – he was, after all, both French and a lawyer). The Greek east is more metaphysical, its piety and morality more mellow. It does not deny the reality of sin, even "original sin," as part of the human condition, but (as already noted in our discussion of the atonement) it is less harsh in its anthropology and much less juridical in its view of salvation. Thus the modern Orthodox theologian John Meyendorff, whom we cited before, has a concept of sin that he calls "ontological" – a tragic circumstance, grounded in a cosmic catastrophe, into which the human race has fallen and for which it or any of its members cannot be held accountable. At most, being compelled to live in this condition, human beings in their struggle to survive have a *propensity* toward evil, which at times, of course, can lead to concrete acts of horrendous evil. Thus sin is embedded in a general "fallen" condition of man and of the whole creation; death is the most important consequence of this "fall." The redemptive power of the risen Christ brings about victory over both sin and death, and this triumph reverberates throughout Orthodox thought and piety. The "fall" has fatally disrupted the relationship between God and man; redemption is movement toward a restoration of this relationship, which Orthodox thought has called *theosis* ("divinization"). There is an almost Darwinian dimension to this understanding, with empirical humanity still caught on a lower rung of an evolutionary ladder. Humanity thus appears more as victim than as perpetrator of its alienated condition; it merits compassion more than condemnation. (I suspect, incidentally, that this greater mellowness of the Orthodox worldview is what attracts many Catholic and Protestant converts – who, as it has been put, "go swimming in the Bosphorus." To avoid misunderstanding, I will take the liberty of saying that I am not tempted.)

To make this point, I will cite a near-contemporary Orthodox thinker, Paul Evdokimov. He was a very attractive figure indeed. Born in Russia in 1901, he spent most of his life in France, where he had an influence far beyond the small community of Russian exiles. During World War II he was active in the Resistance, especially in the efforts to hide and save Jews. After the war he helped found the ecumenical monastic community at Taizé (he himself was married and a father). Here is his formulation of the aforementioned issue:

> The Eastern Church rejects every juridical or penitentiary principle. Her understanding of sin and attitude toward the sinner is essentially therapeutic, evoking not a courtroom but a hospital. Without "prejudging", the Church abandons herself to God, the lover of mankind, and doubles her prayers for the living and the dead. The greatest among the saints have had the audacity and the charism to pray even for demons. Perhaps the most deadly weapon against the Evil One is precisely the prayer of a saint, and the destiny of hell depends also on the love of the saints. We create our own hell in closing ourselves off from divine love that remains unchangeable. (*Ages of the Spiritual Life*, pp. 101f)

(Perhaps only one small footnote is needed here: It should be clear that what Evdokimov means by "therapy" is far removed from the meaning of this word in contemporary psychologism.)

Going all the way back to the third century CE, we come on the impressive figure of Origen, deemed by many commentators to have been the most profound of the Greek Church Fathers, despite the fact that he was repeatedly deemed to be heretical both during his lifetime and afterward.

Origen's thought is multi-faceted, but one of his important concerns was to mitigate the harsh teachings about sin and damnation. Indeed, it was because of two of his efforts in this matter that he was accused of heresy – his views on the "pre-existence of souls" and on the *apokatastasis*. The first issue directly bears on the doctrine of "original sin." Origen was troubled by the question of how human beings could be judged for a sinful condition that cannot be ascribed to their own sinful actions. He taught that all individual souls (of men as well as of angels) were created at the beginning of time, and that it was already then that each of them could make a decision for or against God. Those in a sinful condition now can, therefore, be judged for their primeval decision to rebel against God. (There may be Hindu influences here, with an adumbration of the idea of *karma*. Incidentally, there is a similar idea in Islamic thought, in the notion of the Day of the Covenant, when all yet-to-be-born human beings are commanded to affirm allegiance to God.) Another much-criticized idea of Origen's is that of the *apokatastasis* – the belief that, in the end, all created beings will be reconciled with God; that is, even hell will be abolished. The idea repeatedly resurfaced in later Christian thought (we earlier mentioned Julian of Norwich's somewhat timid statement of it). In the introduction of a passage by Origen, the editor of a modern anthology, the Catholic theologian Hans Urs von Balthasar, thus characterizes Origen's teaching: "The church has never declared any human being to be damned with certainty. Human beings can not and should not judge. Origen is tireless in pointing out mitigating reasons for sinners; and if he has found one grain of good in a soul, he believes that eternal punishment has already been averted" (*Origen: Spirit and Fire*, p. 334). The passage, headed "Unjudgable Guilt," is indeed remarkable for the individuals for whom Origen finds "mitigating reasons" – Cain, the Pharaoh of the Exodus, Judas, Pilate! Origen ends this list of exculpations by saying: "Therefore, let us not anticipate the judgment of God and say that so-and-so is already damned, or, rejoicing, say that so-and-so is clearly saved; for we do not know how to weigh and judge one deed against another" (ibid., p. 335). There is an unstated implication here, highly relevant for the idea of *apokatastasis*: It is not credible that God is less merciful than Origen!

Evdokimov's metaphor of the "hospital" can be spun out: Man is a "sick" creature – that is, he is not what the creator intended him to be. The "sickness" is expressed both by sin and by death; neither is "healthy," in the sense that man was intended to be good and to be immortal, both qualities included in the notion that man was created in the image of God. Put differently, both sin and death are "unnatural," and to be rejected as such. In a quasi-evolutionary perspective, human beings are products of a process which, long before the appearance of *homo sapiens* on this planet, brought about a flawed condition in the universe. The propensity toward evil and the mortality of mankind is thus the consequence of a "fall," and in this sense sin is "original." Further, then, the redemptive action by God is above all one of *healing*, directed equally toward evil and suffering. This understanding can easily be subsumed under the Jewish notion of *tikkun olam*, the "repair of the world." It is also an understanding that allows for a theodicy not tainted by the aforementioned masochism. As the drama of redemption unfolds, human beings are free to help in its work of cosmic repair, or alternatively to aggravate the flaw which makes the repair necessary. (I can visualize this or that theologically educated reader take out his dictionary of heresies. Where does the foregoing paragraph belong? Is it Pelagian? Or perhaps semi-Pelagian? I am cheerfully unworried!)

One further spin on the metaphor is possible: If the overall human condition is one of "sickness," some individuals are more sick than others. Among those, certainly, are the great evil-doers of history. And some, perhaps, are hardly sick at all. As there are "icons of evil," there are also "icons of goodness." It may be appropriate to call these (quite rare) cases "saints." I doubt whether any of those characters are morally immaculate (I am, after all, still a Lutheran). But they can, nevertheless, serve as intimations of what humanity was originally intended to be and what it is to become in the eschatological future.

What, then, about "forgiveness"? I think that, within the view of the human condition that I try to convey here, "forgiveness" is to be understood as part of the great healing process. That is, it is *not* to be understood as a juridical transaction, either between God and man, or between men themselves. Perhaps the term "reconciliation" is appropriate here as a synonym for "forgiveness." Human beings are capable of being *agents of healing*. Those who excel in this task could properly be called "saints." It is clear that Christian faith, with its conviction of being reconciled with God, can be a powerful motive for acts of healing, of reconciliation. But such acts are also possible by individuals without this faith, or for that matter without any religious commitments. There are also "atheist saints."

It is not surprising that Dostoyevsky, deeply steeped in Orthodox piety as he was, provides some of the most impressive portraits of such healing figures in world literature. To mention only the three most famous ones: Sonya, the prostitute who saves the murderer Raskolnikov, in *Crime and Punishment*; Myshkin, the epileptic outsider who tries to do good in the dissolute society of the Russian upper classes, in *The Idiot*; and Alyosha, the young monk who seeks to redeem the raging vices of his wretched family, in *The Brothers Karamazov*. Dostoyevsky, it seems, was drawn toward the most degrading circumstances into which individuals could sink – but always with the intention of showing that even the most degraded individuals were not beyond the reach of redemptive love. Dostoyevsky's characters stand in a long eastern, and particularly Russian, tradition of "holy fools" – saintly characters who cultivated extreme humility by behaving in the most ridiculous manner, thereby showing up the foibles of both Church and society, and pointing toward God who stands above all religious and secular conventions. Such 'fools for Christ's sake" (a phrase going back to the Apostle Paul) are living icons of redemption. Sonya, Myshkin, and Alyosha are such "holy fools." It hardly needs saying that most of us will not aspire to this vocation.

Can everything, everyone be forgiven? I suppose that Sonya or Alyosha would say yes. And perhaps they are right – in the very long run – eschatologically, as it were. In that case, their own exercises in indiscriminate forgiveness may be understood as signals of the ultimate *apokatastasis*. For most of us, ordinary people struggling to live as best we can in a very imperfect world, such saintly behavior is not possible and it should not be required of us. We must live by a rougher justice. One may add here a sociological observation: Any society run on the principle of indiscriminate forgiveness, and *ipso facto* without coercive moral judgment, would very quickly lapse into chaos – or, more accurately, into a Hobbesian jungle in which the most ruthless predators would exploit and destroy those who are weaker or afflicted with saintly scruples. It seems to me that two Lutheran doctrines constitute adequate recognition of these worldly facts – the doctrine of the two kingdoms, according to which the world as it is in this aeon cannot be governed by the rule of grace – and the doctrine of justification, according to which, even though forgiven by God's grace, we continue to be both just and sinful (*simul iustus et peccator*). Having said this, one should immediately concede that both doctrines can be, and have been, misused to legitimate this or that structure of injustice. In this, though, they are not alone in the history of religious thought.

Apokatastasis – the conviction that, in the end, all will be saved and the entire creation will be reconciled with God. Luther once observed that he who does not believe this is a fool, but that he who preaches it is an idiot. One can agree with this sentiment, without agreeing with Luther's implication that people will necessarily misbehave unless they are threatened with hellfire. Rather, some notion of damnation is necessary if one affirms the justice of God in the face of evil. How such damnation may be terminated in the far eschatological future is beyond our grasp.

Nothing short of damnation will be adequate for the perpetrators of the Holocaust. None of us, and certainly none of the victims, should be urged to forgive them. In this world, the moral bill for the Holocaust can never be paid (which is why the Jewish organizations who negotiated the reparations agreements were careful to say that they were making *material* claims against Germany – the moral claims were non-negotiable). Could Hitler ever be forgiven? Can God's grace be *that* victorious? I remember a conversation I had about this question, long ago, with a Protestant theologian (who had just quoted to me Luther's statement about universal salvation). He thought for a moment, smiled, and said: "We cannot know. But I can imagine that, many aeons from now, an unattractive little dog will be running around in heaven. And one of the saved will pat it without much affection and say – 'this used to be Hitler'."

Excursus: On Christian Morality

In Arabic, I understand, the same word stands for "religion" and for "law" – *din*. Thus an Arabic-speaker inquiring about someone's religion will, in effect, ask "What is your law?" The equation of religion with law, of course, makes a lot of sense in the cases of Islam and Judaism, both religious traditions based on elaborate systems of divinely inspired law. It might make sense in some other cases. Does it make sense in the case of Christianity? But leaving aside the question of whether Christianity provides some sort of law, the question could be phrased more broadly:

Is there a distinctive Christian morality?

I daresay that throughout Christian history most theologians and most ordinary believers would have replied with an emphatic "yes." With all due respect for the centuries of this history, I would like to insinuate some doubts into this affirmation.

A few years ago the following question occurred to me: Suppose that I woke up tomorrow and decided that I am an atheist – what would change about my moral convictions? I decided that virtually nothing would change. The only change I could think of would be the moral injunction against suicide, but I wasn't even sure about that (after all, a merciful God could well understand if I could no longer take it). In the meantime, upon further reflection, I would slightly modify what I concluded then. The religious believer recognizes moral obligations toward God, and those would be irrelevant for the atheist. Further, there are moral obligations toward one's own self, and toward both animate and inanimate nature, which would look somewhat different in a religious as against an atheist worldview. But the overwhelming number of moral convictions refer to one's relations with other human beings. As far as these are concerned, I would still conclude what I concluded then: None of them would change.

To mention but two, which now as then I passionately adhere to: The conviction that every form of racial or ethnic discrimination is morally abhorrent; and the conviction concerning the abhorrence of capital punishment. Both convictions are based on a deeply grounded perception of what it means to be human, and this perception does not depend on any particular religious beliefs. Not so incidentally, the empirical record would, I think, support my view on this. There can be no doubt about the large numbers of Christian racists and about many non-religious opponents of racism. And, at least in America, there seems to be a disturbing positive correlation between religious belief and support for the death penalty.

Now, as a sociologist I recognize that my moral convictions have developed in a particular cultural context, that of a civilization profoundly influenced by Christianity. This sociological perspective has come to be widely diffused among people with higher education and, not surprisingly, has led many of them to hold very relativistic views on morality. In certain circles it seems as if the only moral virtue still adhered to is the virtue of tolerance, embracing just about any belief or practice. Nevertheless, even in a cultural situation marked by a widespread understanding of the relativity of moral values, there are what could be called eruptions of moral certainty in the face of certain evils. In my own case, I recognize that my convictions concerning human equality would be different if I had been raised as a nobleman in medieval Europe – or for that matter even today as a Brahmin in a traditional Hindu village. This recognition, however, would only lead to my perception that, in this if not necessarily in other matters, my morality is *superior*. To call this sense of superiority ethnocentric or prejudiced misses this point. By analogy, it is not ethnocentric to say that our modern insights into the workings of the physical universe are superior to the view of other times or places, despite the obvious fact that Einstein was not born in the thirteenth century or in a remote rural area of India. I referred earlier to the Holocaust as an "icon of evil." It is perceived as such by vast numbers of people, who recoil from its horrors and are certain in their condemnation of its perpetrators. The fact that there are some who do not share this perception – neo-Nazis, Holocaust-deniers, anti-Semites of various stripes – in no way undermines the clear and certain perception of the evil inherent in this event. And, of course, there are other, less horrific cases of evil that trigger eruptions of deeply held moral certitude. Among those who share such certitude are both religious believers and non-believers.

It follows that one must doubt the widespread view that only religion, if not a particular religion, can provide a reliable foundation for morality. Conservative Christians have sought to find such reliability in the teachings of the Church or in a literal reading of the Bible, while liberal Christians have tried to do this by relying on the alleged ethics of Jesus. I have argued earlier that these various alleged groundings for certainty are highly dubious. But at this point it suffices to say that the empirical record of what passes for Christian history rather massively falsifies the linkage between religion and morality. To be sure, there have been instances of morally admirable individuals who were clearly inspired by their Christian faith. But on the other side of the ledger there is an endless sequence of morally outrageous acts committed by individual Christians and by Christian churches, and legitimated in terms of Christian theology. I strongly suspect that the latter side of the ledger is by far the larger one.

What we do find in the record is a slow evolution of certain moral perceptions, which, originally and at least in part, were inspired by Christian beliefs. Slavery is a case in point. In Paul's Letter to Philemon we have an interesting document showing the attitude of the early Christian community toward slavery. Paul urges Philemon to be benevolent toward his slave, even to consider him as a brother in Christ, but he does not ask that the slave be freed and nowhere does he suggest that slavery is an evil in itself. Paul's position (very similar to that of rabbinical Judaism) comes out well if compared with the callous attitude toward slaves that was characteristic of Greek and Roman civilization, but it is a position that one could also find among some Stoics. It took many centuries for the conviction to take hold that slavery, the owning of one person by another, was intrinsically evil, no matter how benevolent the owner. It is instructive to recall that, as recently as the mid-nineteenth century, the majority of church people in the ante-bellum American South defended slavery and did so in theological terms. The abolitionist movement, to be sure, was widely inspired by Christian beliefs, but it also contained people who did not share these beliefs while sharing the conviction about the abhorrence of slavery. In other words, this latter group shared a moral perception without sharing a religious faith. I think that the same can be said about many morally admirable movements in more recent times – the resistance against Nazism and the rescue efforts on behalf of persecuted Jews, the civil rights movement in the United States, the anti-apartheid struggle in South Africa, the opposition to Communism in the former Soviet empire. I will add to this list the opposition against capital punishment. The two classic books attacking the inhumanity of the death penalty in the period after World War II were written by Albert Camus and Arthur Koestler, both emphatic agnostics; these books were very influential in the abolition of the death penalty in, respectively, France and Britain – an abolition that has now become normative and binding throughout the European Union. (I will further add the observation that, in this matter if not in others, the EU is morally superior to the United States.)

Is there a distinctive Christian *din*? I think not. The notion, it seems to me, was already repudiated in very strong terms by Paul's understanding of Christ liberating the believer from the burden of the Jewish law, and this understanding erupted once more with enormous force in the Protestant Reformation against the reconstructed *din* of Catholic legalism. (To avoid misunderstanding, let me again say that Paul is not my favorite New Testament author and that I have great reservations about other aspects of the Reformation.) Jewish writers have levelled the charge of "antinomianism" – a utopian rebellion against any form of law – against Paul and even against Christianity as a whole. I don't think that this charge is convincing. Thus we find in Paul's writings long lists of virtues commended to Christians and of vices to be avoided. But these lists do not add up to a new law.

Let me now come to the main proposition I want to make in this excursus: Moral judgments are grounded in *perceptions*. Put differently: Morality is essentially *cognitive*. To say this, of course, is not to deny that one can deduce all sorts of commandments, of normative prescriptions and proscriptions, from these perceptions. The norms, however, will not be plausible if the cognitive presuppositions are absent. I owe this insight to the Protestant theologian Frederick Neumann. In a discussion of conscience, he proposed that it is a misunderstanding to understand conscience as addressing us in an imperative mode – "do this," or "don't do that." Rather, it addresses us in an *indicative* mode – "look at this," "look at that." In the first instance of a moral offence by one human being against another recounted in the Hebrew Bible, the murder of Abel by his brother Cain, God addresses Cain in just this mode. God did not say, "You disobeyed the commandment not to commit murder." What God did say was "What have you done? The voice of your brother's blood is crying to me from the ground." In other words: "Look at this!"

Let me return to the example of slavery. Harriet Beecher Stowe's novel *Uncle Tom's Cabin* was very influential in moving public opinion in the American North toward abolitionism. But Stowe did not preach against slavery. She simply *showed* its cruelties: "Look at this!" And a widespread response was "This cannot be allowed to go on!" In a novel of much greater literary merit if of lesser political importance, Mark Twain's *Huckleberry Finn*, there is a similar response to the perception of the cruelty of slavery. Huckleberry Finn is not moved by some sort of abolitionist propaganda to refrain from turning in the runaway slave. Rather, he does so as a result of coming to perceive the slave as a fellow human being. In other words, what happened was, not conversion by a normative commandment, but rather the result of a *cognitive shift*. I tend to think that such phenomena can be observed in other instances in which one can speak of moral progress, including the aforementioned ones concerning the inhumanity of racism and of capital punishment.

This is not a uniquely Christian insight. In one form or another, it will be proposed by theorists of natural law (something about which I have my doubts). Thus the Chinese philosopher Mencius wrote that even a hardened criminal, seeing a child tottering on the edge of a lake, will be moved to keep the child from drowning. That is, the criminal will look on this scene, and the act of looking will result in the moral impulse. (Mencius, who was a realist, added that the criminal might well overcome this impulse. I don't know whether Mencius might have entertained the idea that some criminals might enjoy the sight of a drowning child. But that is beside the point in the present argument.) But the insight makes sense in the context of Christian faith. This faith leads to *a shift in the perception of reality*. Reality is now perceived as the arena of God's cosmic process of redemption. And, as the author of this process, God is perceived as a loving God. This is a cognitive shift with implications for morality: There is now *a different ontological location* of all moral judgments. The empirical content of each judgment may not be different – for human equality, against slavery, and so on. But morally indicated actions are now seen to have a transcendent dimension, beyond the empirical situation in which they occur – as participating in the "repair of the world" which is God's work of redemption.

Of course, as one traces the historical roots of our moral convictions, one will find that Christianity played an important part in shaping them. But there is a generic fallacy that one should avoid here. That is, the historical origins of a particular definition of reality do not, in themselves, either compel or refute that definition. Put differently, one should not confuse epistemology with historical gratitude. Let me illustrate this with a mundane anecdote. A few years ago I was in London, looking for a bookstore in Bloomsbury that I had been told about; it happened to be a bookstore that specialized in publications from India and I was looking for the English translation of a particular novel by an Indian author. In the course of this expedition I suddenly came across the old building of the British Museum (famous among other things as containing the reading room in which Marx conceived of his theories). I had not previously known the location of the Museum, and the discovery pleased me. Subsequently I had occasion to visit this location again, but there was no need to retrace my steps from the search for the Indian bookstore. That is, the historical origin of my discovery of the British Museum was no longer relevant for further visits: I now knew where it was.

There is a rabbinical saying (it was reiterated by Jesus in different words) to the effect that the essential meaning of Torah could be pronounced by a man while standing on one foot – it is that one should love God above all and one's neighbor as oneself. Leave aside that, for most of us, both these injunctions are quite unfeasible. But the point here is that love for other human beings is linked with love of God. In terms of the present argument, faith in God provides a transcendent meaning, an ontological foundation for all moral judgments and actions.

I have suggested in the previous chapters that there may be "icons of goodness." Some Christian traditions would refer here to "saints". Monasticism from its inception has been an institution for those who aspired, however imperfectly, to such a status. Protestants have criticized the institution for its "double standard," elevating monastics over against ordinary Christians. There was merit to the criticism. All the same, I think that the wholesale repudiation of monasticism by the Reformation was a mistake. Most of us cannot be Alyoshas, but some may have a vocation to try. This vocation need not be deemed superior to that of the ordinary person, who lives fully in the world and gets his hands dirty with its business. But it can still be a very valuable vocation.

Most of us live in the midst of the world and our hands inevitably get dirty. Lutheranism incorporated this insight in the formulation that the Christian (presumably even the one aspiring to sainthood) always remains both justified and sinful – *simul iustus et peccator*. This is a view directed equally against legalism and utopianism, realistic without being relativistic. Max Weber's well-known distinction, in his essay on "Politics as a Vocation" (originally a speech made in 1919 to students at the University of Munich, since then published many times both in German and in English), between an "ethic of attitude" (*Gesinnungsethik*) and an "ethic of responsibility" (*Verantwortungsethik*) is a sort of secularized version of the Lutheran view of morality. The "ethic of attitude" is focused on the individual's quest for moral purity, regardless of consequences. Weber regarded Tolstoy as an exemplar of such an ethic, and, while he showed some respect for it, he finally rejected it. The "ethic of responsibility" focuses instead on the probable consequences of one's actions, even if this calculus enmeshes the actor in morally doubtful actions. Weber approvingly cites Macchiavelli's statement that a ruler must act for the welfare of the city even if he thereby imperils the eternal salvation of his soul. One should recall here another Weberian insight – that most of our actions have unintended consequences. We may desire good ends and employ good means, and nevertheless the results may be unbearably evil. Weber too was an agnostic, and his stance in the face of these lamentable facts of the human condition was Stoic. In the perspective of faith one can make an additional step: Knowing all this, we do our best to participate in the "repair of the world" – and then rely on God's forgiveness when, inevitably, even our best efforts have a way of turning morally sour.

Chapter Twelve

"... the resurrection of the body, and the life everlasting"

The most serious question that human beings can ask is whether death is the final word for both individual and collective life. We know for certain that we ourselves and everyone we care about will die. On the basis of what science tells us, we can be reasonably certain that the earth too will eventually die, be it in ice or in fire. And science also suggests that the entire universe is under a law of entropy, which means that it too is headed for some sort of cosmic death. For the moment, let us stay with the most certain knowledge about death – the knowledge that all human beings must die.

Earlier in this book I affirmed that death is unacceptable. Let me do away, once and for all, with the notion that this affirmation is "selfish." Of course I do not want to die. But, training myself in stoical fortitude, I might accept the prospect of my own death with a measure of equanimity. It is the death of my neighbor's child which I refuse to accept, and there is nothing "selfish" about that. Death is not "natural," except in the most banal sense that it is given in our biological constitution. Death is an outrage. It is an outrage that this child's innocent faith in the goodness of the world will be betrayed, that this child's laughter, which for moments had lit up the sky, will end in pain and will forever disappear from the face of reality. I refuse to accept, to consent to this outrage. What is more, my refusal is for me the acid test for any religious message: Can it, or can it not, endorse my refusal? And does it have any word of comfort for my grieving neighbor?

At the opening of this book I proposed that religious faith affirms that reality ultimately makes sense in human terms. I wrote that, whether true or not, the affirmation is "interesting." Let me list a number of statements about religion that are *not* "interesting." Put differently, if such statements accurately describe what religion is all about, then let us forget about religion.

Religion is supposed to be necessary as the basis of morality, as in the alleged ethics of Jesus. Religion is *not* necessary for morality, and the ethical teachings of Jesus (insofar as they can be distinguished at all from what was taught in the Judaism of his time) cannot serve as a feasible guide for either individual or societal life. *No, thanks.*

Religion provides powerful symbols for the exigencies of human existence. To be sure, it does, but there are other sources for such symbols. *No, thanks.*

Religion demands submission to God's will, regardless of what meaning the death of my neighbor's child may have. Yes, religion implies submission to God's will, but only if God is perceived as being neither the author nor the passive overseer of the child's death. Put differently, I submit to God who does *not* will the death of children. Any other religious submission implicitly denies the goodness of God and the goodness of creation. *No, thanks.*

And religion may seek to console us by saying that all of us, including this child, will eventually be absorbed into some kind of cosmic ocean of divinity. I refuse to be consoled. It is *this* child – unique, irreplaceable, infinitely precious – that I am concerned about. To absorb the child in an ultimate reality in which all individuality is lost is but another version of death. *No, thanks.*

Against all these, thoroughly "uninteresting" religious propositions, Christian faith affirms the unique value and the eternal destiny of *this* child, and of all children and of all of humanity. The affirmation is contained, as compactly as possible, in the exclamation "Christ is risen!" That is why the Resurrection was pivotal at the very beginning of Christian faith and why it continues to be pivotal if we are to entertain the possibility of such faith today. Paul had it right on this: "If there is no resurrection of the dead, then Christ has not been raised; if Christ has not been raised, then our preaching is in vain and your faith is in vain" (1 Corinthians 15:13–14). In that case, Paul – or rather, Saul – go back to Tarsus, pursue a tranquil career as a tentmaker, and cultivate your rosegarden!

Kant suggested that one of the basic questions of philosophy was "What may we hope for?" I'm not sure about philosophy, but it is certainly *the* basic question for religion. We may break it up into two questions:

What hope is there for the individual beyond death? What hope is there for the cosmos beyond entropy?

Jay Robison (in a useful book, *Life after Death?*) uses the terms "personal eschatology" and "cosmic eschatology" to refer, respectively, to these two questions. We will take them up *seriatim*.

Belief in the Resurrection, that of Jesus Christ in Jerusalem and that of all humanity in the eschatological future, has been central for Christian faith. It has also distinguished Christianity from many other traditions. Some years ago I heard a very learned lecture about religious syncretism in Central Asia before the Muslim conquest. There, along the ancient Silk Road, every sort of religion established itself and mixed elements from other traditions with its own – Zoroastrianism, Hinduism, Buddhism, Christianity, Manichaeism, Confucianism, and bits and pieces of Hellenistic religion. I remember two parts of this lecture. To illustrate the exuberant syncretism in the region, the lecturer showed slides. One slide portrayed Jesus – with Chinese features, dressed in the garb of a Confucian scholar, the right hand raised in the gesture of Christian blessing, the left hand stretched out in the Buddha's gesture of compassion. In which tradition was this Jesus to be placed? Then the lecturer remarked that there were many written texts that one also did not know where to place. A text might begin with what looked like a Manichaean argument, went on with Confucian references, then ended with what seemed to be Buddhist propositions. The lecturer observed that there was one thing that allowed one to decide that the text was clearly Christian – any reference to resurrection. (Zoroastrianism also held a belief in resurrection, but this apparently did not enter into the texts analyzed by this lecturer.)

In the religious history of Israel, there was an early period in which there was no anticipation of an afterlife, except in the hardly desirable (and probably temporary) shadow world of Sheol (roughly comparable to the equally unattractive Hades of Graeco-Roman religion). There is much evidence for this in various texts in the Hebrew Bible, so much so that to this day there are Jewish thinkers who maintain that Judaism need not affirm a life beyond death. In this religious worldview, all hope (in the present as well as eschatologically) concerned not the individual but the collectivity of the people of Israel. Slowly, it seemed, a more positive expectation developed. It is possible that Zoroastrian influences were a factor in this. A belief in resurrection may be implied in Ezekiel's famous vision of dead bones being called back to life. But the belief was by no means general. By the time of Jesus there was a clear split between two Jewish factions concerning this issue – the Pharisees affirmed a resurrection of the dead, the Sadducees denied it. In the Qumran texts (ascribed to a Jewish eschatological sect antedating Jesus) there is mention of someone called the Teacher of Righteousness, who will die and be resurrected. But this referred to an event in the future. The Christians affirmed a resurrection that *had already* occurred, thus inaugurating a new age, at the culmination of which all of humanity will be resurrected and there will be a day of judgment separating the saved from the damned – a very different proposition indeed.

From early on in Christian history, there were vivid apocalyptic expectations – that is, expectations of historical and cosmic cataclysms preceding the *parousia*, the return or "second coming" of Christ, who will establish "a new heaven and a new earth." The phrase, of course, comes from the Book of Revelation, the most concentrated apocalyptic text within the New Testament. It was probably written during one of the persecutions of Christians by the Roman authorities, and, not surprisingly, the apocalyptic imagination has always flourished under conditions of acute danger and hardship. Here the hope of a life after death for the individual is linked, in a very Jewish way, with the collective hope of the Church and indeed of all humanity. But, also quite early on, there was an influx of Hellenistic ideas about the soul and its putative immortality. Here the hope for an afterlife is focused almost entirely on the individual. Arguably its noblest expression can be found in Plato's *Phaedo*. The idea involves a depreciation of the body and indeed the whole physical world which is very much at odds with the Biblical view of creation. It is well caught in a Greek play on words – *soma* (body)/*sema* (prison): The soul is imprisoned in the body, and immortality means that it is freed from this imprisonment. I think it is fair to say that, to this day, there is much ambiguity in the Christian imagination as between the notions of resurrection and immortality.

Are these two notions in sharp contradiction or is there a way of reconciling them? A lucid, and very influential, position favoring contradiction was that of Oscar Cullmann – a Lutheran, who taught theology in Strasbourg, Basel, and Paris, and who wrote eloquently in French, German, and English. In 1956 he published an essay on the issue in a *Festschrift* for Karl Barth (a somewhat ironic locale, since Barth is constantly criticized both in the text and in footnotes). The essay was subsequently published as a small book (*Immortality of the Soul or Resurrection of the Body?*). It roused a storm of controversy (which apparently surprised and dismayed the author).

The centerpiece of Cullmann's argument is a comparison of the deaths of Socrates and Jesus. Socrates welcomes death as a friend, Jesus fears it as an enemy. In anticipation of death, both men are in the company of disciples – but what a contrast! Socrates, in Plato's account, serenely discusses philosophical questions with his disciples, then calmly reaches for the cup of hemlock which will kill him. Jesus, in the garden of Gethsemane, is "trembling and in distress," wants comfort from the company of his disciples – who, to his dismay, are sleeping – and he prays to God that this cup of anguish may pass him by. Jesus' terror in the face of death culminates in the cry from the cross which, significantly, is cited in Aramaic within the Greek text of the evangelist – *"Eli, eli, lama sabach-tani?"*, "my God, my God, why have you forsaken me?" We may assume that the purveyors of the tradition were uneasy about thus reporting Jesus' weakness – perhaps the report was doubted or challenged by some early Christians, and the Aramaic citation was intended to verify that Jesus actually spoke these words.

Cullmann argues that Christianity, in continuity with the Hebrew Bible, and unlike Plato and Greek thought in general, takes death with utmost seriousness and without shrinking from its horror. This is in line with its view of the body as an essential part of God's creation, intended by God for eternal life. The resurrection, unlike immortality, is not an act brought about by an innate quality in man, but is exclusively an act of God, who renews His creation. (In this connection, Cullmann discusses the use of the term *sarx*, "flesh," in the Pauline writings: He argues that the term does not refer to the body, *soma*, as such, but, precisely to the corruption of bodily existence through sin and death. And, of course, Paul refers to death as "the last enemy.") In any case, the approach to death is diametrically opposed to that of Socrates and, by extension, that of anyone who accepts death as "natural" or even as a friend.

In Cullmann's own words:

> Only he who apprehends with the first Christians the horror of death, who takes death seriously as death, can comprehend the Easter exultation of the early Christian community and understand that the whole thinking of the New Testament is governed by belief in the Resurrection. Belief in the immortality of the soul in not belief in a revolutionary event. Immortality, in fact, is only a *negative* assertion: the soul does *not* die, but simply lives on. Resurrection is a *positive* assertion: the whole man, who has really died, is recalled to life by a new act of creation by God. Something has happened – a miracle of creation! For something has also happened previously, something fearful: life formed by God has been destroyed. (ibid., pp. 26f)

This is a persuasive argument. To be sure, there is a real contrast here. Whether the contrast is tantamount to total incompatibility remains debatable. Other parts of Cullmann's essay are less persuasive, even if they may well be grounded in valid New Testament exegesis. This is particularly so with the notion that death is the "wages of sin." It goes back, of course, all the way to the story of the "fall" of Adam and Eve as told in the first book of the Hebrew Bible, and it is proposed with particular fervor by Paul. We have previously discussed this issue in terms of the Christian doctrine of "original sin." I argued then that the Pauline version of this notion is very questionable, if only because death antedates the appearance of man on earth – there are all those millenia of animal suffering – but, more importantly, because the notion implies a divinity very different from the God of love, the "Father," affirmed by Jesus and foundational for Christian faith. Let me once more express a preference for the much mellower view prevalent in eastern Christianity. There is a deeper fall, which pertains not only to man but to the entire cosmos, which is temporarily dominated by the "enemy." *Both* sin and death are results ("wages," if you will) of this profound flaw afflicting the creation. And humanity, let alone individual human beings, cannot be deemed guilty of a condition which they did not cause.

Even if one accepts Cullmann's view unconditionally, some troublesome questions remain. There is, for one, the question of the so-called "interim period": What happens between the individual's death and his resurrection? Is the latter experienced immediately upon death, as widely believed (among others, by Barth)? Or is there an interim period of "waiting"? Cullmann takes the view that the departed are still in time, that they indeed "wait" for the resurrection, as some New Testament texts have it (though they may be "sleeping" – whatever that might mean). This raises the general question of the relation of time and eternity: Is eternity simply endless time, or is it a condition in which time is superseded? It is a fascinating question, philosophically as well as theologically. I'm at a loss as to how we can find the intellectual resources to resolve it.

There are also questions to be raised here about how one understands the authority of the New Testament and how one understands the nature of man philosophically. Cullmann is presumably correct in saying that the Biblical view of man is as a unity of body and soul – in life, in death, and upon resurrection. This view is continuous as between the Hebrew Bible and the New Testament. But must we regard this view as binding on ourselves? I think not. After all, there are many other elements of Biblical anthropology and cosmology which we feel free to discount. As before, I would argue that, here and with every other part of the tradition, we must look for and focus on what I have called the nexus between the tradition and our own experience of reality. Such a procedure does not simply rest on the authority of Biblical texts.

Cullmann is also likely to be correct that the Biblical view of man as a unity of body and soul was modified by Hellenistic influences. But what if the Greeks had some insights which are not to be found in the Bible but which can be accommodated by Biblical faith all the same? Roman Catholic thinkers have been much more open to this possibility than Protestant ones. Thus Karl Rahner (in his book *On the Theology of Death*, pp. 24ff) speaks of death as the "separation of body and soul," affirming the possibility of the soul's existing apart from the body. If one takes such a more liberal stance regarding the literal statements in the Biblical texts, there are good philosophical grounds for dissenting from Cullmann's position. Thus Max Scheler, one of the most interesting modern philosophers dealing with the nature of man, makes a very useful distinction: Man, paradoxically, both *is* and *has* a body. On the one hand, I am totally dependent on my body in what I am; as my body ceases to be, so do I. Medical science amply confirmed this in Scheler's time (his basic writing on philosophical anthropology was published in 1927); more recent findings of medical science, especially neurology and genetics, have only added to this confirmation. But on the other hand, my experience of myself leads me to refuse a total identification with my body. This experience is particularly salient in cases of severe illness or crippling handicap: My body is greatly diminished, but I am capable of affirming the integrity of my self despite this diminishment. Thus I find myself able to say: I am not *just* my body. Or, as Scheler could not have said: My DNA does not sum up what I am. In other words: Those Greeks may have had a point!

For a more liberal approach to these issues we can turn again to John Hick, the British Protestant theologian we have encountered before in this book. Hick has written about just about everything; he also wrote a very useful book on the issue discussed here – *Death and Eternal Life*. It is a voluminous and very erudite work, seeking to produce a "personal eschatology" (Hick calls it a "pareschatology") based on a synthesis between Christianity, Hinduism, and Buddhism (I'm not sure whether Hick would like the term "synthesis," but I think it fairly describes what he does).

On the one hand, Hick affirms the notion of resurrection, because some sort of embodiment is necessary for any recognizable self. On the other hand, he recognizes that the self cannot be totally identified with the body, so that the former's survival after the latter's decomposition is at least not unthinkable. A very interesting part of his argument is an attempt to integrate Christian faith with Indian views of reincarnation. Hick discounts an existence of the self before birth, but feels it necessary to posit some kind of reincarnation beyond death, because perfection (presumably the goal of human existence) is not possible in this life (at least not for most people). In this connection he refers to the eastern concept of *theosis* – the long journey of the self toward God. Death is then seen as a necessary stage in this development – and in that sense, at any rate, can be welcomed as a "friend." But this post-mortem reincarnation need not be in this world. In principle (and certainly in the Indian religious imagination) there exist many worlds besides this one, and reincarnation may take place in any of them. (Hick rather ingeniously deals with what may be called the demographic problem with reincarnation: Given the enormous population explosion of the last couple of centuries, where did all these extra souls come from? Well, Hick suggests, they may be born in this world, while other worlds may have been the location of more births in earlier periods. This hypothesis about the sudden popularity of planet Earth in the cosmic machinery of incarnations is less than compelling.)

Another rather curious concept introduced by Hick is that of "replicas". The reincarnated self cannot be identical with the preceding ones, but it relates to them in a recognizable continuity – that is, it is a "replica" of the earlier selves. The reasoning leading to this fanciful notion concerns memory. It would seem that any surviving or reincarnating self would have to be linked by memory with the earlier self, otherwise it would make little sense to say that the self continues. But memory fades. It does so even in this life. Hick compares himself at age 50 (apparently his age when he wrote this page) with what he was at age 3 – which he can barely remember. Yet he assumes some sort of continuity between "H50" and "H3," even if the link of memory is very faint (and never mind the fact that there has been a complete change in physical appearance – "H50" is definitely less cute than "H3"). But if this is true even within the brief lifespan on this earth, how much truer would it be if we suppose many lifetimes in different worlds. What could "H-one million" possibly remember about his life at the University of Birmingham, where he taught in the mid-twentieth century? Hick concludes from this that, even as the replicas of the self continue, individuality fades progressively as *theosis* progresses toward its culmination. It seems to me that Hick adumbrates the cosmic ocean absorbing all of us in the end with this idea – precisely the idea which I regaled with a "no, thanks" a few pages back. (By the way, to forestall the notion that a number of Hick replicas may be marching around simultaneously in different worlds, Hick insists that there can only be *one* replica at any given time. This is reassuring, but not logically compelling.)

Hick gives credence to the idea of *bardo*, presented at length in the Tibetan Book of the Dead – a dreamlike world generated by the individual's own consciousness immediately after death, essentially a world of illusion (pleasurable or not, like all dreams) through which the individual must pass on the way to the next incarnation. In this context Hick proposes what may be called a "soft" version of the Buddhist doctrine of "non-self" – not denying the reality of the self, but disparaging its egotistic character. The final stage in the journey of the self is then a loss of what Hick calls "egoity" – if you will, the nastier bits of the self. In this he agrees, not only with the more personalistic schools of Hinduism (*bhakti* rather than *advaita*) and Buddhism (as in the Pure Land schools), but also with the more moderate versions of Christian mysticism (say, Teresa of Avila rather than Meister Eckhart).

But let me allow Hick to speak in his own words:

> The main weight of the christian [*sic* – Hick has the irritating habit of putting proper adjectives in lower case] tradition has insisted that this earthly life is the only environment in which the individual can either come of his own volition, or be brought by divine grace, to the "saved" relationship with God; and thereafter his individual existence is to be perpetuated in heaven (perhaps via purgatory) or in hell. I have argued that this scheme is unrealistic both as regards what is to happen before death and as regards what is to happen after death. If salvation in its fullness involves the actual transformation of human character, it is an observable fact that this does not usually take place in the course of our present earthly life. There must, then, be further time beyond death in which the process of perfecting can continue. The traditional scheme is equally unsatisfactory on its postmortem side. I have argued that the doctrine of hell is morally intolerable; and that in any case the notion of the immortal ego, the finite person continuing endlessly through time, involves profound conceptual difficulties. (pp. 455f)

Note: This presupposes that eternity is indeed "endless time." The "conceptual difficulties" are much reduced if one posits that eternity is a condition beyond time.

And further: "This hypothesis [that is, Hick's synthesis] accepts both the insistence upon the need for life to be lived within temporal limits and the conviction that the soul can only make progress in the incarnate state towards its final goal. But it differs from the western tradition in postulating many lives instead of only one, and from the eastern tradition in postulating many spheres of incarnate existence instead of only one" (ibid., p. 456). Note: This is a misleading rendition of the "eastern tradition." Both Hindu and Buddhist thought contains the idea of many worlds (or "Buddha-fields").

Here as in other areas of theology, Hick makes a highly intriguing contribution. It has, though, a number of weaknesses: It does not take death seriously enough (as Cullmann would surely have said if he had read Hick). It has no cosmic dimension; in Christian terms, it does not consider the importance of creation, its damaged state, and redemption as the repair of creation. It is overly fixated on a mundane conception of time. And, most important, its distinction between the self and the ego fails to meet the previously suggested acid test of any eschatology – what to say in the face of the death of my neighbor's child.

"Personal eschatology" is not enough. Unless the cosmos has a future other than annihilation, every individual future will eventually be absorbed into an all-embracing nothingness. It is not only humanity but the entire creation that is "fallen" and in need of redemption. In the words of Paul: "The whole creation has been groaning in travail together until now" (Romans 8:22). In line with some of the foregoing considerations, it is of course possible to imagine that, once the work of redemption is completed, God will abandon the entire physical universe, galaxies and all, to oblivion and that the redeemed will exist in other worlds – "Buddha-fields" which at present we cannot even conceive of. Such a hypothesis, however, would mean surrendering the Biblical view of the intended goodness of creation, a view which, I have argued, constitutes an important nexus between faith and experience.

Karl Heim, yet another modern Protestant theologian, has made the dialogue between theology and science the focus of his work over many years. He took very seriously the pervasiveness of death and destruction in the empirical world – most immediately, in the gigantic murderousness of biological evolution, as entire species are obliterated in the "survival of the fittest" – but then also in the foreseeable fate of the earth and of the observable universe as a whole. Heim's opus is by now several decades in the past, and the scientific understanding of the universe has greatly increased since then. The "big bang" theory has given us an awesome picture of the origin of the universe – a minuscule bundle of matter and energy exploding with unimaginable power, giving birth to stars and galaxies – an explosion that continues as the universe expands. As far as I know, astronomers are still arguing about the eventual fate of this drama. Will the universe continue to expand indefinitely, with more and more empty space between its components? This gives us a vista of increasing emptiness, in which whatever conscious life may exist will be increasingly desolate. Or, alternatively, will the universe reach a point of maximal expansion, after which it will collapse again into the little ball of matter-energy? Here is yet another thoroughly depressing vista, strangely reminiscent of the Hindu idea that the universe is created by the Brahman, its divine center, breathing out, and destroyed again as the Brahman breathes in. As to the earth, there are only two, equally depressing scenarios: It will die of cold, as the sun cools down; or it will die of heat, as (more likely) the sun explodes into what astronomers call a nova. Heim gives us a vivid picture of the last days of humanity in the latter scenario: "The tragedy that will be played when our descendants must flee into caverns, and when all human beings throng together in order painfully to prolong their life a little by means of refrigeration, is something which, if our imagination can paint the details even to some extent, must appear so dreadful and infernal that Dante's *Inferno* with its descriptions of the tortures of hell would seem a trifle compared with it" (*The World: Its Creation and Consummation*, p. 99).

A Hindu vision: The Brahman breathing in and out, as the world becomes and unbecomes. A Christian counter-vision, as reported by Julian of Norwich: The whole world held as a little ball in God's hand. Against the prospect of both individual and cosmic descent into nothingness, there is the Christian affirmation that Christ's resurrection has inaugurated the decisive redemption of the world. Its culmination will be the restoration of the creation to what God intended it to be. And this will mean the abolition of what Heim calls the "scheme of this world" – that is, the cosmic *status quo*. In Heim's own words:

> The whole creation . . . that is, not only the human world, and not merely the animal and vegetable worlds, but also the whole inorganic world; not merely our solar system, but also all the galactic systems which exist outside our own and which are all subject to the same scheme of this world, this whole creation will be "liberated". From what? Not merely from the pains and sorrows which sadden our present existence, from the miseries of disease and the fear of death, not merely from the social injustices which cause so much unrest in our community life, but from something which has far more widespread significance, from the "bondage of corruption". (ibid., pp. 116f)

What is this "corruption"? In Heim's view, it is a wound to creation that cannot be attributed to God's will and which cannot be the result of human sin. Rather, there is an adversary power at work in the universe: "From the beginning of creation a Satanic power has been omnipresent in the world, whose aim is to drive God Himself from the throne and to set himself in His place. From this point of view we understand the sinister background of the New Testament view of the demonic world, which prevails not only over the world of humanity, but over the whole cosmos" (ibid., p. 123).

Heim rather cavalierly dismisses the fall of Lucifer as a myth that we cannot use anymore. It seems to me that his own comments on "a Satanic power" contradict this dismissal. Just as God the creator must be understood in personal terms, so must His adversary. It seems necessary to me to conceive of this adversary as an evil power, *willing* all the horrors of this world. But be this as it may, Heim's theology tallies very nicely with that of Gustav Aulen who, as previously discussed, understands the atonement in terms of "Christ, the victor." The resurrection of Christ is the beginning of the end of the adversary's power over the world, and at the culmination Christ's victory will include the entire cosmos. Put differently, at the culmination all the galaxies will join in the Easter liturgy.

By its very nature, all eschatology is a stammering in the face of impenetrable mysteries. The considerations of this chapter are similarly hesitant and, of necessity, leave many open questions. On the level of individual life, there are all the aforementioned questions about the "interim state," if such there is. On the level of history, there are all the questions about the "end time" raised by the apocalyptic imagination. (It seems that, contrary to all theories of secularization, this imagination continues unabated, at least in America. Witness the immense popularity of the novels about "the rapture" – the miraculous removal from the earth of the elect before the onset of the final catastrophes. Only two weeks ago – and in Boston, of all places – I saw a bumper sticker which read "In case of rapture this car will be driverless.") And on the cosmic level, there are the questions about the nature of the "new heaven" and "new earth" which the returning Christ will establish, not least the aforementioned question of whether eternity is to be conceived as being in or beyond time. On all these questions, we cannot possibly know. Nor need we know. I'm reminded here of Luther's reply to a young man who asked him how God occupied Himself in eternity. Luther replied: God sits under a tree and cuts branches into rods, to beat up people who ask useless questions. With all of this, there remains one fundamental Christian affirmation: That God will not abandon any part of His creation. Not the remotest galaxies. Not my neighbor's child.

We began this book with the question of why religion should be "interesting." We can also ask what kind of eschatology is "interesting." It seems to me that we can find a clue in the most searing chapter in Fyodor Dostoyesky's *The Brothers Karamazov*, tellingly titled "Rebellion." It consists of a conversation between two of the brothers, the rebellious Ivan and the saintly Alyosha, about the suffering of children. Ivan tells a number of terrible stories about such suffering. The most awful story recounts the following episode: A feudal landlord has a favorite hunting dog, who is slightly injured by a stone thrown by a eight-year-old boy, the child of a serf. The child is imprisoned overnight, brought out in the morning, stripped and made to run, and then torn to pieces by the dogs before the eyes of his mother. Ivan asks Alyosha what the landlord deserved. Alyosha replies, "To be shot." But Ivan goes on to say that shooting the landlord would not be enough; even hell would not be enough. He suggests that Alyosha might of course say that, in the end, all will be harmony, God's justice will be revealed, and all will be reconciled. Ivan rejects this vision of eschatological truth. In Ivan's words:

"If the suffering of children go to swell the sum of sufferings which was necessary to pay for truth, then I protest that the truth is not worth such a price . . . I don't want harmony. From love of humanity I don't want it . . . Too high a price is asked for harmony; it is beyond our means to pay so much. And so I give back my entrance ticket, and if I am an honest man

I give it back as soon as possible. And that I am doing. It's not God that I don't accept, Alyosha, only I most respectfully return the ticket to Him." (*The Brothers Karamazov*, in the translation of Constance Garnett, p. 237).

We may add that Ivan is disingenuous here. Of course it is God whom he does not accept. Or, more precisely, a certain conception of God. The "entrance ticket" which Ivan returns is membership in what he believes the Christian faith to be.

We know that Alyosha did not return his ticket. Neither, in the end, did Dostoyevsky. But Ivan's rebellion provides a rough answer to the question of what sort of eschatology would be "interesting" – that is, would be humanly acceptable. Here are some propositions (*a priori*, if you will) of such an eschatology:

God does not condemn Ivan's rebellion. Indeed, "for love of humanity," God endorses it. But this means that Ivan's rebellion is wrongly addressed. It should be addressed, not to God, but to God's adversary.

God does not will the horrors that Ivan recounts. The horrors happen in opposition to Him.

God is not a bystander. He is present in the child's and the mother's agony. He suffers with them and with all of tortured creation. This *kenosis* on the part of God is what inaugurates the healing of the world's pain.

All the human beings in Ivan's episode have a destiny beyond this life. Both the child and the mother will not perish, but will be infinitely comforted beyond this life.

Just as importantly, there will be a judgment, beyond this life, of those who perpetrated this horror.

These *a priori* propositions could be subsumed under a heading paraphrasing the title of one of Kant's works: "Prolegomena to any Future Eschatology that may Represent Itself as Humanly Acceptable." But we can follow up these propositions with an *a posteriori* statement: Precisely such an eschatology is at the heart of the Christian Gospel. It provides a nexus – indeed the most important nexus – between the Gospel and our experience of the human condition.

Let me, in conclusion, refer to three Aramaic sentences that were transported into the Greek text of the New Testament. The first are words spoken by Jesus as he raised from the dead the twelve-year-old daughter of Jairus: "*Talitha, cumi,*" "Little girl, arise" (Mark 5:41). The second, to which we referred before, are words spoken by Jesus from the cross: "*Eli, eli, lama sabachtani?,*" "My God, my God, why have you forsaken me?" (Matthew 27:46). And the third (probably liturgical text) was introduced into some texts at the conclusion of the last book of the New Testament, which in the usual English translations simply reads "Come, Lord Jesus" – in Aramaic, "*Maranatha,*" "Come, Lord," or possibly, "The

Lord is coming" (Revelation 22:20). One could say that the entire Gospel is contained in these three archaic sentences, dating from the very beginning of Christian history: With Christ an immensely powerful process of redemption has been released into the world. In Christ's suffering and death on the cross, at the extreme point of God's humiliation (*kenosis*), God both shares all the pain of creation and inaugurates its repair. And Christ will return as victor and restore the creation to the glory for which God intended it.

Bibliography

Anselm, St, *Cur Deus homo*. Edinburgh: John Grant, 1909.

Aulen, Gustav, *Christus Victor: An Historical Study of Three Main Types of the Idea of Atonement*. London: SPCK, 1950 (Swedish original published in 1931).

Baillie, Donald, *God Was in Christ*. New York: Scribner's, 1948.

Balthasar, Hans Urs von (ed.), *Origen: Spirit and Fire*. Washington, DC: Catholic University of America Press, 1984.

Bartsch, Hans-Werner (ed.), *Kerygma and Myth: A Theological Debate* (5 vols.) (trans. Reginald H. Fuller). London: SPCK, 1948–55.

Berger, Peter L., *The Heretical Imperative*. Garden City, NY: Anchor-Doubleday, 1979.

Berkovits, Eliezer, *Faith after the Holocaust*. New York: KTAV Publishing, 1973.

Braaten, Carl, *No Other Gospel! Christianity among the World's Religions*. Minneapolis: Fortress Press, 1992.

Brunner, Emil, *Eternal Hope*. London: Lutterworth, 1954.

Bultmann, Rudolf, *Essays Philosophical and Theological*. London: SCM Press, 1955.

Bultmann, Rudolf, *Faith and Understanding*. New York: Harper & Row, 1969.

Bultmann, Rudolf, *New Testament and Mythology and Other Basic Writings* (edited and trans. Schubert M. Ogden). Augsburg Fortress Publishers, 1984.

Burgess, Stanley, *The Holy Spirit: Medieval Roman Catholic and Reformation Traditions*. Peabody, MA: Hendrickson, 1997.

Cousins, Ewert (trans.), *Bonaventure: The Soul's Journey into God*. New York: Paulist Press, 1978.

Cousins, Ewert, *Bonaventure and the Coincidence of Opposites*. Chicago: Franciscan Herald Press, 1978.

Cullmann, Oscar, *Christ et le temps*. Neuchàtel: Delachaux & Niestle, 1947. English translation: *Christ and Time*. London: SCM Press, 1962.

Cullmann, Oscar, *Immortality of the Soul or Resurrection of the Body?* London: Epworth, 1958.

Dostoyevsky, Fyodor, *The Brothers Karamazov* (trans. Constance Garnett). New York: Signet, 1999.

Evdokimov, Paul, *Ages of the Spiritual Life*. Crestwood, NY: St Vladimir's Seminary Press, 1998.

Graf, Friedrich Wilhelm, "Einleitung: Protestantische Freiheit," in Friedrich Wilhelm Graf and Klaus Tanner (eds.), *Protestantische Identitaet Heute*. Guetersloh: Guetersloher Verlagshaus, 1992.

Harnack, Adolf von, *The Gospel of the Alien God* (trans. John E. Steely and Lyle D. Bierma). Durham: Labyrinth, 1990.

Heim, Karl, *The World: Its Creation and Consummation*. Philadelphia: Muhlenberg Press, 1962.

Hick, John, *Death and Eternal Life*. New York: Harper & Row, 1976.

Hick, John, *Disputed Questions*. New Haven, CT: Yale University Press, 1993.

Hick, John, *Evil and the Love of God*. New York: Harper & Row, 1966.

Hick, John, *God Has Many Names*. Philadelphia: Westminster Press, 1980.

Hick, John, *The Myth of God Incarnate*. Philadelphia: Westminster Press, 1977.

Johnston, William (ed.), *The Cloud of Unknowing*. Garden City, NY: Image Books, 1973.

Jonas, Hans, "The Concept of God after Auschwitz," in Michael Morgan (ed.), *A Holocaust Reader*. New York: Oxford University Press, 2001.

Julian of Norwich, *Showings* (trans. Edmund Colledge and James Walsh). New York: Paulist Press, 1978.

Katz, Stephen, *Post-Holocaust Dialogues: Critical Studies in Modern Jewish Thought*. New York: New York University Press, 1983.

Lindberg, Carter, *The Third Reformation?* Macon, GA: Macon University Press, 1983.

Luibheid, Colm (trans.), *Pseudo-Dionysius: The Complete Works*. New York: Paulist Press, 1987.

Macquarrie, John, *Christology Revisited*. Harrisburg, PA: Trinity Press International, 1998.

Meyendorff, John, *The Orthodox Church*. New York: Pantheon, 1962.

Mullin, Robert, *Miracles and the Modern Religious Imagination*. New Haven, CT: Yale University Press, 1996.

Prenter, Regin, *Spiritus Creator*. Philadelphia: Muhlenberg Press, 1953 (Danish original published in 1946).

Quran, trans. N. J. Dawood. Harmondsworth: Penguin, 1968.

Rahner, Karl (ed.), *Encyclopedia of Theology*. New York: Seabury, 1975.

Rahner, Karl, *On the Theology of Death*. New York: Herder & Herder, 1961.

Robison, Jay, *Life after Death?* New York: Peter Lang, 1998.

Rondet, Henri, *Original Sin: The Patristic and Theological Background*. Staten Island, NY: Alba House, 1972.

Schweitzer, Albert, *The Quest of the Historical Jesus*. London: Macmillan, 1955 (original German publication 1906, English translation 1910).

Swami Nikhilananda (trans.), *The Bhagavad Gita*. New York: Ramakrishna-Vivekananda Center, 1944.

Tillich, Paul, *The Protestant Era*. Chicago: University of Chicago Press, 1948.

Tillich, Paul, *Systematic Theology*, 3 vols. Chicago: University of Chicago Press, 1957.

Troeltsch, Ernst, *The Absoluteness of Christianity and the History of Religions*. London: SCM Press, 1972.

Troeltsch, Ernst, *The Social Teachings of the Christian Churches*, 2 vols. (trans. Olive Wyon). New York: Harper Torchbooks, 1960 (original publication 1912, English translation 1931).

Troeltsch, Ernst, "The Place of Christianity among the World Religions." In *Christian Thought – Its History and Application*. New York, 1957.

Voegelin, Eric, *Order and History*. Baton Rouge: Louisiana University Press, 1956–87.

Weil, Simone, *Waiting for God*. New York: Putnam's, 1951.

Whatley, Arnold, Essay on Anselm, in L. W. Grensted (ed.), *The Atonement in History and in Life*. London: SPCK, 1929.

Index